1/122

The Unfinished Image

Reflections on the Sunday Readings

by
George McCauley

Sadlier

Los Angeles   New York   Chicago

Nihil Obstat
Msgr. James J. Walsh
Censor Librorum

Imprimatur
✠ Edward A. McCarthy
Archbishop of Miami
August 4, 1981

The *nihil obstat* and *imprimatur* are official declarations that a book or pamphlet is free of doctrinal or moral error. No implication is contained therein that those who have granted the *nihil obstat* and *imprimatur* agree with the contents, opinions, or statements expressed.

Acknowledgments
Excerpts from the *Good News Bible.* Copyright © American Bible Society, 1966, 1971, 1978.

Excerpt from *The Documents of Vatican II*, Walter M. Abbott, S. J., General Editor, © 1966. New Century Publishers, Inc., Piscataway, NJ.

Excerpt reprinted with permission of Macmillan Publishing Co., Inc. from *Letters and Papers from Prison* by Dietrich Bonhoeffer. Copyright © 1953, 1967, 1971 by SCM Press, Ltd.

Editor: Norman F. Josaitis
Designer: Gail Schneider

Home Office:
11 Park Place
New York, NY 10007

ISBN: 0-8215-9903-8
123456789/9876543
Library of Congress Card Catalogue Number: 82-061134

For my sister Mary

Contents

Introduction

Reading the Scripture puts us to the test. On the one hand, the people we meet in the Scripture seem so foreign to us. They force us to learn a strange idiom drawn from a revered religious heritage that often seems alien to us. The landscape of Scripture is full of odd place-names for which we have no familiar point of reference. Behavior is reported in Scripture that seems quaint and exaggerated to our technological age.

On the other hand, the issues, problems, and hopes that Scripture deals with are almost painfully similar to the ones we experience as Christians today. Scripture poses all the human questions. Scriptural characters manifest the same spiritual orneriness, confusions, and energy that we do. They *are* us—written in a painstaking and old-fashioned hand.

For people who get their Scripture only in the liturgical setting of the Sunday and feast-day readings, the situation can be even more puzzling. People are not always familiar with the rationale governing what readings they hear. They don't know why there is an Old Testament reading on some days and not on others. They may not spot when readings from John's Gospel interrupt the readings from Matthew, Mark, or Luke that they had been hearing all along. Above all, they don't know whether they're supposed to see some thread running between the readings, or whether they are to take each reading on its own merits. This is not very easy either, since what they are getting in liturgy are abrupt excerpts from Scripture, snippets without lead-in, context, or elaboration.

Scriptural readings, even when proclaimed in a liturgical context, do not work of their own power. They do not necessarily touch people in rich ways. There is still much that can and should be done to make the hearing of scriptural readings a fruitful experience.

The essays that follow originated as a series of weekly commentaries on the liturgical Scripture readings for *America*, the national Jesuit magazine. They have been honed and polished since their appearance there, and many others have been added to cover the whole liturgical cycle. But their purpose remains the same, namely, to offer people some insight into the scriptural readings.

The essays were guided, moreover, by two convictions concerning the way insight into Scripture is achieved. The first conviction is that people have a wealth of concrete experience on which *they* can draw, if encouraged to do so, in order to make sense of their faith. Religious language has a way of becoming unmoored from such concrete experience. We talk of salvation, mystery, union, redemption, transfiguration, creation, purification, repentance, community, sanctity, and so on, yet the words seem to float in the air. We fail to see their connection with our real lives, even though there are a thousand points of contact between them and our ordinary experiences in life. True, our profane experience is not the measure of God's action in the world, but it is the measure of how we come to understand and talk about what God has done in Christ. So, in the essays that follow, attention is paid to the ways people behave, to how they fare, and to what they often feel. When these normal experiences of people are brought near the word of God, light is thrown not only on them but on the word of God as well.

The second conviction is that the key to understanding Scripture is to work through—gradually and without anxiety—the image of God with which we are presented. We have to ask incessantly: What kind of God emerges from the descriptions given by the different scriptural authors? What kind of person is the Jesus that is being described in Scripture, and does that correspond to my experience of Jesus? What kind of Spirit are we saying is at work in the church? The essays zero in on such questions; that is the common denominator that links them together. The most promising question we can ask ourselves when we hear Scripture read at liturgy is: What kind of God is being presented here?

Our images of God, like our images of ourselves, never exhaust the realities in question. The images are always unfinished. Other people help us finish them; so does God. My hope is that these essays will help people explore the Scripture with some excitement and relish, and with the confidence that God's own image, Jesus, is taking shape in them by the working of the Spirit.

A thematic index has been added to this publication of the essays. I notice that people use the liturgical readings in many other settings: for informal reflection, for liturgy team preparation, for private and communal prayer sessions, discussion groups, weekday liturgies, retreats, and so forth. I thought the index would facilitate that kind of usage.

George McCauley
October 15, 1982

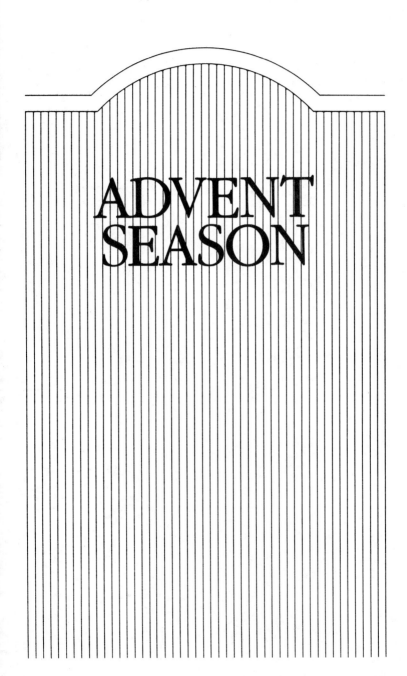

ADVENT SEASON

Isaiah 2:1–5
Romans 13:11–14
Matthew 24:37–44

Seeing Is Believing

"Take up the weapons of the Lord Jesus Christ, and stop paying attention to your sinful nature and satisfying its desires" (Romans 13:14).

Advent originated, we are told, as a period of prayerful preparation for the Christmas–Epiphany festivities. Just as Lent prepared people to celebrate the resurrection of the Lord, Advent looked to the celebration of God's incarnation in our flesh.

Strange, then, that our flesh gets such a raking over in today's readings: "Stop paying attention to your sinful nature and satisfying its needs." *Sinful nature*, in this case, is a translation of the Greek word for "flesh." Again, we read: "In the days before the flood people ate and drank, men and women married, up to the very day Noah went into the boat; yet they did not realize what was happening until the flood came and swept them all away" (Matthew 24:38–39). Texts like these make it look as though God takes on our flesh only to run it down!

The fact is that *flesh* is used in Scripture in two senses. In the best sense, flesh means our human condition in all its fragile splendor. That God has personally identified with this flesh in the incarnation is our reason for celebration and joy. In the negative sense, flesh is used to signify spiritual obtuseness, or a lack of spiritual

15

alertness and concern. When Saint Paul talks about not satisfying the desires of our sinful nature, he refers not only to gross, physical sins but to spiritual ones as well: "Let us conduct ourselves properly, as people who live in the light of day — no orgies or drunkenness, no immorality or indecency, no fighting or jealously" (Romans 13:13). Flesh can mean the most artful and subtle devices the human spirit makes use of to dull its perception of God. Alas, this negative sense of flesh in Scripture carries with it a common prejudice against fat people who, of course, may be as spiritually alert as the next person. (Those who can, take a bow.)

The point is made. In Advent, the Christian is urged to be alert to the inroads of the flesh. "The time has come for you to wake up from your sleep" (Romans 13:11); "If the owner of a house knew the times when the thief would come, you can be sure that he would stay awake" (Matthew 24:43).

Many might argue whether, as a general rule in life, alertness is all that desirable. It seems to unveil layer after layer of depressing realities. Ask those people who have stopped reading the newspapers. Who wants to read accounts of rip-offs, rapes and murders, the rich stealing from the poor and the poor stealing from each other, political triviality, runaways, slick deals by big business, urban rot, monosyllabic mobsters, incompetence, righteous self-interest, international upheavals, the human preference for pets over people, demented heads of nations, religious fakery, and on and on?

Is the gospel inviting us to be alert to all that goes on around us; to the shifting fears and feelings, the anger and confusions within us? What happens if we let all this into our consciousness? Isn't it better to block it out, to numb ourselves in the various ways at our disposal?

To be sure, the alertness we are called upon to have as Christians ranges more widely than this depressing vista. This alertness also brings into view the delicate heroisms and massive charity at work in the world. It lets us see where faithfulness and humor and the creative use of talent in the service of others abound. It allows us to see the sustaining presence of God in all things and for all things.

Advent, then, is a time for keeping our eyes open. Who would have thought that "seeing is believing" could turn into such an energetic pastime?

First Sunday of Advent — B

Isaiah 63:16 – 17, 19; 64:2 – 7
1 Corinthians 1:3 – 9
Mark 13:33 – 37

The Future Within Us

"No one has ever seen or heard of a God like you, who does such deeds for those who put their hope in him" (Isaiah 64:4).

Advent is a season of expectations. But expectation is taken in two ways by the Advent tradition. In the first way, Advent reviews expectations that people had *before* the actual coming of Christ. It goes back over the situation of humankind before that event and measures what people hoped for against what they got. In the second way, Advent calls us to examine what we expect for the *future* in the light of all that happened in Christ. If you find yourself confused by the liturgical readings, then, it is not your fault. Some of them concentrate on expectations that have to do with the first coming of Jesus. Others highlight expectations surrounding the second coming. For example, today's epistle and gospel are clearly dealing with the second coming. Saint Paul says: "You have not failed to receive a single blessing, as you wait for our Lord Jesus Christ to be revealed. He will also keep you firm to the end, so that you will be faultless on the Day of our Lord Jesus Christ" (1 Corinthians 1:7 – 8). And Saint Mark goes on about the appointed time, being on the watch, and so on.

The Advent tradition wobbles between two emphases and leaves us room for choice. We ourselves prefer to consider Advent from the earlier point of view and thus to meditate on events leading up to the incarnation. We will try to picture the expectations, neediness, reversals, hopelessness, and surprises that preceded the coming of Jesus in the flesh.

The amazing thing was that humankind had any expectations at all. We ought to think twice about Israel's expectation of a savior. To expect a solution, let alone a solution in human shape and form, took great faith. Believing in the ultimate comforting providence of God is one thing; believing that God's providence will proximately and creatively influence the flow of human history is another thing.

We Christians tend to take such an expectation for granted. We have seen Jesus at work. But imagine for a moment that Jesus had not in fact come. What would our hopes and expectations be? Who would expect relief or solace in the midst of so much greed, triviality, stupidity, malice, indifference, psychological handicaps, selfishness, and superstition? Why wouldn't the same old routines persist? If virtue can be laughed out of the councils of the powerful, why should anyone be confident? If it can be redefined at every turn by people who can't even follow a logical argument, why should anyone expect anything?

Israel, however, rose above cynicism and sour despondency to hope. It took seriously the promise built into life by God. This promise was not written down in any one place or uttered at any one moment of time. It came to a multitude of individuals through the ordinary and extraordinary events of their lives. It invaded their dreams and their waking hours. It spoke to them in their prayers and their political upheavals, in their hero worshiping and their sinning, in their child making and their children. Israel collectively solidified its conviction that God would effect something marvelous out of humanity, because God had promised to do so and had given such constant signs of promise.

But people cannot have faith in a promise unless they can see that what is promised is a real possibility in and for themselves. This is the thesis of the theologian William Lynch, S.J., in his *Images of Faith*. Promises, Father Lynch maintains, must meet a kernal of expectation within people. Where people expect nothing, nothing can happen; the promises will fall on deaf ears. If a Hollywood mogul promises a beautiful young woman a career, it won't work if the young woman cannot picture herself as that future actress. If a school promises a football scholarship to a sturdy young man, it doesn't help unless the young man sees in himself some glimmer of possibility for playing football.

Time and again, Israel was called upon to look into itself to find such seeds of possibility. It was asked to trust that God could create *in* it the capacity to produce wise kings and heroic judges, prophets and healers. And through such faith, Israel has become the spiritual teacher of us all.

It could have gone otherwise. Israel could have settled for the miserable self-image of itself that is described in today's first reading: "All of us have been sinful; even our best actions are filthy through and through. Because of our sins we are like leaves that wither and are blown away by the wind" (Isaiah 64:5– 6). Instead, it clung to the belief that God could transform humanity as surely as he formed it: "We are like clay, and you are like the potter" (v. 8).

We cannot comment here on the sequel to Israel's faith. Perhaps it was too much to bear when all the potter came up with was a solution in the shape of a small child named Jesus who would, in the eyes of many, grow up to be part of the same old failed human project. Father Lynch also warns us that faith must expect the unexpected.

In any case, during Advent Christians might review their own expectations. What do we hope for here on earth? What horizons do we sweep and search? Have we looked into ourselves to find, despite all our misshapen and tortuous ways, our God-given capacity for healing the world and making it flourish? Advent would be a good time to start all over again to enter and take hold of our own humanity. After all, that's what the finale to the Advent season will be all about.

First Sunday of Advent — C

1 Jeremiah 33:14 – 16
1 Thessalonians 3:12 – 4:2
Luke 21:25 – 28, 34 – 36

Comings and Goings On

"In this way he will strengthen you, and you will be perfect and holy in the presence of our God and Father when our Lord Jesus comes with all who belong to him" (1 Thessalonians 3:13).

"What is it all coming to?" the chorus goes. Future shock waves roll over the land and people are unsure. Job security, mortages, health insurance, pensions are everyday anxieties. Even in success we fear that the future, like some new toy, will go stale. Youth is relentlessly bad-mouthed — a sure sign of what we think about our own hope.

Jesus, too, sees the grim side of things, the fretful sky-searching and the general distress. "People will faint from fear as they wait for what is coming over the whole earth" (Luke 21:26). But for him all this terror is not prelude to more terror. That is the difference between Jesus and us. His forecast is liberation.

People are not cheered by this news. They will not give over their morose squinting at the horizon. Why bother avoiding the trap of indulgence, drinking, and worldly concerns (Luke 21:34) when God seems to spring the larger trap of death on us? Why bother about anything when we seem to be dealing with a God who uses death as a warning lest something *worse* happen? Besides, the gospel sometimes sounds like Catch 22: "If you're in a trap, you can't get liberated on the day of liberation; so avoid traps and wait for the day of your liberation from your trap."

Naturally, if God is suspect, less can be expected from the guy on your block, from the woman next to you in the pew, from your broker or your government.

Jesus, according to everybody, overcame these depressing thoughts by faith. The rest of us often seem unconvinced about a liberating future. We have to be teased and argued out of our chains.

This is precisely what a new liturgical cycle does. The cycle that begins with the First Sunday of Advent is not the esoteric creation of the initiated: the X readings rather than the Y or Z readings. Put simply, the liturgical year is the retelling of the story, in the expectation that we will find therein conviction for our hope of liberation. It is a technique for conducting the larger spiritual argument that even believers are engaged in: Has God ever really freed anyone? Is God that kind of God?

So the record must be consulted. The whole thing must be replayed, this time with more attention to the lyrics. We survey the way it has gone with God in the past: See where it took a sudden turn, there. Notice that long squiggle. See how people looked, how this one was disappointed, how that one was surprised.

Many words get said in the liturgical readings. We hear from all kinds: sarcastic, stuttering prophets; shaggy warrior kings given to a fitful tenderness; prostitutes-turned-civic-heroines; dull holy men; dumb apostles; cagey interpreters of God's will; bellyachers; raconteurs; breathtaking truthspeakers; frustrated intellectuals; haranguers; and some, too, who speak an impressive silence.

But there is one Word that captures God's foreign accent best. Jesus' fate is central to the liturgical cycle. He is God in our skin, so let us see how he wears it. Can he really walk in our shoes and make our way credible? Can he really take our side? His story is not just history. It is a story in which we are involved. It is addressed to us and stirs us to prayer. We are part of the plot, and the good news is aimed right between our eyes.

No wonder the liturgical cycle displays all the characteristics of an argument. People have to argue themselves into freedom, and Advent is the beginning of the argument. As in any good argument, we begin with a rousing, unnuanced thesis: Advent stubbornly announces a rosy liberating future under God's aegis. It teaches us that we can be convinced of this future only by looking back and retracing God's actions in the past. This swivel-headed back-and-forth can be exhausting. But it is a standard therapy.

Genesis 3:9– 15, 20
Ephesians 1:3– 6, 11– 12
Luke 1:26– 38

A Talented Lady

"I will make you and the woman hate each other; her offspring and yours will always be enemies" (Genesis 3:15).

Where problems of peace, world hunger, or sheer survival are to the fore, the attempt to understand, let alone to get excited about, the Solemnity of the Immaculate Conception might seem superfluous. Others would applaud the effort. Either they like to concentrate on Mary as an untouched and untouchable oasis amid the general squalor, or they enjoy replaying the part where she crushes the serpent's head.

The feast, we suggest, has a different message. It deals with the relation between talent and getting things done, even in the kingdom of God. The ordinary believer is rightly pressured to affirm that it is God (not you, you sinner) who makes the kingdom come. What is often left unsaid is how God does this, namely, by equipping humanity (you, you sinner) to face the forces in its midst that militate against the kingdom.

These contrary forces we usually call *original sin*. If Mary's exemption from that condition is to make any sense, we have to be clearer about what original sin means. Many think of it in terms of a personal stain, an uncleanness that renders us distasteful to God. Under our breath we add that, after all, it is God who needlessly perpetuates this blight. Sentiments of humiliation and of hostility toward God are right beneath the surface of our original sin language. But rather than staying with recriminations, how about recomposing the main doctrinal themes about original sin in the following way?

First of all, our situation is such that we are haunted by the unwavering promises of God to make us happy. The Book of Genesis hints at the areas of our unhappiness. We could be on familiar terms with God. No strained conversation, no games around the fact that God is God and we are creatures; we could make as little of this fact as God does. We could be fraternal with each other and forego the violence. We could be less strident and ill at ease sexually, instead of smarting with shame all the time or being so cautious that it comes to the same thing. We could work together without the babel. We could avoid the ecological slum that rises about our ears. We could find many more cures than we do. We could pull ourselves together and align our emotions better with our purposeful selves. But—without actually pointing the finger at anyone—we are not doing so and, as a race, we never have. And that's such a sin that we seem to be damned without God's promises and doubly damned with them.

Second, our situation has built into it an acceleration factor: the more time spent doing nothing, and the more people doing it, the more magnified is the difficulty of doing anything about anything. It is like the difference between organizing your street and organizing your city. It's a crime that it all gets so complicated. Ask any big city mayor.

Third, while our situation is promising as far as God is concerned, we still require delivery on the promise. This, too, is gift and is not yet in our hands. So our situation remains one of utter dependence.

It is important not to moralize too much about the threefold situation just described. In fact, a Jesuit philosopher friend suggests that much of our situation is just our evolutionary bad habits showing their effects. Too many millenia on the mountainside swishing flies off our rumps; stomping on smaller, slower things that might feed our latest hunger sensation; sniffing for hostile presences—the toll was taken. The call to love one another, to love *any* other, runs so counter to our prehuman instincts that no wonder it all seems uphill.

In any case, it takes talent to face our original sin squarely. Sometimes this talent sits awkwardly on people. There is the old joke about Billie Burke, the aging actress, arriving at customs with eleven suitcases. When asked what was in them, she huffed, "*That* is Billie Burke." Her virtues were candidly appendage. Christians aren't much different. Saint Paul even talks about suiting up in the virtues as though they were belts, breastplates, shoes, shields, and so on (Ephesians 6:13 – 18).

But what of the warrior within? What of the character and capacity of the person? Sometimes, at this deeper level, people are talented in a silent and substantial way. Call it instinct, style, or flair: they have it. It does not protect them from the roughness of life, but they bring greater resources to living it. Mary is preeminently in this class. The papal bull establishing today's feast says she is "loaded with charisms" (*copia charismatum*). Original sin, look out.

Second Sunday of Advent—A

Isaiah 11:1 – 10
Romans 15:4 – 9
Matthew 3:1 – 12

To Do or Not to Do

"The spirit of the Lord will give him wisdom and the knowledge and skill to rule his people" (Isaiah 11:2).

In your ordinary conversation, keep mentioning performance and doing, efficiency and action, effectiveness, output and results, and you will soon find yourself surrounded by a lot of people with nosebleed. Such productivity seems beyond our capacities. In our achievement-oriented culture, there is a special pain attached to such emphasis on visible accomplishments. Not only social dropouts, but many good and exhausted people are sullenly skeptical about exhortations to "produce." They want to know: Produce by what standard? What yardstick of effective human performance is being applied? Am I "producing" if I am trying, or is that not enough? Am I showing results if I am a loving person within the limited range of friends, job, and family, or is there more I am supposed to be doing?

The questions are particularly acute today when, in and out of religious circles, "doing" is equated with social action. For nowhere more than in issues of social injustice (housing, hunger, education, discrimination, economic opportunity, political repression) do we feel so powerless to act. It would require so much changing: by the poor, who rip off welfare systems; by the middle class, who play games with taxes; by better-off people, who invest modestly in rapacious, profiteering companies; by the high rollers, the Neanderthals who go straight for power and unrestrained wealth—no matter who stands in the way.

In the face of all this, Christians are concerned to know what standard of performance Jesus is applying to them. Personal relationships, after all, demand this sort of clarity. When we constantly have the feeling that we are not doing what is expected of us by another person, the relationship can be frustrating. What effectiveness, then, does Jesus expect from us?

Saint Matthew's Jesus is big on getting results. Today's gospel contains key themes of Saint Matthew's theology, which lays great stress on the observance of Jesus' commandments. The Pharisees in today's gospel join the pious pilgrimage to John the Baptist's revival meeting by the Jordan. John hits them hard: "Do those things that will show that you have turned from your sins" (Matthew 3:8). When John gets around to describing Jesus, we have an intensified impression that action is called for: Jesus is going to lay axes to trees that do not bear fruit. He is going to clean house, apparently on the basis of who is performing and who isn't. In his wild, shaggy dress, John would be threatening enough to deal with. So, when he describes the baptismal program of Jesus as an even more spirited and firey one, the emphasis on performance—and the nosebleed—are complete.

Simply stated, the problem is to see how God can be "the source of patience and encouragement" (Romans 15:5) when axes are being laid to the tree. God seems to have conflicting standards: one of mercy and forebearance, the other of bearing fruit or else.

The anxiety lessons, however, if we consider the following. First, the Lord does not give commands without at the same time offering vision. Today's first reading details a stunning program of world rehabilitation. "On Zion, God's holy hill, there will be nothing harmful or evil" (Isaiah 11:9). This visionary quality is central to the gospel, as well. If Jesus seems to be issuing commands, it is not without having clued his followers into an exciting vision of better times. So we can be sure that, where people are calling for our performance without giving us any vision at the same time, the gospel is probably being twisted.

Second, many holy people have told us that when Jesus calls to performance, he calls individuals to it. That is, his yardstick takes into account our individual talents, backgrounds, graces, situations, and so forth. Faith is a matter of doing what we are capable of doing, given who we are and where we have come from.

What scandalizes us is that so much of our Christian activism seems to consist of catching up. We hate to see our full-time job as one of picking up the pieces, of healing somewhat parochial interpersonal rifts, of getting up the gumption even to try. Yet, this is where most of us personally are. We cannot subconsciously interpret Jesus' "bearing fruit" to mean "never having problems in the first place."

If we look on Jesus' call to action in this light, we can at least free ourselves from some of our more transparent excuses for inactivity: I won't do anything until and unless others do something; I won't do anything unless I get instant recognition from others for doing it; no one can do anything anyhow; other people have more talent for doing than I have; if God wants it done, why doesn't God do it?; I've done things before, but they always seem to get undone.

Perhaps Advent could be a time for coming alive with spirit and fire to where we really are, without excuses and with a minimum of nosebleed.

Second Sunday of Advent — B

Isaiah 40:1 – 5, 9 – 11
2 Peter 3:8 – 14
Mark 1:1 – 8

Big Man

"Get the road ready for the Lord; make a straight path for him to travel!" (Mark 1:3).

To rise above the sense of our own self-importance is no small achievement. We may even wonder whether everyone thinks it is a sound idea to begin with. The street scene is ever revealing. People of varying shapes and sizes, gender and nationality, status and education scurry around seeking to maintain a slender hold on their dignity. This one sneaks a glance at a dirty store mirror to reassure himself. That one bristles as she is cut off at the market counter. Some wear uniforms, but not lightly. Others read amidst the chaos of a subway; they do not yield to the greatest scholar. One person boasts of the sausage he sells. In the most fleeting glance, a passerby stares back a challenge: "I can do whatever you can do." Another person argues that his rotgut is the best available. All are poignantly serious—about their hair style, their car, their turf, their utterances. The banality of their lives dogs them, but they rebound. Arrest them, yes, but don't push. Hire them for peanuts, but don't look down on them. Heal them, to be sure, but treat them like the rich patients upstairs. People take pride in the way they fold a napkin or roll up their cuffs, the way they lean on a building or sit in a chair. Greatness is tied to their knowledge of this technique or that shortcut. Like a constant, surging tide, the voice of the people, its gesture and mein, all assert a fundamental claim to self-importance, to the uniqueness of me.

To say the least, the whole business of uniqueness is a complicated one. No one likes to be compared to someone else (except favorably). But culture is built on such mutual assessment. Grades are given in school. Some make the team; others don't. Jobs are allotted on the basis of competence. Despite all the complaints about nepotism and who-you-know, expertise becomes the criterion for advancement. Opportunity is never really equal, and not everyone gets canonized. How, in the face of this obvious pressure to compare, can we take our uniqueness as some absolute and unarguable point of reference? Is valuing our individuality simply the defense mechanism we use against the harsher demands of reality? Are we kidding ourselves?

Now John the Baptist—he was different. "The man who will come after me is much greater than I am. I am not good enough even to bend down and untie his sandal" (Mark 1:7). This hero of Advent, this rugged and blunt symbol of the urgency of God's kingdom, was himself a magnetic crowd pleaser (Mark 1:5). Yet he could defer to another. He could see in Jesus something different, something better. His own unique talent became in that circumstance a nonissue.

How do we explain such humility and self-forgetfulness? John himself gives us the answer: "I baptize you with water, but he will baptize you with the Holy Spirit" (Mark 1:8). To get the point of his remark, we have to recall the special significance of baptism in the Holy Spirit for New Testament writers. Commentators point out that the Spirit was seen by them as someone full of surprises. Like the fickle wind and the brusque gale, the Spirit kept people off balance. The Spirit of the new creation brooded over the baptismal waters in much the same way as he did over the waters of the creation. Out of the vast sameness of things, the Spirit again created diversity. Jew found himself in the same pew with Gentile, free man with slave. Contours once thought clashing now meshed. The Spirit obviously graced the community with a diversity of talent, skill, background, temperament, and appeal. The community came to see this very diversity as a sign of the Spirit. Comparisons became not only inevitable but unthreatening, since a positive purpose could be served by them: to explore the rich diversity of the one Spirit of God.

John the Baptist caught something of this Spirit from Jesus. He became able to see his own task and talent as different from that of Jesus. So he could say the truth about Jesus and his own truth in the same breath. He could postpone commentary on his own uniqueness, because he found himself in the company of someone like Jesus, who set store not on uniqueness but on diversity of talent.

We should welcome the emergence in others of their special selves. We should foster it even if we feel a bit left out in the end. This habit of expecting great things from others and of controlling our own anxieties about our uniqueness is a difficult one to form, but it might help us to recognize someone like Jesus when he comes.

Second Sunday of Advent — C

Baruch 5:1 – 9
Philippians 1:4 – 6, 8 – 11
Luke 3:1 – 6

You Are There

"I am sure that God, who began this good work in you, will carry it on until it is finished" (Philippians 1:6).

We surround important beginnings in life with frames of time and place and high personnage in order to fix them more firmly in the course of history, and perhaps to increase their scale. Saint Luke does this to the initial preaching ministry of John the Baptist. The apparently insignificant revival launched by John suddenly takes on a portentous tone: "It was the fifteenth year of the rule of Emperor Tiberius; Pontius Pilate was governor of Judea, Herod was ruler of Galilee, and his brother Philip was ruler of the territory of Iturea and Trachonitis; Lysanias was ruler of Abilene, and Annas and Caiaphas were high priests. At that time the word of God came to John Son of Zechariah in the desert. So John went throughout the whole territory of the Jordan River, preaching, 'Turn away from your sins and be baptized, and God will forgive your sins' " (Luke 3:1–3).

Many beginnings in our lives do not merit such lofty landmarks. A college graduate starts a summer job and no trumpets blare. A portly citizen starts to diet, and no one remembers who happens to be governor. A postman heads out on his rounds without fanfare or notice. It is only when we are beginning something that will impact on ourselves or on society in momentous ways that beginnings are enshrined with elaborate trappings.

The difficulty is in knowing what will turn out to be momentous and what won't. A certain nervousness attends all beginnings. The future resists our efforts to live it all at once; it remains opaque and a bit threatening. We wonder what will happen to our resolve, let alone to our luck. We are vaguely anxious that the future might call for a talent and capacity in us that just aren't there. A beginning is a kind of dare. Great events in Christian life—baptisms, weddings, ordinations—all have this quality of adventure in them.

It is people who get us through such perilous beginnings. They cheer us on; they prod us with promise; they instigate and foster the step we are about to take. They say they will resource us in the future. They will not simply remain the passive adornments of our beginnings, but will press on with us to the end. Our faith in the future is possible because of them. This holds true especially of the One of whom Saint Paul speaks today: "I am sure that God, who began this good work in you, will carry it on until it is finished."

Third Sunday of Advent—A

Isaiah 35:1– 6, 10
James 5:7– 10
Matthew 11:2– 11

A Good Look Around

"The desert will rejoice, and flowers will bloom in the wastelands. The desert will sing and shout for joy" (Isaiah 35:1 – 2).

Today's gospel deals with two people, John and Jesus, who shared a soaring vision about God's kingdom coming into this world. They wanted to make all the talk about a nice God, peace, healing, and so forth, come true *now*. But this vision demanded, in turn, that they take the measure of each other. We learn visions from one another, but we also have to look closely at each other to see whether, realistically, we are representatives and authentic agents of the vision. We have to read one another's mettle and behavior and heart. This can get tense.

John the Baptist saw something in Jesus. Most probably, Jesus began as one of John's disciples. In fact, historians argue that it was probably through his association with John that Jesus came more and more to discover his own role in the kingdom's arrival. Today's gospel, however, indicates that the Baptist's vision of Jesus was not all that unclouded. That new times had arrived, John was convinced. He was also sure that Jesus was to have some special role in developments. But that Jesus was to be the *central* cog in the kingdom did not leap out, neither for some of John's more partisan disciples nor for John himself. "When John the Baptist heard in prison about the things that Christ was doing, he sent some of his disciples to him. 'Tell us,' they asked Jesus, 'are you the one John said was going to come, or should we expect someone else?' " (Matthew 11:2 – 3).

Recall that both John and Jesus are clear about the larger vision. They can use its pregnant, shorthand language with each other and know what is meant. "The one . . . to come" meant the shrouded messianic figure of Old Testament prophecies who would not, like some new Elijah, merely announce the kingdom's arrival, but would actually usher it in. It's pinning this figure down to real people like Jesus that worries John.

What can Jesus answer? He is aware that prisons are not the best places for vision. He knows that John wants to weigh what's happening to Jesus "on the outside." The only response Jesus can make is to testify to the signs that are taking place in and through him. The kingdom is starting *to work*. A vague enough answer, and perhaps not the most satisfying one for John.

Jesus, on the other hand, is generous in his measure of John. In fact, he's gushing. He praises his mentor for sharing in the work of beginning the kingdom, and especially for John's realistic acceptance of suffering as part of the process. By his high accolade, Jesus enshrines once and for all in the memory of his own followers the rough-hewn and ascetic John.

In a sense, though, Jesus can't worry about John. He has to go on with his own work. This is another aspect of maintaining the larger vision in the real world: We have to know when others have had their day—or when we ourselves have. We can't take time out to prove ourselves to the satisfaction of everybody. If we get flak from others, sometimes the only way to get down to work is to repeat our allegiance to the larger vision, and then do what we have to do.

In today's church, we need large visions for sure. But even more, we need the capacity to envision in other people their real possibilities for doing worthwhile work in the service of God's kingdom in today's world. We have to play John to their Jesus and bring out the best in them. If we run each other down, who's going to act on the vision? So we must seek out signs of greatness in others, however faint. We must fan whatever timid aspirations they might have. We must look for harvests in their somewhat sere landscapes. We must not carp at each other with a depressing quest for exactitude. Above all, we must not keep silent with each other about whether we share the larger vision at all!

Isaiah 61:1– 2, 10– 11
1 Thessalonians 5:16– 24
John 1:6– 8, 19– 28

Cause for Joy

"Jerusalem rejoices because of what the Lord has done. . . . God has clothed her with salvation and victory" (Isaiah 61:10).

The grimness and tense manner of many religious sects today are surely signs of sickness rather than of salvation. Someone comes up to you with eyes fixed and jaw straining. He chatters monotonously but with aggressive insistence about the love of God or the purity of your organic body fluids. What you are beginning to feel is how it's like living on the boundary between religion and mental illness. The obsessive and morose versions of life that thrive in many sects are a dead giveaway that something is amiss in them.

It is unfortunate that the more established religions cannot name out loud exactly what is amiss. They themselves too often have shied away from publicly exploring the boundary between faith and the findings of psychology. So when bizarre sects hit the headlines, the established religions can't say very much. They might have to apply a lot of what they say to themselves. Too often, the official position is that the spiritual is some kind of hermetically sealed province apart, with its own morphology and with rules that are not subject to psychological analysis. That way, grace can continue to deny the existence of nature whenever it is convenient.

This is not to say that the findings of psychology add up to some kind of gospel of their own. On the other hand, today's epistle advises us to "put all things to the test: keep what is good" (1 Thessalonians 5:21). If this expression means anything, it means that faith might have to learn a lot from psychology. Perhaps if we believers could do this learning more openly and less grudgingly, we might be better able to address ourselves to the question of counterfeit faiths in our world.

What the established religions do contribute that distinguishes them from morbid and obsessive sectarianism is a sense of joy in the midst of life's complexities. For example, today's Advent liturgy programs in such determined pursuit of joy: "Be joyful always, pray at all times, be thankful in all circumstances. This is what God wants from you in your life in union with Christ Jesus" (1 Thessalonians 5:17– 18). It is not easy to set one's sights on joy. So many things depress and trouble us. To carry out Saint Paul's injunction, we must vigorously put aside our favorite angers. We have to give over deploring this or that. We cannot give free reign to self-pity; we must check it firmly. We have to shrug off the miseries and literally talk to ourselves about the reasons we have for joy. The risk of artificiality in this attempt is minor compared to the somber alternatives to joy of which we are capable. Even though it may seem odd to practice recalling things that make gratitude and joy swell up in us, that's exactly what must be done.

It really isn't too hard, either. Some examples might help. . . .

We rejoice in God. We are exhilarated by the wild ride of creation, as the Father sends us off on solar winds like some atomic starburst, full of flesh and blood and knowing soul. We are flattered that the Father has likened us to himself, and that to prove the point he has identified us with his Son, Jesus. We are uplifted by the Spirit who gasps and marvels at us as images of the Father.

We rejoice in spiritual and corporal works of mercy whenever the lowly get good news and the brokenhearted are healed, whenever captives hear about liberty or prisoners are released. Today's first reading shows us how to get excited about such things.

We rejoice in prophets, the give-'em-hell kind and the give-'em-heaven kind. We rejoice especially in those prophets like John the Baptist who cry out for justice even when their own ratings go down. We are glad, too, that prophets aren't always right.

We rejoice in small children, in the questions they ask about God, and in their crooked drawings of him; in their solemn conclaves and feverish machinations; in their bodies, worn lightly by them and without trace of dissoluteness; in their sane judgment that ogres and monsters have the edge on them; in their play-acting and their massive leisure; in their ability to watch things—including themselves—grow.

We rejoice in silly things, such as jokes that fizzle, bake sales that replace sacraments, and collection envelopes stuffed with confetti.

We rejoice in the newness of relationship that is always possible with gods and other people. We rejoice that we are not locked into last week's image of each other and can still find freshness in each other by a process of mutual discovery and sharing.

Many people are too threatened by their image of God and of his last judgment to indulge in this kind of rejoicing. They dourly suspect that God will have the last laugh. But when you think of it, what if the last laugh were really a laugh?

Third Sunday of Advent — C

Zephaniah 3:14– 18
Philippians 4:4– 7
Luke 3:10– 18

Living It Up in Jerusalem

"Sing and shout for joy, people of Israel! Rejoice with all your heart, Jerusalem!" (Zephaniah 3:14).

What they didn't tell you that Zephaniah said was that Jerusalem in his day was a mess. The joyful thought expressed above comes only at the end of his long tirade against the religious performance of his contemporaries. This sequence—attack/console—captures the problem with Christian rejoicing: the smile after the tongue-lashing. It sounds like "Knuckle under and you will be happy." Think of all those movie villains whose greasy "exhortations" to joy made your skin ripple.

The epistle and gospel offer a more sophisticated analysis of Christian joy. They stress that it is the return of the Lord which is the radical source of our joy: "The Lord is coming soon. Don't worry about anything" (Philippians 4:5– 6). A different sequence is urged: first, the sense of God's nearness; then, a surge of joy; then an outbreak of unselfishness on our part.

Even this analysis leaves us uneasy. The Spirit of Jesus will indeed make us do nice things, but it will all seem like purging fire (Luke 3:16). Jesus will make a clean sweep, but everyone—the wheat with the chaff—will feel as if they were hit with a shovel (Luke 3:17). Peace will break out, but sentries will have to be posted anyway (Philippians 4:7).

Lest this joyful day of Advent (Gaudete Sunday) seem like a forced or programmed grin, let us consider the matter further. What kind of God is drawing near to bring us joy? Isn't it true that many of us try to be joyful *despite* God, who has somewhat the reputation of being a killjoy? Or, like Homer, do we suspect the gods of having private jokes among themselves, while we hack and toil at each other on some windy plain down here?

If God draws near, it is not to engage us in a kind of aimless banter. Nor is God one of those tightbrowed people who glumly approach you and say: "You look glum." Neither does God simply add an outer coating of joy to cover over a deeper grimness within us. What he does is tell us things about joy that we already know but rarely attend to. No one has to tell a tax collector that he would feel less like a louse if he stopped gouging his already burdened customers. No one has to tell soldiers that they would be more comfortable with their spit-and-polish bravado if they didn't use it as another weapon against the weak. And people are quite well aware that they would feel better after feeding the hungry or giving someone needier the shirt off their back. God simply reminds us that joy is tied to a generous heart.

But the gospel characters (Luke 3:10–14), like ourselves, are so tentative about joy. There is such an awkward air to our good deeds. We spoil even our successful attempts at justice by a cloying righteousness that, to our surprise, sours joy.

The nearness of God promises an abiding integrity, one that is relatively free of such creaking stops and starts. Forgetting this promise, we force God to prod us along convusively with worldly lessons. Like Edith Piaf's streetwalker, God has to wheedle us out of our disillusionment and stuffiness with prompting smiles and much jaunty self-deprecation: "Allez, chantez Milord/ Voilà, c'estça Milord/ Smile for me . . . a little more/ Go on, dance Milord."

It takes great faith to admit that God is steadier than we are in sustaining joy, that he is the one who has the generous heart. "May you always be joyful," says Saint Paul (Philippians 4:4). Oh, what a Jerusalem that would be, to realize that God wants to laugh it up with us in the depths of our being! Small wonder that we might then break out in a rash of generous, practical goodness toward our neighbors.

Isaiah 7:10–14
Romans 1:1–7
Matthew 1:18–24

Facts of Life

"A virgin will become pregnant and have a son, and he will be called Immanuel (which means, 'God is with us')" (Matthew 1:23).

The New Testament narratives about Jesus' infancy are trying to make a simple point, namely, that there were signs of greatness in Jesus even before his public ministry. We've seen this done elsewhere: George Washington and the cherry tree, the verbal prowess of Lord Macauley even in the cradle. (When a dowager who had scalded him with hot tea was anxiously fussing over him, he is said to have calmed her, saying: "Thank you, madam, the agony is abated.")

Biblical scholars, however, with their severe brows, are always after us to verify such narratives, to ascertain whether they are just pious legends or constitute accurate reporting about factual happenings. Take today's gospel about Jesus' virginal conception. Fact or legend? It doesn't help to say, "I don't care whether the mystery can be historically proven, because I take it on faith in a teaching authority." For that same teaching authority admits that Scripture is normative for *its* faith. Scriptural scholars are asking us: "Are you sure that the scriptural authors even meant for you to take it *as a historical fact?*"

Why everyone gets so uptight at this question is itself a mystery. In a way, it is predictable that the One who takes on our human condition be subjected to the normal human tendency of others to make legends of him, to embroider the description of his life and works, or otherwise mix fact and fantasy about him. We may suppose that God can survive this aspect of being incarnate as he did other aspects.

But the nervousness remains. It leads one group of Christians to greatly reduce any detailed historical claims. This group argues that after all it's not this or that factual detail of Jesus' life that is important. What matters for faith, they say, is that the Son of God became human for us in Jesus; that he lived a life of holiness (consisting of faith in his Father and concern for others); that he died for his troubles; that he was vindicated by his Father, who raised him from the dead; that now risen he is an effective force in the life of others who seek holiness. Notice that nowhere in this list will you find the virginal conception, Saint Joseph's dilemmas, or the Magi, for according to this first group, other items are only of peripheral interest. They would refer us, for example, to today's epistle, where Saint Paul speaks of Jesus this way: "As to his humanity, he was born a descendent of David; as to his divine holiness, he was shown with great power to be the Son of God by being raised from death" (Romans 1:3–4). They would note there the scant detail about Jesus' life and the great stress given to his impact on others, beginning with the resurrection.

A second group would sidestep historical questions completely. For them, it is the "story" of Jesus that has impact on their lives. They would be less interested in the factual nature of Jesus' divine origin, in his actual behavior, his resurrection, or present whereabouts. The "story" of these things, however, would have great significance for us. It would enable us to organize our lives in healthy, humane ways. While we may, out of curiosity, ask whether the original storytellers took the details literally, at its core "faith" would not require such information.

We agree that this second view seems to be little more than a crowd-pleasing capitulation. It tells people what they want to hear, namely, that their fate is even more interesting than Jesus' fate. It makes stories out of people. It expects faith to feed on edifying sagas.

The first group's view, while certainly more substantial, seems very cavalier about some cherished beliefs people in the pews have. Where, then, does this leave the matter of today's gospel?

From its literary context, it is clear that the main point of Saint Matthew is not to underscore the relationship of Mary to Jesus. Still less is he taking a stand on the merits of virginity. He is trying to establish Jesus' unique relationship to the Father, and hence to underscore Jesus' unique authority. His reference to Isaiah bears this out: Jesus is Immanuel, God-with-us. But Saint Matthew also gives some deliberate play to the virgin who conceives. For this reason, Christians, officially and otherwise, have interpreted his faith as extending to the fact of Jesus' virginal birth, as well as to its significance.

Motley as the church is, it is not surprising that official and unofficial versions of faith don't always coincide. Nor do people always cling to official teaching for the best of reasons. Even when they do, it is no guarantee that they are catching thereby the intended significance of the teaching. But let us not underestimate the people in the pews—or official teachers, for that matter. They have much experience in sensing which items in a personal history are important and which are not. They also know, with Cardinal Newman, that we believe because we love. They grant that love can be blind, that it can exaggerate, but they also know it can be unerring in its instinct about facts. Perhaps we all ought to concentrate more on loving, and then our debates about history might fall into place.

Fourth Sunday of Advent—B

2 Samuel 7:1–5, 8–11, 16
Romans 16:25–27
Luke 1:26–38

Sweet Talk

"God sent the angel Gabriel to a town in Galilee named Nazareth. He had a message for a girl promised in marriage to a man named Joseph, who was a descendant of King David. The girl's name was Mary" (Luke 1:26–27).

Whether or not Mary was aware of all the implications of her motherhood, she stands first and foremost as one who waited on God with trust and love and the conviction that God could deal with her very flesh. In her there seems to be a deep realization that God deals with us by making us enter the rhythms of our own humanity more fully.

Scripture tells us elsewhere (John 1:13) that salvation comes not from the automatic processes of the flesh, nor from people's ingenuity, but from God. This could lead one to think that salvation is foreign to the flesh. But Mary's openness to God locates salvation much more squarely in the midst of our flesh. What is especially impressive about Mary is that she even put her motherhood in the service of her God.

In some ways, motherhood has a built-in potential for a contrary reaction. Motherhood is made for possessiveness, as a woman finds within the walls of her own body another person who is hers to carry and to build. In her inner space the massive nurturing process churns on as the form, cells, extremities, nerve networks, capillaries, heart, eyes, and brain of another person gel and expand. It all seems to create some special title of ownership.

But this is precisely what a mother must gradually forego. The pain of letting go is first and most forcibly exhibited in childbirth. The mother's own salvation and safety requires that the child leave her body. While the arena of nurture and care now changes, the same process of having-and-yielding-up is repeated as the child grows into adulthood. A mother cannot be content with just one part of this process. Just as she fosters what she has while she has it, so, too, she must foster the leaving and promote the freedom of her child to exist apart, with its own life and interests.

A recent television program on unwed mothers painted a different picture. The girls who were interviewed all gave the impression that, in their initial view, motherhood was a matter of having. This possessiveness proceded, no doubt, from intense personal need, loneliness and anxious clutching, or from a frail desire to show off. One could only sympathize with their disillusionment and young pain, but they provide a kind of reverse testimony to the truth of today's gospel, in which Mary's words "May it happen to me as you have said" are firmly preceded by her own conviction, "I am the Lord's servant" (Luke 1:38).

A mother like Mary cannot balance off the having against the yielding up unless she sees the having as gift in the first place. If mothers do not recognize and appreciate that they are seeded in love by others—by gods or husbands, it does not matter—they will only be able to see motherhood as a matter of having. If on the other hand they realize that the life in them is the expression of someone else's love, possessiveness will never be a problem. So, even when angels address mothers-to-be, they make sure first to reassure and compliment them that they are loved: "Peace be with you! The Lord is with you and has greatly blessed you!. . .Don't be afraid, Mary; God has been gracious to you" (Luke 1:28, 30). Mary's response is one of simplicity, of surprise at this favoring. There is no trace of gloating or of personal victory.

Mary's love mirrors the kind of love that God has for the world. That is why her actions form such a crescendo for the Advent season. In perfect, blissful, encompassing possession of the Son, the Father yields up the Son for others with awe-inspiring ease. Mary learned the lesson well.

Micah 5:1– 4
Hebrews 10:5– 10
Luke 1:39– 45

He's the Greatest

"Here I am to do your will, O God" (Hebrews 10:7).

Whoever put together the three readings for to-day came perilously close to giving us the makings of a liturgical soap opera. First, the Hometown Crowd: parti-san and proud of it, anxious for it to be known that the champion is from their bailiwick, rooting in unison for themselves. Then, God: bored, even irritated, by the sac-rifice-boys, by the endless succession of heifers, pi-geons, goats, cats, and cows, whose burnt smell is so annoying to him. Then, the Kid: a great body, deter-mined concentration, itching to be let loose. Then, the Women-Folk: intimate, caring, chatty about wombs and such.

This is all fine, as long as it doesn't distract us from the higher drama that surrounds the theme of do-ing God's will. What is this "will" through which we have been sanctified through the offering of the body of Jesus Christ once and for all? (Hebrews 10:10). On the face of it, having Jesus die in fulfillment of the Father's will sounds like the same old sacrificial butchery. Deep-seat-ed problems with the will-of-God language begin to stir in us. These problems are numerous.

First, the will-of-God language seems coercive. Our native instinct is that it is not polite to work one's will on another person. We have seen people done in by parents and other potentates who, by working their will, produce a cowed and resentful population whose humanity looks more like a gutted slum than the grand edifice originally intended. Nor is it immediately evident that such coercion becomes permissible just because one happens to be God, however many religious people line up to tell us so. A sullen mood sets in. We seem to be mainly engaged in a contest of wills. Painted in the colors of an adversary, we also feel cut off from that part of ourselves which seeks peace. It's a pain.

Second, the will-of-God language seems to lend itself to a kind of infantilism. The case is pressed that parents can legitimately work their will on a child for the good of the child. Papa spank if baby touch hot stove. Can such a comparison ever serve as a way of understanding how the will of God functions in our regard? Maybe, but only because we presuppose that God wants to treat us as children on an ongoing basis, so that we never reach an understanding of his plans and purposes. We are wedded to this picture of the 5-year-old child of the 35-year-old parent. The image of a 35-year-old son dealing with a 57-year-old father would scare our pants off; we might have to talk together with God as grownups.

Third, the will-of-God language seems needlessly murky and enigmatic. This "will" is something to be discovered and deciphered. Although there is truth to this, it can easily turn into a hide-and-seek spirituality, a frustrated quest for a peek at the Big Plan, a frantic anxiety about always doing exactly the right thing.

Does Jesus simply cut through all these conflicts? We certainly have no reason to say that he does not feel them. We would do better to suppose something like the following:

The Father looks for someone lathed mentally and physically to join him in his cause. Jesus, according to Hebrews, fits the bill instinctively. He credits his Father with sense and sensitivity. So he puts his energies into the kinds of things that excite the Father: healing, forgiving, arguing about what love really is, getting serious about it all, discovering his own worth and seeing through the dross to the worth of others. He then urges people to relate to the Father and to others this way. These are the things that get Jesus killed. He pays with his life for *them*, and not for some prearranged, edifying game plan.

Let's hear it for class.

CHRISTMAS SEASON

Isaiah 9:1– 6
Titus 2:11– 14
Luke 2:1– 14

Winter Thaw

"A child is born to us! A son is given to us" (Isaiah 9:6).

Christmas is a feast of sentiment. The midnight liturgy bears this out. Isaiah reflects palm-slapping merriment and rejoicing. Saint Paul captures the titillating, happy-humble sense we have when we are up for favorite treatment. The gospel speaks of tender solicitude, of bands of angels radiantly urging bands of shepherds that the news is all good. The liturgies at dawn and during the day continue these themes: "When the kindness and love of God our Savior was revealed, he saved us. It was not because of any good deeds that we ourselves had done, but because of his own mercy" (Titus 3:4). A festive mood excites cities and nations (Isaiah 62:11– 12, 53:7– 10). The Maiden takes it all in with expanding heart (Luke 2:19) and, all around, there is the bursting sense of new life (Luke 2:16– 17; Hebrews 1:4– 6).

All this is brought about by a Child. How foreign a child seems to our Lebanons and OPECs, to our faceless political bombings ("They never really paid attention to ME"), to our jut-jawed hedonism. Is a child the only thing left that can free up sentiments within us, that will make the world a better place? God seems to think so. "A Child is born to us." Omnipotence in low profile, and not begrudging it.

A fantasy suggests itself: I go into the boardrooms and bars, the prisons and bourgeois strongholds of Gotham. I place in the arms of every person present a fragile, cuddly baby. (Don't ask where I got the truckload of babies for this mission. You don't have to explain such things in fantasies.) Then, I just wait 'em out. How long before the barstool patriot stops hurrahing other people into war and devastation? With my baby in his arms, when will the droning executive (who happens to be advocating maximum corporate profits) begin shifting from foot to foot with an uneasy sense of his own transparent nonsense? How long will the shrill lady with the used eyes continue to lament all those comfortable demands on her to conform?

Can the presence of this helpless Child save us from the violence we do to ourselves and to one another? If not, then who is going to save the children from *our* agitated hovering? Who will protect them from being enfolded in our cheerless arms or, worse, from the menace of our suction methods?

The problem is not that we lack sentiment completely. It is rather that we sheathe ourselves only in hard, impermeable sentiments: anger, fear, revenge, indignation, and grasping bitterness. The danger is that we damn up in ourselves the wellspring of more tender sentiments, the ones of which the Christmas liturgy is unabashedly full.

There is no inevitable logic that leads us from minor compromise to mass mayhem. But we have to let ourselves feel more. In the Spirit of this Child, we have to experience other kinds of sentiments than our flinty ones. Look around. The world is full of such

Christmases: A nurse's aid laughs a patient into a little more hope. A guard writes a letter for his prisoner. A cleaning lady straightens out the boss's desk because, you know, he's worried this month. A social worker gives his lunch money to some joker of a client whose scars, after all, stand out most. A terrified teacher coaxes a horribly deformed child closer to oh what possibilities. A cop in the emergency room tells a funny story so no one else will cry. A priest apologizes for coming up empty-handed in someone's spiritual need. An old parent climbs unsteadily once more into the harness, because who else will care? A soldier runs with, yes, a child to safety.

Christmas Mass at Dawn

Isaiah 62:11–12
Titus 3:4–7
Luke 2:15–20

Treasure Room

"Mary remembered all these things and thought deeply about them" (Luke 2:19).

Shepherds have to get back to work sometime. And a baby, after all, is a baby. When it's sleeping, there's a lot of time to stare off into space and wonder. Radiant joy fills that wonder, a sense of freshness and excited hopes. But Mary also experiences the perils of wondering: You let people into your heart and, suddenly, their fragility becomes your imminent danger. They get hurt, and you wince. They shine, and you rise up in splendor; they sink, and you go down and down.

It's like slowly building a precious treasure room in your heart with the beloved details of another person, and then finding that you have a massive security problem on your hands.

Mary reminds us that it is not enough to bring God into your heart. When God comes, he never comes alone. He has strange friends, hangers-on, causes, and projects. He fidgets, for all his individual love, if we try to close them out. He seems to invite us to take them into our hearts, to enshrine them as our treasures, just as we are his.

This, after all, is what got his Son in trouble. The Baby would grow up. He would take a lot of people to heart and suffer because of his love for others. He would not treasure them in that modern, generalized way "as persons." He would take them to heart in their concise, concrete humanity: their lopsided resolve, their pettiness and isolation, the specters of guilt and violence that inhabit them, their unpredictable bodies and shrill memories, their jobs and lusts, their in-laws and thin aspirations. Sometimes, his heart would look more like an infirmary than a treasure room. We may assume that his mother taught him a thing or two about love.

Christmas is a time for treasuring. Sometimes we get it backwards. We give gifts, not always as a sign that we treasure, but as an alternative to letting people, in their concise humanity, into our hearts. The world is calling for a more intimate kind of charity. Who will take on the poor and the elderly, the prisoners and the sick, the cripples and the Scrooges as the proud adornments of their own treasure rooms?

There are, indeed, many who do precisely these things. Christmas has always seemed to be a day of their special shining. They succeed where the innkeepers of the world fail. They seem to need no return on their love. They watch and wash the shaking decay of old age. They breathe in the smells of poverty. They do not run from its menacing violence, but live in its shadow with kindness. They nurse, and fetch, and listen, and gather other people into their quieting arms. They bring funny jokes into the grim halls of hospitals, orphanages, mental clinics, prisons, flophouses, and to victims of war and broken homes. They tease out the good in people and shrug off the sullen snarls they get in return.

They seem to have caught the spirit of God's love, which is so indifferent to the quality of what it takes in: "When the kindness and love of God our Savior was revealed, he saved us. It was not because of any good deeds that we ourselves had done, but because of his own mercy" (Titus 3:4). Unlike Santa, God does not ask if we were good boys and girls this year. The real spirit of Christmas takes the risk of love, as Mary did.

Realizing this, the rest of us are humbled. We admit at last that we'd treasure more things in our hearts if we were convinced we had a heart. We doubt our capacity for sentiment and feeling. We ask: Who could make a treasure room out of our barren stables? The answer is born again today.

Holy Family

(Sunday in the Octave of Christmas)

Sirach 3:2 – 6, 12 – 14
Colossians 3:12 – 21
Luke 2:22 – 40, 41 – 52

Ups and Downs

"This child is chosen by God for the destruction and the salvation of many in Israel. He will be a sign from God which many people will speak against" (Luke 2:34).

Not only this Child, but every child presents to its parents' generation a challenge and sign. To be sure, children take in their parents' values. They learn attitudes toward country and race, money and clothes, health and leisure. They pick up mannerisms and manners. From their parents they get the feel of things such as love and prejudice, fear and ambition. They first come to know what it is like to talk freely, to be held warmly, to depend, and to trust.

But in each of these areas children soon branch out on their own. They have a way of dismissing some of the most cherished aspects of tradition. And while they sometimes do this to their own embarrassment and impoverishment, their curiosity and initiative equally often lead to healthy developments within society at large.

Take Jesus. The pious parents of Jesus, we are told, fulfill "all that was required by the law of the Lord" (Luke 2:39). An idyllic picture of family life is also hinted at: "The child grew and became strong; he was full of wisdom, and God's blessings were upon him" (2:40).

But this same Jesus ended up in the same Temple, flailing about in an angry rage. In the shadow of the Temple, he argued heatedly with leaders of his day. He broke their laws and defended his disciples for doing the same. Those dear characters Simeon and Anna—those symbols of so many energetically religious old people who frequent our churches today—would have been shocked.

It would be nice to think that Jesus' later thinking came out of his own family, but is this fair to assume? It is neither necessary nor edifying to credit Joseph and Mary with the seeds of all Jesus' thinking and feeling. Families can at best create a backdrop of seriousness, piety, and integrity against which children will have to work out their own lives in their time. Always full of surprises, children will take new directions that outstrip anything parents dream of.

What seems crucial to family life is that channels of communication be fostered and used. We are told that children have felt like strangers in their own house. Children have to have the confidence to bring their troubles and plans to their parents. Familiarity, ease, mutual access, and openness should reign in families.

Everybody, no doubt, would like to learn techniques and steps that would guarantee such familiarity. For some strange reason, family counseling is a last resort, despite the fact that there are many agencies that specialize in such support systems. Family problems are brought instead to the doorstep of religion; solutions are sought there. In many ways, families have the information they need to solve their problems of communication. They know the deadfalls, the silences, the withdrawings that prevent such communication. They know the work to be done. Very often it is conviction and motivation, strength and enthusiasm that need to be supplied. Families often think religion has something to offer. But what?

If anything can be learned from the Holy Family (and sometimes we have tried officially to get more mileage out of it than seems right), it is that nothing moves without some kind of centering on God. This centering sustains all the other rhythms of family living. Notice in today's epistle that Saint Paul's remarks on family living are prefaced by his reminder of how Christians are supposed to see themselves in relation to the Lord: "You must forgive one another just as the Lord has forgiven you. And to all these qualities add love, which binds all things together in perfect unity.... Christ's message ... must live in your hearts.... Sing psalms, hymns, and sacred songs; sing to God with thanksgiving in your hearts. Everything you do or say, then, should be done in the name of the Lord Jesus, as you give thanks through him to God the Father" (Colossians 3:13 – 17). The tenderness and sensitivity that are found in the relationship with the Lord are to carry over into family life. Parents should not victimize their children with dull, horrendous, creepy, militaristic images of God. Then perhaps they will not communicate to their children similar images of themselves.

(Octave of Christmas)

Numbers 6:22 – 27
Galatians 4:4 – 7
Luke 2:16 – 21

No Match

"When the right time finally came, God sent his own Son. He came as the son of a human mother and lived under the Jewish Law, to redeem those who were under the Law, so that we might become God's sons" (Galatians 4:4 – 5).

Today's feast is called the Solemnity of Mary, Mother of God. Before we get too solemn, however, we should recall a bit of history. *Mother of God* was a phrase that churches—and armies—went to war over.

The fighting was not so much about Mary as about her son: Was he God? What was he basically up to? What signs of godliness did he show? Relatives inevitably get dragged into these things, and not without distortion. They are either exhalted (solemnized) or downgraded. It all depends on what you think about the main party to the dispute.

An earlier, more peaceful stage of the tradition is caught in the passage above, which comes from today's epistle. Saint Paul mentions that the Son is born of a woman. His point is to express the condescension of God's Son, who takes on our simple humanity, who "levels" with us in order to show that all people, men and women, are precious to his Father. Saint Paul's point could hardly have been made if his readers failed to see that Mary was, in a way, just another woman. So it is possible to express her enormous role in our salvation and, at the same time, her utter normalcy.

But many have found this hard to do. In teaching and in pious practice, they have distanced Mary from our humanity. In fact, some seem to use Mary to distract everyone from pressing issues that arise in the church's life. They make suspicious cause of her just when the church at large is poised on the edge of other business. They seem to be waiting in the wings with new adjectives to apply to her list of accolades. The accolades aren't suspicious, but the timing is.

None of this should be surprising. Jesus himself is subjected to such solemnization by us, contrary to the obvious intent of his incarnation. We are greatly threatened by a God in our midst, rubbing shoulders with us, speaking his piece from within our ranks. If we like to keep him at a safe distance, it's consistent, at least, to do the same to her.

But in Mary's case, there is a special consideration. Is our elevating of her a sneaky way of getting "woman" closer to us and on a grander scale? Is it our aim with her to fill ourselves with a massive sense of nurture and protection? That is, do we load her up with all our expectations about being taken care of in divine matters?

We do this so often to women generally that it would not be surprising if we do it to Mary, as well. We assume that it is the role of women to be accountable for our feelings of well-being. Women, to be sure, set a great precedent for this assumption in our infancy. We know them first as nurture, warmth, and protection. We carry over a lot of this experience in our later dealings with men and women. Even in religious matters, it may be that we do not trust the Father or Son to do what the mother used to do for us. So Mary must take on that role.

In contemporary culture, women are revolting somewhat against the pressures that make them accountable for good feelings of all-around nurture and niceness. They are refusing to sway, smile, lean, smell, puff, glow, yield, exude, or otherwise sell their souls for men's benefit. They will no longer be exalted, posed, paraded, or kept in comforting readiness, if this means they are going to lose a sense of partnership in work, talent, choice, status, or reward. If all this looks somewhat belligerent to the men, then the men are going to have to examine themselves and ask: Belligerent by what standard? By making women supernurturers, have we unfairly ruled out legitimate behavior in them that only looks belligerent to us because of our prejudice?

Women do not simply want to gain recognition for their true talent and potential. They want to unload some of the responsibility for keeping the emotional levels of the world euphoric. Or, if they are going to be made so very responsible for a balanced emotional ecology, then they want a say in how to structure the world to maintain that balance.

That these movements are at work in the church, as well, is clear. The puzzled cleric who can't seem to keep the sisters in line, the layman who balks at receiving communion from a woman, the horrified bishop who hears the slogan "Ordination or bust," the chairperson who can't get the gals out for the sacred cake-bake —

all are feeling the effects of the growing consciousness on the part of women of their evolving role. Anyhow, it would all make a wild topic for a Sunday sermon.

And what if the women join forces with the mother of God? Not a bad idea. It would be impossible to caricature Mary as some steely-eyed, withholding woman, firmly bending herself and us to her son's tasks in the world. Mary will always be the poet's delight and our own consolation: "I sing of a maiden that is matchless." Mary shows us how to rejoice in God our savior. But she also shows us that rejoicing can be man-killing work.

Second Sunday After Christmas

Sirach 24:1– 2, 8– 12
Ephesians 1:3– 6, 15– 18
John 1:1– 18

Wisdom's Way

"No one has ever seen God. The only Son, who is the same as God and is at the Father's side, he has made him known" (John 1:18).

Today's first reading pictures the eternal wisdom of God as the architect of creation. It is truly a majestic wisdom, reclaiming whole continents from the waters, setting celestial backdrops of sky and stars, filling an enormous landscape with marvelous works of nature. But for all that, wisdom is a bit bored. It is weary of its distant labors in clouds and ocean depths. It longs to come down from the mountain mists. So it comes to rest on the plains of man.

Not all ancient traditions put the matter this way; in some of them wisdom descends, takes one look around, and "wisely" goes back up in haste! But Sirach describes wisdom as a sojourner. It resides in the shrines and temples, the Law and customs, of an otherwise nondescript Jewish people. Sirach's picture is certainly benign. By the time the author did his preaching in the early second century before Christ, there wasn't much left of the old glories. Even former enmities between the northern kingdom (noted for shrines) and the southern kingdom (noted for the Temple) were exhausted. So kudos for wisdom could be passed out generously to everyone. On the other hand, it was at this period of Jewish history that people discovered the link between wisdom and hope. Without the latter, the Jewish people taught us, wisdom can look pretty foolish.

This is borne out in the New Testament readings. The Spirit of wisdom is now given to a new people (Ephesians 1:17). They manifest that wisdom in the hope they have in Jesus Christ (1:18). This hope commits them to a new form of behavior. They discover the radical necessity of cultivating in themselves the Spirit of God's own Son. All their energetic striving, all their do-goodism, all their pursuit of holiness is stamped now with the attitude of Jesus, at the heart of whose activities and conflicts is his presence to and devotion to his Father (John 1:18; many translations have Jesus merely "at the Father's side," but more is implied). Christian wisdom consists in discovering the role of the Father, Son, and Spirit in one's own endeavors and in trying to place oneself with the Son.

But don't our own lives mirror, in fact, the progressive stages of wisdom that we see in today's readings?

At first we, too, tried our hand at nature. We explored it and tamed it. In our own creations we aped it, making castles like mountains, fountains like streams, clothing like nature's own colorful array. We mimicked its rythyms in our calendars and clocks. We drank in nature's rays and the fruit of its vine. We hunted its wild life and marked out fields for food.

But then something more seemed called for. So we poured our talent into human institutions. We busied ourselves with culture, law, government, and even religion. We struggled with issues of human and divine rule.

Finally, we get closer to the heart of the matter. We end up asking ourselves more simple questions: Who can you lean on in life? Who is trustworthy? Who loves you and who is worth loving? Is there light for our individual and corporate darkness? What will give some spirit to our labors and enliven our relationships?

In these questions we are gradually being drawn to the Father, in whom we, too, would do well and wisely to rest.

Isaiah 60:1 – 6
Ephesians 3:2 – 3, 5 – 6
Matthew 2:1 – 12

The Camels Are Coming

"Nations will be drawn to your light, and kings to the dawning of your new day" (Isaiah 60:3).

What does your average churchgoer remember of this Solemnity of the Epiphany from year to year? The readings make its central point obvious enough: God's salvation is intended not only for the people of Israel but for all peoples (whom the Scripture calls "the Nations" or "the Gentiles"). Today's epistle describes this intention as God's secret plan, something he was cooking up all along. And in the gospel the Magi symbolize the non-Jewish world coming to Jesus the Israelite to pay homage and to discover joy. All fine and good. But we suspect that what the man or woman in the pew remembers more distinctly are the camels.

All right, let's work with this. The camel, we are told, started out as a horse, but the committee who made it acted like any other committee: jostling, mishearing, competition, crucial documents misplaced, hidden agenda, perfectly timed trips to the bathroom, misquoting, lost threads of thought, woolgathering, flirtations, resurfacing issues that were closed, irrelevant outbursts of emotion, anxieties, pet projects, broken pencils, rereading, incipient feelings of madness—the usual stuff.

What stands out, then, are the difficulties we have in dealing with our differences. Can the Lord bring the nations together when he doesn't seem able to bring committees to effective corporate action? The talk of cosmic togetherness rings hollow when we have such trouble getting lesser acts together.

No feast of the church solves all our problems. Sometimes it even sharpens our troubled vision. But each feast gives us a handle on hope, a facet of faith, a clue as to where the way of charity lies. Epiphany, along with the whole Christmas season, shows us how one major difference at least—that between creator and creature—has been overcome. Even that difference, the Lord teaches us, should not be the basis for domination and triumphalism. It is to be *ignored* in the interests of love and peace. No wonder God is so optimistic about our resolving our other differences! If only we could get off our high horses, or high camels, or whatever.

Baptism of the Lord
(Sunday after January 6)

Isaiah 42:1–4, 6–7
Acts 10:34–38
Luke 3:15–16, 21–22

Want Ad

"You are my own dear Son. I am pleased with you"
(Luke 3:22).

Anyone familiar with the intricate ritual of the job interview knows what a sweat it can be. A resume lies there on the desk, the neat and compelling account of one's accomplishments. In flattering, if not also inventive, terms it states the year-by-year progress of one's life. Gaps naturally are covered over. Plumed and pedigreed titles adorn it; prestigious names and places abound. Competence is spelled out and qualifications urged. Still, the throat is dry and the palms moist. One tries not to look the beggar, not to show the strain, not to crumble beneath fantasies of rejection and defeat. It is indeed a baptism of fire.

We wonder what qualifications are needed to work for God. Jesus' baptism is certainly the point at which he lands a commission from his Father. He gets the job of ushering in the eschatological age, when the Father takes a final initiative to bring justice and life to all in the world. A special anointing of the Spirit endows Jesus for this task (Acts 10:38). The whole scene is set in imagery borrowed from Isaiah: the rending of the heavens and the descent of God from above in some tangible form (Isaiah 64:1). In the heavenly voice, there is also an expression of confirmation and affectionate congratulations.

Fine, but what are the qualifications? Without them the whole thing will look like another case of nepotism. To see them, however, we have to look at the earlier part of the scene, the baptism of Jesus by John. It is there that Jesus proves his mettle for the job. He does this by affirming his willingness to be identified with a struggling, sinful, cursed humanity. He determines to identify with their neediness and their hopes with the explicit awareness that their common fate is death.

There is, of course, altruism in the gesture; his respect and concern for the mangled lives of people move him. But altruism is not the present issue. The present issue concerns what he is willing to do himself now that he has entered (however unwillingly and altruistically) the human condition. Is he up to taking on the full implications of incarnation? Even a divine altruism is not spared that question once incarnation is underway.

It is easy for us to think the scene went otherwise. We are convinced that people get high level jobs because of connections, or for their readiness to use power and take every advantage. Or we see their achievement as the automatic, painless overflow of their sheer talent. We tend not to notice the personal human price they pay in terms of simple courage and dedication in the face of limitations.

When Jesus gets the job, his Father's voice is not just the announcement of what was worked out previously in a backroom conclave. His Father is reacting to an impressive qualifying gesture of his Son. And anyone interviewing for a place in the Son's operation will have the same question put to him or her: Are you willing to take on your human condition with faith and love?

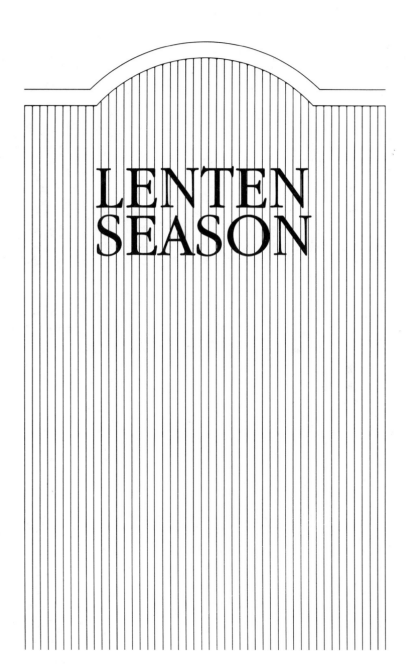

LENTEN
SEASON

Genesis 2:7 – 9; 3:1 – 7
Romans 5:12 – 19
Matthew 4:1 – 11

The Oldest Temptation

"The snake replied, . . . 'When you eat it, you will be like God and know what is good and what is bad' " (Genesis 3:4 – 5).

The argument the snake uses runs something like this: Being God basically consists in having experience of good and evil (*know,* in the above phrase, is the Hebraic expression for our "experience"). The snake represents the view that God is simultaneously the author of beauty and malice, of virtue and sick deeds, of darkness and light. Thus the snake can argue that if poor Adam and Eve get no experience of evil, how are they going to be anything but second-rate compared to God?

In today's gospel, where we find Saint Matthew's version of Jesus' temptation in the desert, Satan's approach is the same as the snake's. God is described to Jesus in an ambiguous way that would make Jesus suspicious of him. There is just that annoying hint that the God to whom Jesus is trying to be faithful is himself untrustworthy. After all, a God who can turn bread into stones might be asked why he doesn't do it more often. And a God who would send angels to save Jesus as he plunges from the Temple pinnacle seems to be the sort who indulges in such histrionics in the first place.

By the third and most blatant temptation, Jesus has worn Satan down. Satan has failed to confuse Jesus with innuendoes about God's goodness. So Satan tries a more frontal approach. He suggests that Jesus embrace evil for the sheer profit and joy of it. The confrontation with God is naked, and perhaps this was Satan's aim all along. But Jesus is, according to Saint Matthew, the new Israel. Like Israel of old, he will have none of it. With the Book of Genesis, he maintains that God's goodness is to be defended with fidelity and joy.

There is great irony in humanity's conviction that it must experience evil before it can become like God. When it gets to do the evil, it loses even the good it once had.

There's a parable in Albee's "Zoo Story" : A deranged young man lives on the same floor as a huge dog, and has to pass it frequently in the hall. He maintains good relations with it. At one point, however, he decides to poison the dog in order, as he says, to see what their continuing relationship might be after such an action. The dog survives. The young man is surprised and a bit disappointed to find that their relationship has grown somewhat cooler. He and the dog pass in the hall with only a distant nod. According to the story, the young man had to try out evil; otherwise he could not appreciate what seemed to be good.

Many people experiment with drugs, sex, and violence from this same mentality. And it is God who gets blamed when they get burned. The ridiculousness of all this dickering about God's goodness appears in today's epistle. Saint Paul is clear about who is evil and who isn't. He pictures God not as authoring evil but as allowing it to pile up in the world, only to show how his way is to acquit the guilty in his mercy. So humanity is left with the embarrassing realization that the very evil it commits in resentment of God is graciously overlooked by God!

With these readings we begin the Sundays of Lent. Traditionally, Lent is a time when we take on the evil in ourselves in a great ascetic outburst. Our customs in the matter are at once serious and simple. Cut down on the cigarettes and sweets, cork the bottle, attend Mass more frequently, dedicate greater amounts of time to our children or our work. These resolutions can be improved if we get down to basic attitudes toward God. At the same time as we deprive ourselves, we cannot be agreeing under our breath with the snake that God is in the depriving business. Nor can we pretend that God will be nice if, and only if, we become high Lenten achievers. Our Lenten disicipline is in the service of love. It is our attempt to get ourselves in better shape to meet the demands of love in us and around us. It is a time to reflect on Jesus' kind of love and to fire ourselves with enthusiasm for the needs of others. It is, after all, the lack of love that leaves the taste of ashes in our mouths.

Genesis 9:8 – 15
1 Peter 3:18 – 22
Mark 1:12 – 15

Lenten Landscape

"Wild animals were there also, but angels came and helped him" (Mark 1:13).

Of the many devils that beset us as we head off on another Lent, there is none so troublesome as the one that keeps repeating to us with a knowing and condescending smugness: "Why bother? Others aren't really interested in improving themselves. So why should you be the only one who is?" This appeal capitalizes on our cynicism and self-pity. Clearly it implies a low view of the efforts of others. It paints us, like Jesus, as surrounded by wild beasts. The jungle is out there. We know we can get bitten, stung, devoured, infected, and picked apart. Nor do we notice, as Jesus did, an angel waiting on us. So, we think, maybe the devil has a point. Why offer the beasts an improved version of ourselves? Better they choke on what they get.

Somehow we have to confront this temptation to make our own conversion wait upon the conversion of others. We have to get past this view of our fellowmen as beasts. Why, real beasts seem to come off much better. Today's first reading even has God making a covenant with the beasts that accompany Noah on the ark: "I am now making my covenant with you and with your descendants, and with all living beings—all birds and all animals—everything that came out of the boat with you" (Genesis 9:9–10). Although many have given up on Noah's descendants, they continue to think kindly of real beasts. *Beast* is a dirty word only when applied to people. What can we do, then, to improve this image of others as obstacles to our own effort at conversion?

In his *Spiritual Exercises,* Ignatius of Loyola offers a fascinating demonstration of how personal conversion gradually changes the landscape around us. He, too, begins with the image of beasts. Early in the book, he bids us consider ourselves surrounded by wild animals: "The mental image will consist of imagining. . .my entire being in this vale of tears as an exile among brute beasts." His point, however, is not literally to characterize others that way. It is to get inside our feelings toward others. Then, in the light of a subsequent review of our own case, we gradually discover how unfair we are being to others.

The personal review of our case includes looking at our own sins. We parade them before us. We watch with embarrassment and anxiety from the reviewing stand. We discover that beastliness is not simply or solely a quality in others. There is a lot of the hawk and the snake, the hornet and the bull, the porcupine and the cold fish in us.

On the other hand, our sins do not seem to defeat us as they march by. Some wave at us, some wink; some blow noisemakers at us and make faces. We get a few ho-hos, and some glide by us with quickened pace and averted eyes. Some are brawny and sullen; they stare us down, but they keep moving nonetheless. What we mostly notice, to our great surprise, is that we are still on our feet. No one has chomped us or bitten us. Especially not God. The beasts turn out looking suspiciously like Bert Lahr as the Cowardly Lion.

This realization is meant to lead us to a different view of things from the one we started out with, in which we were surrounded by brute beasts. As though an apology were due real beasts for his original remarks, Ignatius now bids us to be "struck with amazement and filled with a growing emotion how creatures have suffered me to live and have sustained me in life. . .how birds, fishes and animals have all served my needs."

People, too, begin to come into more benevolent focus as the individual gives over his or her prejudice and disordered judgment. People are now viewed with greater sympathy: "I will see all the different people on the face of the earth, so varied in dress and behavior. Some are white and others black; some at peace and others at war; some weeping and others laughing; some well and others sick; some being born and others dying." It is as though personal conversion has induced a vast and sharp sense of the struggles and mystery of others. They are no longer beasts.

More than this, Ignatius invites the individual "to consider how God dwells in his creatures: in the elements. . .in the plants. . .in the animals. . .in men." He puts the issue squarely to us whether God is present or absent, friend or beast. It is our ambivalence over this point, he thinks, that is the clue to every other judgment we make or every other action we take in life. For Ignatius, God is not simply friend but someone who works at it. We are told "to consider how God works and labors for me in all created things on the face of the earth, that is, he conducts himself as one who labors." It is easy to grow from here into the sense that angels are waiting on us, since practically everything else we can think of is being done for us as well.

All this starts, however, when people begin to exercise themselves about their own spiritual condition. Even membership in the Christian community is no guarantee of much of anything without this personal exercise of responsibility. The baptism whereby we enter the community of faith is no magic. As today's epistle says, "It is not the washing off of bodily dirt" (1 Peter 3:21). It introduces us to a long process of dealing with ourselves, with our personal relationship with God in Jesus. Lent is a time for accelerating this process. May the beasts be kind to us all.

First Sunday of Lent—C

Deuteronomy 26:4–10
Romans 10:8–13
Luke 4:1–13

When the Spirit Hits You

"If you are God's Son, order this stone to turn into bread" (Luke 4:3).

Some people fast in order to make the world go away, but they are fooled. The experience of privation brings on thoughts about what to do next. In this respect fasting makes us like infants who, pausing at the breast, take one look around at the big wide world and begin to wonder. When we're deprived of basic consolations, we ask: What will happen next? When we realize our basic dependencies, it's natural to be nervous about who will nurture us now. Fasting doesn't make us better so much as it clears the air for real issues like these to be raised. It promises divine visitations, but we usually end up on a guided tour of all the psychological trouble spots in the kingdom of God.

Jesus gets a large dose of reality after his long fast. The common denominator of his temptations is the teasing prospect of shortcutting reality by some razzle-dazzle solution. Behind the desire for such shortcuts is, presumably, an annoyance at having to do it the normal, human way. The Father is expected to collude in this magic, at the risk of losing Jesus' cooperation. Each of Jesus' temptations raises questions about whether a kingdom of God built on faith is worth it. In Luke's theology, these temptations center on how Jesus will cope with his own messianic role within the kingdom. But it is understood that the issues raised for Jesus are raised in a way for every believer.

The first temptation concerns *bread.* As in modern slang, *bread* means "material provisions." The gospel is not referring to the sicker excesses of contemporary consumerism: ermine paw-warmers for your Poopsie, musical toasters, obscenely priced jewelry—these have to do more with the guilty game the rich play to see how far they can push the poor and get away with it. Rather, *bread* refers to laying in even normal provisions. The issue is whether they are layed in before or after the matter of God is brought up. Are they in fact serving as a cosy nest egg in case speculation in God's kingdom doesn't work out?

In this connection, Polanski's film *Rosemary's Baby* held a powerful lesson. The young couple in it was pictured having just the right things: address, wallpaper, dress, chinaware, magazines, furniture, and so forth. All the while, the camera seemed to comment: "This kind of thing could only happen to people living at this superficial level."

Jesus was tempted to base his messianic appeal to others on the material well-being he could provide them. The bread/stones theme occurs elsewhere (Matthew 7:9), and there Jesus' point is that our concern for bread should not make us cautious and untrusting about God's competence. We cannot shout helpful instructions to God, such as: "Go easy there. Watch this obstacle coming up on the right. Can you navigate that turn?"

For himself, Jesus resolves to be bread rather than to base his platform on it. That is, he chooses to nourish people with his own person, his thoughts, his concerns, his fidelity and challenge. He will not waltz them with tales of shortcuts to glory.

To take this position, Jesus first has to trust his Father. The second and third temptations are further attacks on this relationship of trust that Jesus has in the Father. The second temptation (Luke 4:5–8) runs, "Why not admit that sin has more effective power in the end than love?"

In the third temptation (Luke 4:9–12), Jesus is invited to find out in effect whether the Father himself might be killer rather than savior. Jesus' trip to Jerusalem would be suicidal enough, even without Satan's proposed swan dive from the Temple pinnacle, because preaching a universal kingdom in that parochial hotbed would hardly win him friends. Will his Father back Jesus' unpopular teaching when the going gets rough?—a question that pursues Jesus to the end (Luke 4:13).

An unsubstantial, incompetent, and possibly malevolent Father? These are the issues raised when Jesus is driven by the Spirit into his personal desert. How easy was it for Jesus to turn aside these temptations? Did trust in the Father come automatically to him? Probably not. That's why he could be tempted in the first place.

Second Sunday of Lent—A

Genesis 12:1–4
2 Timothy 1:8–10
Matthew 17:1–9

Me, Myself, and I

"Jesus took with him Peter and the brothers James and John and led them up a high mountain. . . . As they looked on, a change came over Jesus: his face was shining like the sun and his clothes were dazzling white" *(Matthew 17:1–2).*

How conscious was Jesus of his divinity? This is a gigantic question. It requires more extensive treatment than it ever could get here. Even so, it is difficult to speak of the subject of today's gospel, the transfiguration, without saying something about Jesus' awareness of himself. Many Christians will tell you that in the transfiguration Jesus was carefully and deliberately pulling back the veil that covered his divinity, clueing his disciples in ever so slightly to what he was so constantly and fully conscious of, his own identity as eternal Word of the Father.

Why do people insist on such awareness in Jesus? They are not always motivated by divine or ecclesial revelations in the matter. Some simply wish for a Jesus who serenely knows his way through the human maze. They hope *somebody* does.

Others feel that the Scriptures direct them to think that way. But they are unfamiliar with a fairly basic principle of reading the Scriptures: Much gets said about the historical Jesus by his evangelists only after his resurrection and only after they had come to certain realizations about him which, while factually true, may not have been clear to anybody, including Jesus, at the time the events occurred. If we take the Scriptures as a blow-by-blow account of events in the life of Jesus, then Jesus is not only divine, he is also vividly conscious of the fact. But this latter conclusion is one we cannot draw, given the way Scriptures were written. While Jesus may indeed have been conscious of his divinity, the scriptural accounts cannot establish that fact of themselves.

What would probably help us all is to imagine what kind of consciousness someone might have who is fully human and at the same time whose identity is that of God's own Word. We can only suggest a comparison. Without being overly cute or profound about it, we can ask ourselves whether, even in our own case, we know the ultimate "I" of who we are. In what way do we know our own identity?

Actions, creativity, longings, sins—all tumble out of me marked as *mine*. But they are not marked as *me*. My human conviction is that I am more than I did or said or failed or strove for. There is some ultimate source or center in me that is my uniqueness. When I ask myself, "Who am I?" the source is there in knowing silence. Its vivid proximity reminds me that, yes, there is such a thing as my responsibility. Yet its distant stillness makes me hesitant to blame or praise myself too much. Sickness and health often hang on whether I see myself as radically cursed or blessed. Nonetheless, I am always more distant from myself than I thought, like a traveler coming closer to a mountain that only seems to recede as its real dimensions become sharper. When and to the degree that I can say "I," it is not with a sense of pride or vanity. "I" am discovered, like a landfall or a clear, spreading vista. I am suddenly called by a strange name, and all my old cronies sit up and allow that they knew me by this name long before I heard it. Yet what others tell me of myself doesn't always seem to fit. A poem of the theologian Dietrich Bonhoeffer puts it well:

> Who am I? This or the other?
> Am I one person today and tomorrrow another?
> Am I both at once? A hypocrite before others,
> And before myself a contemptibly woebegone
>   weakling?
> Or is something within me still like a beaten
>   army,
> Fleeing in disorder from victory already
>   achieved?

Our struggles to be conscious of ourselves are paralleled in our attempts to know who others are. When we try to reach them—spouses, friends, whatever, it's a long journey, indeed, full of sudden places of scarred rock and shining mirage, dead ends and turnings. It gets elusive.

The transfiguration is a matter of getting closer to who we are. It is a time for entering into our actions more fully with our uniqueness. It is a moment for discovering and revealing the mystery of ourselves in a way that suspends interest in those very actions. We know our name best when we are loved, and it is being loved that transfigures us most.

We have seen tiny transfigurations, awkward ones, all around us. A teenager breaks free from family stereotypes of him and everyone is taken aback. A man who used to come to heel easily suddenly says, "No more." A woman's conscience cracks the phalanx of dos and don'ts that were expected of her. A bum picks himself up and throws his hopeless feelings back at others where they belong. A shy person comes to life when someone smiles warmly at her. In each case an individual starts to take form, a name begins.

Was what Jesus saw on the high mountain something like that? Did he find that all his doing and planning were suddenly referred back to a source in himself that scared him, tore him from the earth where he was so rooted? Was there widening surprise, an uncomfortable hint of. . . what? Was there the beginning of a word that could not be uttered? If the thought is frightening for us, imagine what it was for him.

Genesis 22:1– 2, 9, 10– 13, 15– 18
Romans 8:31– 34
Mark 9:2– 10

Isaac's Dilemma

"When they came to the place which God had told them about, Abraham built an altar and arranged the wood on it. He tied up his son and placed him on the altar. . . . Then he picked up the knife to kill him" (Genesis 22:9).

There is a sick strain in many of us that pleads the reasonableness of killing off what is beautiful in us or in others—lest we offend. But who is this self-destructiveness supposed to placate? Who is being offended? Some have traced this attitude in us to our fear of the gods' jealousy.

Others interpret it in more Freudian terms. From the first, this theory goes, the child is a rival to one or both of its parents and thus learns quickly to keep a low profile. It feels guilty about anything in itself that might fan the rivalry, so it learns to view the destruction of what is alluring in itself as a normal requirement for survival.

Notice that neither of these explanations has us giving over what is dear to us for higher, more noble purposes. They depict, rather, cautious and cringing reactions to life and to its beauty. The season of Lent is not intended to reinforce such negative attitudes. But it takes quite an effort not to get sucked into them.

Stories like the one in today's first reading don't help in this matter. Its God can only look like an arbitrary madman. His testing of Abraham doesn't even seem to be motivated by jealousy. It seems to resemble the surreptitious sadism that goes into college hazing ceremonies. Abraham is not much better. He seems to act on the theory that at any given moment everything hinges on whether his own loins are teeming with potential descendants. This was great stuff back in the days when we brought to our reading of Bible history the same critical disinterest that we brought to comic books. After all, Daddy Warbucks was in tighter corners than Abraham. But things look different with our grown-up heads on. We are not blind to the reasons for pairing the Abraham story with today's other liturgical readings (Abraham willing to give up his son; the Father willing to spare his Son; son beloved in both cases). But there is no reason to transport the limitations of the Old Testament scene and apply it to Jesus.

The Old Testament God is basically one who runs experiments, who "plans" things for our edification. But we cannot have the Father "planning" Jesus' death in any sense. We cannot even have him "allowing" that death in a roundabout way that sneakily comes back to the same sort of "planning" after all. Still more insensitive is the view that because God plans the rescue, he can also plan the death. You wonder how people can endure hearing it said in *any* sense that God "plans" their own death!

If the Father plans anything, it is that the Son share in solidarity our human condition. But this means that the Son takes on the mystery of human freedom, or lack of it. It means that in acting, interacting, and being acted upon by others, the Son is surrounded by risk, co-incidence, fate, windfall, surprise, accident, chance, chemistry, and chaos. These things are intrinsic to our human lives. Jesus gets caught like the rest of us in the middle of crisscrossing human freedoms. He did not die, we must keep repeating to ourselves. He was killed, put to death, done in. His death was not something to be embraced with some subtle joy. To be unsheathed of our body in one tearing, terrifying wrench is an awful thing, no matter who it happens to, no matter what sentiments accompany the event. His death, like ours, remains the stinking, grief-ridden, crushing thing that all death is. Let's not try to dignify it by having the Father plan it.

Perhaps the Father's role is better captured by looking at all those real-life parents who send a son or daughter forth into the big bad world. They flinch at the vulnerability; they scan the horizon anxiously; they bravely choke back the urge to interfere. They pray, too, and stand ready to support. But they respect the mystery of their children's lives and they never take responsibility for everything their children might experience by way of pain and suffering in this world. You would never say, for that reason, that they "plan" the pain and suffering. Like Jesus' Father, their stance is one of solidarity. The spiritual gumption they need is to let their children enter the human condition.

Some readers might tire of these remarks, recognizing that the considerable iceberg of predestination, providence, and so forth, lies beneath the mere tip we are discussing here. Fair enough. Only consider Isaac's dilemma.

Genesis 15:5 – 12, 17 – 18
Philippians 3:17 — 4:1
Luke 9:28 – 36

The Best of Both Worlds

"This is my Son, whom I have chosen — listen to him!"
(Luke 9:35).

What a sight. Abraham hunched over the carcasses of his animals, shooing scavengers away from his sacrifice — all for one purpose: to know whether Yahweh delivers on his promises (Genesis 15:8 – 12). It is an age-old pursuit. Today, too, Christians (not to mention others) sit staring at their sacrifices to see if they can catch a spark of divine corroboration in them. A housewife regularly goes without a hairdo to provide for her family. A graduate student does the bus-subway-bus-walk routine to be able to get a better education. A cop walks away from a cushy compromise and gets a sneer for his troubles. A husband turns down a sure-fire step to the corporate top so he can give his children more time. Are their sacrifices worth it? The gods are not always clear with their answers.

Sometimes a spirit of sacrifice makes us feel like foreigners and aliens in a worldly environment. Saint Paul, for all his political realism, admits: "We. . .are citizens of heaven." (Philippians 3:20). Things were bad enough when Catholics were accused of holding dual citizenship here on earth, when they were charged with allegiance to foreign lands. It gets worse when they are accused of having no real investment here on earth because of their celestial citizenship.

Today's gospel—that of the transfiguration— surely says something about this problem of being between two worlds. The transfiguration has been called a lot of things by scholars: a misplaced resurrection story, an alternate version of Jesus' baptism, a pious legend which expresses that believers gradually came to see Jesus as the fulfillment of Old Testament prophecies. A strong case can be made, too, that its main affirmation is the Lordship of Jesus all through his earthly life.

But the real issue is just how much Jesus capitalized on the fact of his Lordship during that earthly life. If that Lordship was constantly and consciously lurking beneath a facade of his humanity, then it would indeed be difficult to find in him someone who could identify with our struggles and sacrifices. It would make his life on earth more of a charade.

One commentator meets this problem head-on. He considers the transfiguration, too, a crisis point in Jesus' life. The synoptic writers locate the event shortly after Jesus' first prediction of the passion. In Luke's narrative, there are indications that the passion is still on Jesus' mind. Moses and Elijah, for example, speak with him about the "passage" (*exodus*—that is, death) which he was to fulfill in Jerusalem. Moreover, this is a route that Jesus feels he must go alone. So he rejects Peter's suggestion that they all settle down in glory on the mountain. For all the glory, there are a lot of reminders of the sacrifices ahead.

But if Jesus doesn't get an untarnished vision of glory, neither do we get an unrelieved experience of sacrifice. There are those moments when we, too, make peace with the lawgiver and prophet within us. There are times when the argument stops and the briefs are set aside. There are situations when fervent commentary or fiery exhortation are no longer called for. There are oases where we glimpse the glory in the sacrifice. Tiny transfigurations, you say.

Well, Jesus became the best of our world by accepting his glory in small doses. For the rest, he had to live in the faith that sacrifice and love would triumph.

Third Sunday of Lent—A

Exodus 17:3–7
Romans 5:1–2, 5–8
John 4:5–42

Downpour

"Jesus, tired out from the trip, sat down by the well"
(John 4:6)

What's in a symbol? Some claim that symbols such as water, wind, fire, mountain, earth, and rock automatically touch nerves deep in our humanity. They stir us to feeling and thought; they remind us of things undone, of needs and possibilities. They express our personal histories in enigmatic ciphers. If you stare into fire, if you let the waters wash over you, if you run with the wind or sense the massive density of rock, you supposedly will experience levels of your psyche that are otherwise seldom reached. You will discover the rhythms of life within you and be gripped by them.

Moreover, symbols are said to contain uncertain and shifting meanings. They make an ambiguous and conflicting reference to reality. Water, for example, conjures up a sense of refreshment, of buoyant newness. But in the water there are creepy crawling things, serpents and suffocation, decomposing processes. Was that a refreshing tingle as you swam or was it. . .Jaws? Wind is soothing; it is as brisk as a late autumn hike. But it also barrels in at lethal speeds, churning up concrete, iron, and flesh in its way.

But others argue that symbols must be deciphered, that they are not all that spontaneous and full of natural significance. They mean different things to different people. You learn what they are saying only by asking the person using them what he or she specifically intends to say by them. When contemporary advertising heard the news that symbols were ambiguous, it rushed off to sell cigarettes, insurance, beer, and hair spray by means of symbols. Harnessing the world's great symbols this way to such prosaic commodities takes a special talent for aesthetic pandering. But it proves the point: symbols, even religious symbols, need to be read in the context of the specific traditions in which they appear.

The symbol of water runs like a rivulet through today's readings. The first reading has Moses, at the Lord's behest and to save his own hide, striking the rock with his staff: "The water will come out of it for the people to drink" (Exodus 17:6). (The rock and the staff also went on to future fame as symbols, but we can't go into that here.) Saint Paul describes the realization of God's love for us as a flood of refreshing water. The gospel absolutely revels in the image of water. A well is plunked down center stage (with a moutain and spreading fields of earth for a backdrop). The dialogue swirls in the midst of this imagery: "The water that I will give him will become in him a spring which will provide him with life-giving water and give him eternal life" (John 4:14). Jesus' personal counseling of the Samaritan woman (did she *look* as though she had had five husbands?), his playful fencing with her over the relative theological merits of the Jewish and Samaritan persuasions—these never get too far away from the central image of living water.

Indeed, some commentators take the whole incident as more representative of a late first-century baptismal homily than as an actual event in the life of Jesus. Yet there is no reason to exclude this kind of feel for symbol from the fertile imagination of the preacher, Jesus. And today's gospel is full of accurate information about Samaria, its locale, its customs, its religious bias. So the whole incident might well be more historical than some would admit.

More important, however, is to catch the special nuances that are given the symbol of water in this reading. For only from these will we learn the meanings Christians attach to water, however others might understand that symbol.

In the gospel Jesus calls us to surmount the usual nitpicking religious debates. He reveals the irrelevance of our personal past to our present potential for being loved by the Father. He promises us a Spirit who will convince us that we are personally valued and loved by the Father. Notice how all these meanings serve to pin down the sense of the Christian symbol of water: They state that we are plunged into a relationship with God. They promise a certain amount of floundering in dealing with others in our community. They call for creativity in us to flood the world with a new vision.

The woman went back from the well to town with the news of her meeting with Jesus: "He knew my whole life story and was still nice to me." She probably took special delight in telling all her old husbands about it.

Third Sunday of Lent — B

Exodus 20:1 – 17
1 Corinthians 1:22 – 25
John 2:13 – 25

Dog Days

"Jews want miracles for proof, and Greeks look for wisdom. As for us, we proclaim the crucified Christ, a message that is offensive to the Jews and nonsense to the Gentiles; but for those whom God has called, both Jews and Gentiles, this message is Christ, who is the power of God and the wisdom of God" (1 Corinthians 1:22 – 24).

How many times has this conversation been repeated: "That's a very cynical remark," says the first person. "No," says the other person, "I'm not being cynical; I'm just being realistic." The line between cynicism and realism is thin, almost imperceptible. It depends, doesn't it, on what reality really is. In any situation, the realist tries at least to assess the degree to which faith, hope, and love are present. The cynic, if he or she doesn't altogether deny the existence of such qualities, says that most likely they are not around in any abundance.

What are we to make, then, of Jesus in today's gospel? "While Jesus was in Jerusalem during the Passover Festival, many believed in him, as they saw the miracles he performed. But Jesus did not trust himself to them, because he knew them all. There was no need for anyone to tell him about them, because he himself knew what was in their hearts" (John 2:23 – 25). The statement seems to totter along the thin line between cynicism and realism. It brings us up short, because it makes Jesus sharp-eyed and slightly sour, while it leaves us as the naive ones. Perhaps we thought the opposite was true.

What would happen if we all went around with the same attitude toward human nature that is expressed above? It would be terrible. Why, students would not be believed when they complained of excessive homework. Husbands would not be able to convince their wives how exhausting the executive luncheon was. Politicians would be laughed at when they said how much they respected the voters. The media would not be able to claim impartiality or artistic integrity. The man-on-the-street would be told that his opinion is important only to the extent that it is informed. Religious leaders would not be able to invoke mystical obedience for run-of-the-mill decisions concerning the day-to-day operations of their organizations. The views of people on wage and price control would be measured against their willingness to disclose their actual incomes. Pro- and anti- abortionists would discuss their favorite topic only in conjunction with a discussion about having sexual relations in the first place. Why, a dark view of human nature could be downright disruptive!

In today's first reading, the Ten Commandments seem to take direct aim at such overt kinds of human sham and fakery. We are told not to be ungrateful, not to curse the gift of life we have received. We are warned against grinding on greedily and restlessly, with no thought of God. We are not to indulge in blood lusts or to fool around with someone's wife. We are not to be sneak-thieves or malicious snipers. We should not exhaust ourselves with envious thoughts of what might have been.

But the case in the gospel is different. There, it is almost as if Jesus' idealism gets him in all the trouble. When he kicks up a scene in the Temple precincts, it is because he has expected too much. Did he really think that people could carve a sanctuary out of life for something so amorphous as prayer? Did he really believe the hucksters would stay away from the guaranteed market that pilgrims provide? No wonder he blows up.

We have to go back to the point made earlier about how things like cynicism, idealism, and realism are always being measured against some invisible and unspoken standard of reality. Perhaps the fact is that, given his standard, Jesus is engaged in some fiercer kind of realism than the one we are ready for. Saint Paul has a stunning expression that gets us closer to the kind of realism for which Jesus stood: "For what seems to be God's foolishness is wiser than human wisdom, and what seems to be God's weakness is stronger than human strength" (1 Corinthians 1:25). He is saying that the idealism of Jesus is the smart—real—way to be. He is saying that if Jesus' weak attempts to better things look like a gigantic flop, they are nevertheless endowed with an indomitable strength.

This realism of Jesus stems from his having made a firm, personal place for the Father in his own life. That is his standard of realism. His brashness is based on the trust that this relationship gives him: "Tear down this Temple, and in three days I will build it again" (John 2:19). The supreme realist is, for Jesus, the one who tries to keep God real in his or her life. His apparent cynicism, on the other hand, turns out to be a sympathetic reading of human hearts. For he is merely saying that God is better company than a lot of people you'd meet.

Third Sunday of Lent—C

Exodus 3:1–8, 13–15
1 Corinthians 10:1–6, 10–12
Luke 13:1–9

A Good Word for God

"At that time some people were there who told Jesus about the Galileans whom Pilate had killed while they were offering sacrifices to God" (Luke 13:1).

Does God show what he thinks of people by having them executed? Does he express an opinion about them by having them die accidentally? On the face of it, such questions are grotesque. It is terribly insulting to

God even to ask them. But today's gospel recounts an incident in which Jesus was asked just these kinds of questions.

Put the same questions in modern garb and see how vicious they can be: Were those men executed recently at _____ (fill in your latest political execution) proved to be sinners because they were put to death? Were those people who died recently in _____ (fill in your latest tragic accident) proved to be sinners because they died? Who could ask such questions? How do people get that way?

In Jesus' case, there seems to have been personal hostility behind the questions: "Maybe Pilate would add one more Galilean to those whose blood he had already spilled. Maybe a tower would fall on Jesus, too, and everybody's problem would be solved." But even granting this subtle hostility, and granting all the learned commentaries which point out that some of Jesus' contemporaries saw innocent suffering as a punishment for sin, it still doesn't explain how people can so blithely ignore the terrible picture of God implied in their questions.

A frightening conclusion might be that this *is* the picture of God people generally have. Some, to be sure, might have such an opinion, but more likely a certain amount of projection is going on. That is, people are giving away how they would act if they were God!

Another explanation is that even well-intentioned people use this rather sick picture of God to coax a little better performance from one another. In today's epistle, Saint Paul might be accused of this very kind of exaggeration: "We must not complain, as some of them did—and they were destroyed by the Angel of Death. All

these things happened to them as examples for others"
(1 Corinthians 10:10–11).

It seems that we live with many presuppositions
about God that need regular weeding out. We all have
met people whose god is pictured in ways that make our
hair stand on end, or whose god seems so petty and bizarre that no one would reasonably want to be bothered
with religion.

We all have our pet peeves in this matter: A god
who whispers in ears. A god of special confidences and
secret winks. A competitive god whose pastime is to take
on all comers at spiritual arm-wrestling. A god whose
chief concern is picking spiritual lint off people, telling
them, like your least favorite aunt, "Don't cross your
legs. Sit up there. Don't be gawking out the window.
Where's your wristwatch? Who was that you were just
talking to?" A god, finally, who stares into your eyes a lot.

Whatever. It is certainly the work of more than
one Lent to explore the many faces of God. Today's readings, however, bring out one face of God that is difficult
to keep in focus. For we find there God's interest in social justice and in action. "I have seen how cruelly my
people are being treated in Egypt; I have heard them cry
out to be rescued from their slave drivers. I know all
about their sufferings" (Exodus 3:7). "Look, for three
years I have been coming here looking for figs on this fig
tree, and I haven't found any. Cut it down! Why should it
go on using up the soil?" (Luke 13:7).

This face of God is frightening. First, it calls up
the image of all those flushed and sinewy prophets who
have flayed us with our social responsibilities: world
hunger, slums, housing, blacks, women, industry, chil-

dren, media, on and on. Second, it implies that we can do something about it. So we fear the annoyance and impatience we might find when we look squarely at our God.

But let's be honest. It is not the face of God that wears the violence. It is the face of humankind. We know that there will be other faces set against us, should we get involved: hard ones, dead-set on pure greed and profit; bigoted ones; pampered ones that couldn't care less; defeated ones, unable to cooperate in their own liberation; conveniently confused ones; sharp-eyed and wincing ones. Then, too, there is the face in the mirror.

When God calls to action, however, he is not frenzied. He is compassionate and kind. Would there be more social action if we realized this?

Fourth Sunday of Lent—A

1 Samuel 1:6– 7, 10– 13
Ephesians 5:8– 14
John 9:1 – 41

Born That Way

"One thing I do know: I was blind and now I see. . . . I have already told you, and you would not listen. Why do you want to hear it again? Maybe you, too, would like to be his disciples?" (John 9:25, 27).

Today's gospel recounts the story of the man born blind. It is a literate and endearing account in which the little guy takes on the big shots and makes them very uncomfortable, indeed. We are in a time of conflict between Jesus and his enemies. But try as they may, they cannot get at Jesus through the blind man he cured, because the man won't budge. He even seems to be having a good time bearding them, like the old-time comedian Lou Costello at those rare times when he had an edge on someone else.

The gospel also plays on the man's blindness to make the point that it is the enemies of Jesus who are spiritually blind—those who, like Jesus, subordinate law to love have really seen the light. The use of the blind-seeing imagery is somewhat obvious. We would prefer to credit the evangelist rather than Jesus with its symbolic overkill. To the degree that Jesus' enemies were sincere, they could use the same imagery against him: He claims to see, but he doesn't, and so on.

Some commentators on this gospel think that the passage, with its heavy reference to seeing-blindness, reflects a highly developed, late first-century liturgical practice of baptism. By that time baptism had come more and more to be viewed as a spiritual illumination, a point of discernment of life's real values. Today's epistle makes a similar reference to a baptismal illumination: "Wake up, sleeper, and rise from death, and Christ will shine on you" (Ephesians 5:14).

If this baptismal reference of today's gospel is correct, there is one other detail in the story that deserves special mention. It is the word *born*. Some biblical commentators see behind that word the conviction of early

Christians that baptism gets at the *root* problems of life, the situations that seem to afflict humanity from its *origins*. Like the man "born" blind, humanity is weighed down from time immemorial by the regularity of ignorance, the relentlessness of greed. It is entangled with hopelessness and pathos. Self-centered and indulgent, it seldom lets up its metaphysical grousing. It is haunted by miasmic memories of ancestral evils, real or imagined. It spews up generation after generation of bigot, bully, huckster, village atheist, sloth, and sulker. In a simpler age, this morose situation was called original sin.

In universities and barrooms, Christians have debated for centuries how deep the rot runs. Opinion hovers between a kind of optimistic cynicism and darker views cast up, for example, by some Reformation writers.

This might all sound pretty grim. And it might seem a lot to read into the statement in the gospel that the blind man was "born" that way. But the point is that Christians think their baptism does something about the direst and most radical conditions of humankind. They take fair measure of the odds against them and see Jesus as candidly facing *those* odds. They believe he takes on such fundamental forces and overcomes them.

The same Spirit of the Lord that rushed upon David in today's first reading and made him the unlikely hero of his people is the Spirit Christians expect at baptism. It is the kind of Spirit that allows a person to attack Goliaths with a slingshot. It allows them to twit the entrenched and the satisfied, as the blind man does in the gospel. Baptismal faith lends enthusiasm.

Goliath, watch your marbles.

2 Chronicles 36:14– 17, 19– 23
Ephesians 2:4– 10
John 3:14– 21

Double Exposure

"Anyone who does evil things hates the light and will not come to the light, because he does not want his evil deeds to be shown up" (John 3:20).

Normally, when we think of having our wicked deeds exposed, we think of other people finally catching on to us. We envision a moment when fingers wag at us, when eyebrows arch, half in discovery, half in glee, as others spot our hand in the great cookie jar of the world. We feel the hot, sweaty blotch on our cheek that marks the spot of our compromise and of our loss of integrity in others' eyes.

Not that others are being judgmental toward us. Any surprise or recognition they may register, any identification they may too enthusiastically make is due less to their being judgmental than it is to our own abortive attempts to be secretive and conspiratorial about our behavior in the first place. Having our sins exposed simply means that the cover-up has failed.

Today's gospel gives a peculiar twist to this scenario of exposure. For in it, a cover-up is carried on not so much to prevent others from knowing the truth, but so that we ourselves may not have to admit the truth about ourselves. Saint John makes our personal conscience the arena in which the big lie and the straight story do battle.

He says that people know all about the truth of Jesus but they cover it up. (Actually, Saint John is talking about nonbelievers. The speech of Jesus to Nicodemus in this section of the gospel probably reflects a baptismal catechesis from the late first century. At that time, a fairly bellicose attitude toward nonbelievers characterized Christian literature. But we have learned enough since then about the nonbelief hovering in the midst of belief to legitimately apply Saint John's insights to ourselves!) They know what Jesus is all about. They know he is light. He is the kind of light that invades Rembrandt's paintings; it serves to heighten the sense of pain, of nervous self-searching, of ill fitting and cumbersome presence to one's surroundings that Rembrandt conveys in his self-portraits. Jesus is the kind of wincing glare that erupts at the end of the late-night cabarets, dispelling all illusion.

Saint John's point is that we know very well those dark, shifting forms that live in us; our lust for money and power; our readiness to use people; the bitter, vengeful memories that we keep chained up in us like so many half-starved and alert watchdogs; our knowing indifference to the poor and hungry of this world; our double standards and cultivated misuse of reason; our envy of other people's talent. We feel that these things had best be kept obscure in us, so we do not even let ourselves see them with any clarity.

Saint John sums up the matter this way: "This is how the judgment works: the light has come into the world, but people love the darkness rather than the light, because their deeds are evil" (John 3:19). Though he seems to revel just a bit too much in this observation, there is no question of John running us down. He does not make Jesus look good by making us look bad. Any new order of things begins with what we really are — slightly wicked and loath to admit it. John is convinced that the world, for all its moral squalor, is the object of God's love: "For God loved the world so much that he gave his only Son, so that everyone who believes in him may not die but have eternal life" (John 3:16). God shines his light on us only in order to be better able to get down to the work of creating a new order of things. Like anyone else, God needs light to work by.

Fourth Sunday of Lent—C

Joshua 5:9,10–12
2 Corinthians 5:17–21
Luke 15:1–3, 11–32

The Prodigal Father

"When anyone is joined to Christ, he is a new being. . . . Our message is that God was making all mankind his friends through Christ. God did not keep an account of their sins, and he has given us the message which tells how he makes them his friends" (2 Corinthians 5:17, 19).

In our normal usage, *reconciliation* does not simply mean that the fighting is over. It is not a begrudging kind of truce. It means that active peace replaces hostility. People change and exchange. New ways of dealing with each other are established. Old, happy ways are reestablished.

The heart of New Testament reconciliation is the fact that an explosive situation between God and man has been defused by God, to the point that a new familiarity is possible between them. When you finally can be familiar with people, especially people once considered stiff, aloof, or forbidding, everything looks different. This accounts for the sense of newness Saint Paul speaks about. The new creation has the same quality of freshness and unspoiled grandeur about it that the first creation had.

One difficulty we have with divine reconciliation is to admit its necessity in the first place. It is as though someone were to say to you, "Hey, peace has been declared," when you weren't sure you were at war. When you hear that God now wants to be friends, you can only shudder at the thought of ever having had God for an enemy. We associate many sentiments with normal human reconciliations: the fantasized hurts, the short fuse, the mutual blurring, the jittery memories, the insecurity ahead. It is frightening to think of these in relation to God.

Reconciliation might even have been a poor word for Saint Paul to use to describe God's dealing with us. (He is the only one to use it.) The word presupposes that at one time friendly relations prevailed. Many people haven't existentially experienced these in the case of God. So the announcement of God's reconciliation at first seems abrupt and puzzling.

Today's gospel captures with masterly imagery the true sentiments of God-the-reconciler. The parable of the Prodigal Son brooks very little commentary. The most we can do is to underline elements of its plot and character. The major conflict is between the father and the elder brother. The father's character leaps out: anxiety to normalize relations as soon as possible; no concern for revenge; no attention paid to what people will say; no insistence on his rights; no probing demand for an accounting; no naivete. Rather, he is quick to change the subject, lest things heat up. He is physically affectionate. He has a good instinct for when a party is needed.

The elder brother is more bent on recriminations. His futile reconstruction of past rights, wrongs, merits, and claims is maddening. His arithmetic is impeccable. His righteousness leads to a gigantic pout and from there to a frustrated sullenness.

You wonder how these three men were ever from the same family. But take another look. In a way the parable collects in its three characters the struggling parts of each one of us: part rake, part big-hearted person, part picky calculator of our own rights.

It is the elder son in all of us that poses the major obstacle to reconciliation in the world. Saint Paul says that God has entrusted the message of reconciliation to us. Literally, he has "placed in us the word of reconciliation." It is there as a speech we are to give about God's graciousness. But how can we give that speech if we are unsure that God really is that way? And how can we give that speech convincingly if we do not manifest in our behavior some tangible sign that we believe God to be that way? This requires that we embody in our relations with others a spirit of reconciliation. Looking back at the qualities of the father in the parable, this is a tall order. Reconciliation is a technique to be learned and practiced.

Some can do it with style. Saint Thomas More's departing remarks to those who condemned him are classic: "I verily trust and shall therefore right heartily pray, that though your lordships have now here on earth been judges to my condemnation, we may hereafter in heaven merrily all meet together, to our everlasting salvation." The rest of us have to approach reconciliation with our smiles fixed and our hopes high.

Fifth Sunday of Lent—A

Ezekiel 37:12–14
Romans 8:8–11
John 11:1–45

Resurrection Now

"I will put my breath in them, bring them back to life, and let them live in their own land" (Ezekiel 37:14).

Tolstoy said that anyone over thirty-five who didn't give a lot of thought to dying was a fool. Death is eternity's edge pressing inward, crowding our thoughts, crimping our desire, confining us in all that we do. No wonder we get anxious. In what way, then, are we to take the measure of our death? We hear it said that death is God's way of testing us. On the contrary, death is one more event in which God indulges our nagging practice of testing him. It is our last chance to gripe, our final challenge to his trustworthiness. Perhaps that is why we don't like to think of death now, because we'd have to think about the kind of God we're dealing with.

Today's gospel seems to be saying that God is the kind of God who favors not death but resurrection. The details of the story of the raising of Lazarus bear this out. Martha has just expressed to Jesus the pious belief in a final resurrection that was popular in late Judaism: "I know. . .that he will rise to life on the last day" (John 11:24). Jesus corrects her with the statement: "I am the resurrection and the life. Whoever believes in me will live, even though he dies; and whoever lives and believes in me will never die" (John 11:25– 26). What he is in effect saying is that we must redefine living and dying entirely. We must view them not only in relation to the last day, but in relation to today, to the daily deaths we undergo with family sorrows, lost loves, gloating enemies, with our incompetent selves. If we believe in him, we will see that kind of death and suffering in a new light. We will see that resurrection is already here. These daily deaths can be integrated into a life-giving, spirited pattern of loving and being loved. Instead of muttering and moaning, we are to trust the power of God's love in our midst as an unfailing source for our renewal.

The other two readings are also full of dead bodies that get enlivened now by the Spirit of love. "When I open the graves where my people are buried and bring them out, they will know that I am the Lord" (Ezekiel 37:13). Saint Paul holds death and resurrection in a more precarious balance. It's never just Spirit or just death; the two are at work in us all the time. "If Christ lives in you, the Spirit is life for you because you have been put right with God, even though your bodies are going to die because of sin" (Romans 8:10).

Our culture is currently fascinated by death and dying. Pulpier stuff, such as *The National Enquirer*, is usually good for an account or two of someone who died into some amorphous beyond, some blissful brightness, and came back to tell it all, an exclusive to our reporter. It is difficult to tell whether this preoccupation stems from the desire to make a killing from death, or whether it catches sentiments abroad in the culture. Sometimes it seems as though we are beckoning to death, mimicking the way it beckons to us. This kind of concern for death is somehow tied into the transcendental trip our culture is on. Films like *Star Wars* and *Close Encounters of the Third Kind* sell tickets for such a trip. There does seem to be some effort underway to test the boundary of God.

In some ways, these cultural manifestations seem so unchristian. Jesus calls us back rather to encounter life and death on a day-to-day level, in familiar surroundings and without much fanfare. This can be an energetic venture, as we see in the gospel when Jesus weeps and groans and shouts before the tomb of Lazarus. Jesus' raising of Lazarus may be a somewhat gaudy way of making his point, namely, that the power of God is at work now. But that is his message. Much of our Lenten striving should be to let that sense of resurrection now grow in us. And, where we can, it wouldn't be a bad idea to invite some of our friends out of their tombs for a day.

Jeremiah 31:31 – 34
Hebrews 5:7 – 9
John 12:20 – 33

Far Cry

"Because he was humble and devoted, God heard him"
(Hebrews 5:7).

If you just take the dictionary definition, *reverence* comes out looking slightly pale: "A feeling or attitude of deep respect tinged with awe." We would do better with concrete images: a burly husband is caught up in an unfamiliar wonder as he watches his child grow in his wife's belly; an audience listens motionlessly to a heroic missionary's tale of endurance; a hunter is caught by the beauty of morning mist scattered by the sun; an architect sees the towering realization of what was once a set of his blueprints.

These images don't do very well, either. Reverence implies that we have fully tasted the difference of something from ourselves; not simply the beauty and majesty of something, but the fact that it so utterly shows itself to us on its own terms. Reverence is a response in which we appreciate the other for itself, in all its striking dimensions.

Commenting on the verse from Hebrews cited above, Saint Thomas Aquinas remarked: "What we easily repel we do not fear. And hence it is plain that no one is feared except for some pre-eminence." He is explaining the sense in which Jesus can be said to be reverent. He sees in Jesus' human experience this tasting of what it is to come in the flesh before the mystery of the Father. The surging, eternal response of the Son to the Father is now marked by that nervousness we all experience before the infinite.

But with Jesus there is not merely a grudging acceptance of the Father's greatness. Grudging acceptance is not reverence. Neither is self-conscious cringing. Reverence does not simply mean that we step gingerly. Reverence is full of affirmation and, finally, of self-forgetfulness. It respects the preeminence of someone or something over oneself. A commitment to live with the difference is involved, a desire deep in the heart to credit the other with all the other has and is. It includes the calm realization by us that the other is not measured by a standard we are familiar with.

That is why Jesus' reverence for the Father is so impressive. The Father seems to him in his humanity to be the kind of person who makes death a condition for life; now that is *really* different. But Jesus never loses reverence for that reason. He even thinks up supporting arguments of his own: "A grain of wheat remains no more than a single grain unless it is dropped into the ground and dies. If it does die, then it produces many grains" (John 12:24).

Isaiah 43:16– 21
Philippians 3:8– 14
John 8:1– 11

A Fine Point

"Whichever one of you has committed no sin may throw the first stone at her" (John 8:7).

The Lenten liturgy continues to hammer away at the theme of forgiving. So we will, too. The story of the woman taken in adultery (today's gospel) floated around the early church for quite a while before it was inserted into John's Gospel and made a part of the canonical writings. Its difficulty in finding a home stemmed, it is suggested, from a certain hesitation on the part of Christians to officially accept the cavalier manner with which Jesus lets the adulterous woman off the hook. If this is so, it is just another indication of the general difficulty we have in seeing God as forgiving, or in seeing ourselves as forgivers.

Forgiving seems such a complicated art. Religious philistines ignore it. Their first instinct is to stone the sinner. "We have a law, and by that law she must die." Amateurs at the art are less vindictive. But they feel that they can be forgiving persons only by blotting out any consideration of moral law. The best way to judge people favorably, they say, is never to judge them at all, neither their personal sincerity nor the ethical quality of their actions. They insist that the logic-chopping analysis of good and bad behavior is what gets us into trouble in the first place. And they add under their breath that the reason God is such an accomplished forgiver is probably because he cares a lot less about laws than we do. They try to find support for this position in Saint Paul's vigorous rejection of law as a basis for relating to God: "I reckon everything as complete loss for the sake of what is so much more valuable, the knowledge of Christ Jesus. . . .I no longer have a righteousness of my own, the kind that is gained by obeying the Law" (Philippians 3:8– 9). Forgiving, they say, is not a moment of moral debate. It is a vigorous concentration on the *person* of the sinner, and what that person can become. It is rhapsodic as in today's first reading: "Do not cling to events of the past or dwell on what happened long ago. Watch for the new thing I am going to do. It is happening already—you can see it now!" (Isaiah 43:18– 19).

There is much truth and a certain appealing quality in this position. But it also runs the risk of a kind of dualism; that is, the amateur forgiver separates the person from the sin to an excessive degree. The person is no longer touched, as it were, by the seaminess of sin. It is as though a person would actually *become* unforgiveable if he freely got too close to what were clearly wicked actions. Forgiveness in this instance is something you do for a person to the extent that he is good, but not if he is bad.

On the contrary, we must intellectually and emotionally confront and embrace his badness. We have to let it enter into us in all its grimness, there to forgive as it is. Like Jesus, we somehow have to be "made sin" (a literal translation of 2 Corinthinas 5:21) as part of the process of forgiving sin.

Jesus is the professional at forgiving. What does he do? The woman taken in adultery is brought into his presence. He does not deny that adultery is adultery. He does not use the occasion to argue how extramarital sorties might even help strengthen the primary marriage bond. He is as alert to the tawdry shape of adultery, to its smell and shameful afterglow, as are the woman's accusers. It is this real person who is at the same time a real adulteress that Jesus forgives.

A fine point, you say. A nicety which overlooks the fact that we forgive sinners because they have dignity as persons. And we don't want to approve their sin, do we? (Or be envious of it!) Approve no, but neither should we intellectually and emotionally pretend it never happened. Otherwise, we end up forgiving persons for being persons, and the real sinners with their lopsided dignity have to fend for themselves. All of us.

Passion Sunday (Palm Sunday)

Isaiah 50:4–7
Philippians 2:6–11
Luke 22:14—23:56

True to Form

"He always had the nature of God, but he did not think that by force he should try to become equal with God" *(Philippians 2:6).*

By that artificial division the liturgy makes in the paschal event, we move into the week of the passion. At least there was nothing artificial about the passion. It seems to have been one continuous boil: the grand entrance and its parade of ironies. Jesus and his enemies snapping at each other in the final exchanges. The gathering anger at his popularity. The Great Feast looming just at the moment when everyone was feeling least religious. The first signs of his own team cracking. The deals made behind his back. Going through the motions of hope despite the obvious inevitability. The shambles of a supper. Slaughtered lamb with mint jelly. What if they twacked *him* that way? Where's the glory, anyway?

The long speeches telling his own that they are really worth it, really. No, really.

How do you die for what you believe without making your less competent friends feel guilty?

Clearing the air on treachery, as though it were one man's issue. Fighting down his gorge at the pious incomprehension. Powerless remarks about where real power lies. "You see, don't you? Don't you?"

Then, breakdown. Nerves on the brink, unmanly pleading; close friends catching a few winks. Maybe it will all go away. But it doesn't. That kiss really twists the knife. The smirks now on faces that used to get squinty and all tied up with his logic. The righteous fists. The shuttling begins. Who was that? Officious zealots meet entangling bureaucrats, to a finish. The waiting. The legal runaround. The waiting. Glimpses of life as usual. Noticing the way others cannot enter into your tragedy, as though there is room on life's stage for only one person to be dispatched at a time. Faces averted. Pass the political football. Innocence assaulted with dutiful violence. Fighting back the bitterness. Not playing to the crowd for pity.

Provision, yes, there are things to be done. How do you bow out? Mothers find this sort of thing hard. How stop *that* pain? Hurried arrangements. Will the bowels hold up when it comes?

Then, the silence. The mounting absurdity. Digging in. The baleful eye under a crown. Say something nice now to this miserable onlooker; don't make him pay for what you are paying. Curiosity coming toward him from shadowy passersby. Catcalls and the rougher stuff when the mob smells a killing.

The review in his head of all that led to this place. Could what He said have been said better, clearer, kindlier, more insistently? Did he miss something? What makes people pick the sides they pick anyway?

Finally, the time for no more thinking, hurting, being.

Passion seems to be relentless, once it's underway. Do we think his was real? Or do we think that the love which inspired him made him less alert and sensitive? What of those who pray themselves into a rosy oversight of these gory details?

It is difficult to know how to meditate on these events. Is it false to isolate the passion? Are we allowed to peek ahead at the resurrection? It is more likely that we are to steel ourselves mentally and emotionally, to let ourselves feel the events of his passion. But to what purpose?

The words of Philippians above capture the point of the passion better than anything. It is part and parcel of that acculturation process whereby God becomes one with us. When you are in the form of God, they don't push you around the guardroom or spit in your face. They better not. But just to show us that he can get inside our passion, that he can feel along with us, he takes the form of man. He enters our culture. He picks his way down our dangerous streets. He listens to the strange accents of our violence. He shares our scars. He doesn't lean on his rich and powerful friends back home. He lives with our jarring standards. He lets himself be judged by them. He even accepts death because, in our culture, death is a big thing. He brings us, however, his own kind of question: Can you still believe when the passion comes?

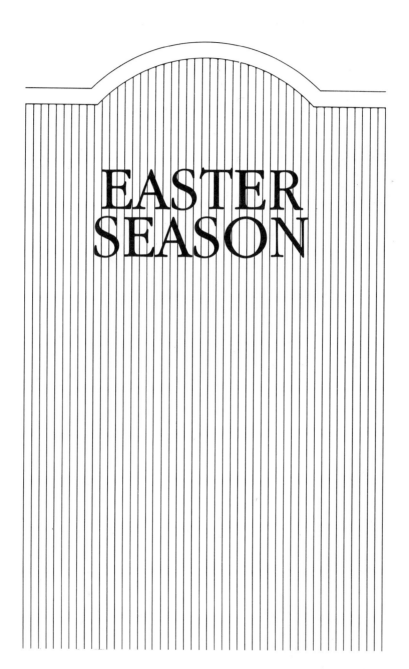

EASTER
SEASON

Isaiah 54:5– 14
Romans 6:3– 11
Matthew 28:1– 10
Luke 24:1– 12

Son Rise

"My love for you will never end; I will keep forever my promise of peace" (Isaiah 54:10).

You have to love something very, very much to bring it back from the dead. It is self-hatred and disdain for others that keep our slums the way they are. It is a lack of somebody caring that locks whole populations into cycles of poverty, starvation, joblessness, and lost hope. If someone loved enough, rivers could be blue again, stars would reappear, trees could be green. The endless dead relationships that occur in families, work settings, schools, and offices; the ennui and edginess; the sullen, sour distances between people—these wait only for a word of joy or humor or love. Who can love enough to resurrect the earth and its people?

And what about the majority of the population, those beneath the earth? What kind of love can front death itself, the marauder who cows us and leads us off like pigs to the precipice of cold silence and terrifying nothingness? Who can brighten the lot of the elderly, who wait helplessly for the marauder, frail and faltering, no longer able to run, having trouble even concentrating on the detailed sequences of dying?

There is a great love that can handle all this death and more. It is the subject of our Easter celebration. It is the Father's love for his Son, Jesus Christ. Actually, it doesn't apply directly to us. We don't fit into that special relationship, and death really ought to have its day with us, sinners that we are. But we can watch anyway as the Father, concentrated, concerned, and deeply moved, roars out his affection for Jesus in a resurrection. With a swelling rush, the Father's Spirit sweeps into Jesus and he stands anew, smiling, shaking his head in stunned gratitude, rubbing his painless wounds, full of peace, ready to reminisce about his tilt with death and how he had the last laugh on it. He even seems more relaxed now about being human, more at ease with being one of us, even though he is one of them. It's a great scene and we really believe it. It's just too bad it wasn't us. But good for Jesus.

The truth of the matter is that this glorious scene is not for Jesus alone. For Jesus has associated us with himself. He evokes from the Father the same kind of creative love for us that the Father has for him. Who can knock Jesus' friends? He presents us to the Father not for our great virtue, but for our humanity. In the Easter epistle Saint Paul reminds us that we have been crucified with Jesus through baptism and therefore will be raised by the Father with him. The first part of that remark is one of those statements to which we give lip service, but would be surprised if it were really true. What does it mean? Well, baptism certainly isn't a simple matter of getting your forehead wet, or our fanny, either. It means entering a community that is trying to love and is getting crucified for its efforts. In a way the whole world is trying to do this (which is why, after all, we can talk of baptism of desire in the first place). We all bear scars on our humanity where we have been hurt trying and straining in the service of love. You don't have to arrange to be crucified. It's part of the process of trying to fend off the many deaths that plague our humanity. Even though we have done our share of crucifying, too, Jesus draws the Father's attention away from that. He spruces us up, rearranges our tatters, fluffs us out, and introduces us to the Father as old friends, human people he used to know. We played together for the Christians against the lions—really good, too—fellow sufferers, that sort of thing. How gracious of this Conqueror of death to make cause for us.

All this pleading, of course, is not all that necessary. For the Father loves and has always loved us. The readings in the Easter Vigil service form a panoramic display of the history of his love. They are worth much reflection and prayer. You'll find there occasional nagging about our sinfulness, but it's the normal kind of demanding perfectionism that fathers tend to exact from children they love. As it is, we hope to stand with Jesus, comparing fates and fortunes, kicking up a good time, in love forever. Not a bad Easter message for Christians to bring to each other and to a world still gripped by so much death.

Acts 10:34, 37 – 43
Colossians 3:1 – 4
John 20:1 – 9

When a Body Rises

"You have been raised to life with Christ, so set your hearts on the things that are in heaven" (Colossians 3:1).

What do you say to someone who has risen from the dead? Congratulations are certainly in order. Gratitude, too, since His rising is a sign to us of God's faithful love for us as well. Astonishment at it all is probably a truer reaction.

The personal resurrection of Jesus, however, might well lead us to consider how his "other" body, the church, is faring. The Easter liturgy traditionally includes a remembrance of our baptism, whereby we became members of Jesus' movement. There was a promise of life in that baptism, a call to rise together with Jesus to new heights. How have things gone?

If you were to ask people whether they associate real life with their baptism, you might get some raised eyebrows. Many would hesitate to trace their capacity for friendships, their hard work, their humor and doggedness, their talents and hobbies to a rite called baptism. It was all too long ago.

Even when they see past the external rite to the fact that baptism, after all, was simply the point of their entering the church, they are unsure whether that church has been a source of life for them. True, in the church they encounter Jesus in the eucharist. That is a high form of life for them. But many other things in the church they find deadening, uninspiring, and trivial. What, then, does the church bring by way of resurrection and life?

There are two ways of answering this question. The first is frankly apologetic. It insists that a lot of life can be found in the churches, if only people get over their petulant bias and emotional hang-ups long enough to look for it. It points to the work of the churches in hospitals, homes, and schools, and it ridicules the suggestion that such work is carried on merely as some kind of pious indoctrination. It reels off the numbers of people touched by the churches' low-cost concern: orphans, cripples, the hungry, prisoners, the aged, strikers, rebels, lepers, prostitutes, homeless bums, outcasts.

It underscores the countless life-building actions that are inspired by a prayer to Jesus, by the memory of an odd word read here or there (in however garbled a fashion) from the Scriptures, by devotion to a stirring tradition of sanctity, by the fear of ending up selfish and unloving, contrary to the gospel.

It is unimpressed by people who, preferring instead the right Sunday brunch or the newspapers, have no time for church attendance. It asks what the majority of critics have done lately for the developing countries in terms of volunteer personnel, shoestring living, loneliness stubbornly borne, and cultural adaptation. It invites a comparison of what the banks, the unions, the professions, and corporations are doing in our urban ghettos with what a handful of holdout nuns, priests, and ministers with their families are doing.

When overheated, it argues that—by and large, on the whole, in the long run, with higher statistical probability—the churches have kept more people more human, less dangerous, more kind, more in the right frame of mind (not to mention in the right beds) than all the critics put together have done.

It does not deny that Christian performance has been dismal at times. But it refuses to be measured by some catty and illogical standard that requires the churches to be simon-pure before they can be judged favorably, while everything else naturally is expected to be flawed. It sees in all this not a chance for the churches to blow their own horn, but a chance to proclaim how Christ is risen in them.

The second way to answer our original question is to admit, with equal frankness, that much in the churches needs to be raised from the dead. In many areas we have settled for the tomb. Rather than rolling back the rock, we try instead to make the tomb snug: fix it up a bit, a splash of paint here and there, some oils, perhaps drapes, a few pin-ups of their various excellencies, a mimeograph machine, many candles. The image is tempting.

The revitalization of the churches today does not mean that they should rise above mundane matters to some kind of self-satisfying spiritualism. It does not mean that we may pretend to the triumphal, serene, and privileged qualities of Jesus' risen state. What, then, should our revitalization look like?

According to the Acts, Jesus is "the one whom God has appointed judge of the living and the dead" (Acts 10:42). His life is now life for God. But life "for God" is, as it always was for Jesus, a matter of expressing God's love for the world: freeing prisoners, preaching the good news to the poor, helping orphans and widows, caring for the sick and the weak, confronting religious pretense and legalism, energetic forgiving, trusting that the Father will bring all this to pass.

Can we rise to that occasion?

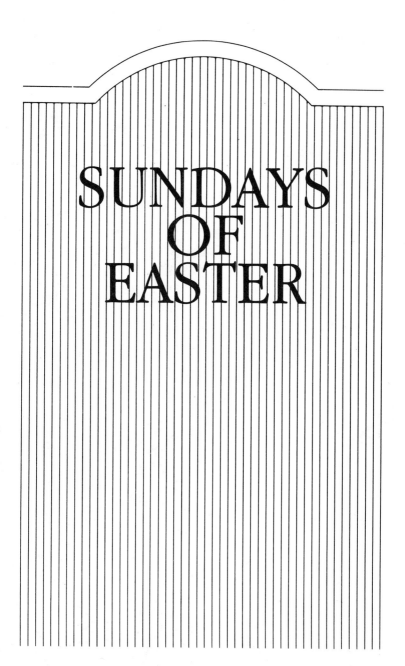

SUNDAYS
OF
EASTER

Acts 2:42–47
1 Peter 1:3–9
John 20:19–31

Show and Tell

*"Jesus came and stood among them. 'Peace be with you,'
he said. After saying this, he showed them his hands and
his side" (John 20:19–20).*

The big question these days is whether we have
gotten it together. We are Jigsaw, a Rube Goldberg con-
traption made up of emotion, intellect, body, plans, relationships, hopes, and haunting memories. Our goal is to
arrange all these elements or at least to manage them,
with a degree of aplomb and a minimum of self-
destruction.

First, however, we have to get in touch. Then, in a
questionable image, we are to let it all hang out. We may
even have to defend belligerently the presence of con-
flicted and ambivalent parts in us. Mastering our inner-
dynamic mechanisms and psychic circuitry is the next
step, and this can be done only in relational settings.
Those who can, pay for such settings; those who can't,
rap. It all takes a lot of experimentation, but hope in that
one day out will pop a total person.

It is difficult to assess these aspirations. Do you
trust someone who builds up trust levels so tentatively
and in such a complicated fashion? Is the process itself
self-perpetuating, so that the unwritten law is that one
never finishes? Is it really all some kind of stale
reprocessing? No one can deny that getting in touch with

one's own identity, with one's own reality, is a praise-worthy goal. But there is a fine line in here somewhere. To be aware of all the stuff within us—the noises in the attic, the rumbling below, the sudden rushes, the voices at the door—that is one thing. To be surprised that it is all going on is another.

Faith tries not only to cut down on the element of surprise but also to anticipate it. It is hard to make this point when so many people look on religion as an escape from the realities going on around them. Or when they see faith as a secret kind of haven where they can dismiss much of what is going on in themselves. This kind of denial is sometimes fostered by religion itself. The first reading today, which is taken from the Acts of the Apostles, presents an idyllic picture of faith. The primitive community seems to have had a rosy time: "They had their meals together in their homes, eating with glad and humble hearts, praising God, and enjoying the good will of all the people" (Acts 2:46). But anyone who ever read the rest of Acts will tell you that things gradually came apart at the seams. Confusions, bickering, simony, rivalry, treachery, and accusation tumble out in the sequel. Saint Luke records in Acts the maturing realizations of the primitive community as it comes to see the prices to be paid by the believer. But you would never get this from today's reading.

The second reading, dating from a much later period, makes no bones about prices to be paid. "It may now be necessary for you to be sad for a while because of the many kinds of trials you suffer. Their purpose is to prove that your faith is genuine. Even gold, which can be destroyed, is tested by fire; and so your faith, which is much more precious than gold, must also be tested, so that it may endure" (1 Peter 1:6– 7). More poignantly, mention is made that Christians are operating in the dark. They do not and have not seen the Lord. That makes their faith tougher, in both senses.

In today's gospel we see that faith inevitably is a matter of sharing scars, not concealing them. It is open about the pain that exists in the midst of dealing with God. To doubt this or to be surprised at it is a sign of a struggling faith. The usual thing to say is that Thomas was having trouble believing that Jesus was alive. But he was also struggling with the seemingly stupid necessity of dying to begin with. Thomas is, after all, the one who brings up the subject of wounds and nail marks!

Through all of this, Jesus is the man of peace. He has, as they say, gotten it all together. But he challenges us about the way in which getting it together takes place. His Holy Spirit reaches into the deepest interior of a person, but it does not settle there. It makes the person look outward to see the needs of others. It gets us to see that others are hurting, are bound. If we don't forgive them, if we don't unbind them, then they are trapped. We get it together by freeing these others, not by an excessive preoccupation with ourselves. We do have to face the suffering in ourselves but we do not have to be hypnotized by it. Like Jesus, we have to take our scars more lightly. That's one of the big disadvantages about being risen from the dead. You have no alternative but to go around cheering others up.

Acts 4:32–35
1 John 5:1–6
John 20:19–31

Taking Inventory

"The group of believers was one in mind and heart. No one said that any of his belongings was his own, but they all shared with one another everything they had. With great power the apostles gave witness to the resurrection of the Lord Jesus, and God poured rich blessings on them all" (Acts 4:32 – 33).

Fantasies about power preoccupy people. We are using *power* here in a precise sense: the access one has to resources. Internal resources are things such as talents, charisms, and endowments. External resources are things such as possessions, connections, experience, and repute. In many cases one can have these resources but remain powerless, because one does not have access to them. My personality is warped, so I cannot get at my musical talent; my funds are tied up in litigation, so I cannot get at them. Access is essential to power. Nations, organizations, governments, and individuals are all judged powerful or weak on the basis of the access they have to resources.

But what do we mean by "fantasies about power"? We mean that people, when they are insecure about their own access to resources, begin to imagine certain things about other people's power. They wonder whether others will share the resources they have; they fear others will use their resources to dominate them;

they envy the resources others have; they exaggerate and idealize the actual extent of others' resources; they ignore how others might have come by their resources (for example, by luck, by hard work, by circumstance, by channeling one resource into the development of another, and so on); they pay no attention to the question whether the resources others have are committed to the common good, or designated for specific purposes, or are on reserve for some predictable eventuality. They simply lick their lips and feel hurt at the sight of the power others have, compared to their own.

It comes all the more as a shock, then, when we read the scriptural verses above. There, power is associated not with things such as envy or depression but with joy and sharing. The Christian paradox (master is servant, high is low, death is life) is stretched to the limit. We have here people actually feeling they will become powerful (gain access to resources) to the degree that they share the resources they have with their neighbor.

What has happened here? Simply that the Spirit of God has taught them that *God is their resource*. With such faith, they do not need to engage in the usual fantasies they have about power. What further access to resources do they need when they have been promised resourcing by God? It makes you kind of irresponsible and profligate with the resources you have on hand, the way a big winner at the track tends to drop money all around freely.

If there's a problem at all, it is in believing that God's resources are in fact promised us. We can and do entertain the same fantasies about God's power that we saw ourselves having about the power of other people:

Will God share the divine resources? Will God use them against us? And so on.

Resurrection faith considers these questions answered.

Second Sunday of Easter — C

Acts 5:12 – 16
Revelation 1:9 – 11, 12 – 13, 17 – 19
John 20, 19 – 31

No Further Evidence

"Jesus said to him [Thomas], 'Do you believe because you see me? How happy are those who believe without seeing me!' " (John 20 – 29).

Today's gospel passage originally served as the finale to John's Gospel. Throughout that gospel, themes of blindness and seeing are interwoven in gradually more and more ironic and startling ways. Some see, but they really don't. Some who are blind actually see. Some can pick up the signals (or "signs" as John calls them); others miss what is right under their noses and blindly clamor for further evidence. The wonder-worker himself appeals to the works he performs as indications of his authority. But he also taunts his enemies that the only sign they will get is that they cannot kill him for good.

The issue behind the signs is: What to make of Jesus? Could he really be the chosen one of God, the hinge of history, the point to which Israel's erratic wanderings led? Was he perhaps even more than all these things?

The figure of Thomas demonstrates how far the church had come in its answer to the question: What to make of Jesus? Thomas's words "My Lord and my God" contain an allusion to Hosea (2:24), where it is said that Israel always is to find its promised fulfillment in God. If the church now sees Jesus as the fulfillment of the promise, it consistently is saying that Jesus is God.

Moreover, Thomas illustrates the difficulties faced in holding to this faith. Just as people could overdo the demand for proofs and signs during Jesus' earthly life, so, too, they can overdo these demands now that Jesus is risen.

This holds doubly for the communites for whom John wrote late in the first century. It was even harder for them to face squarely the question of Jesus. Out of sight, out of mind. And the mind plays tricks, doesn't it? Perhaps further evidence should be sought once more for their faith that God was in Jesus and that Jesus lives. John allays their nervousness with the example of Thomas. The believer is advised that the desire for signs can be a dangerous and deceiving business.

With this realization, the church was giving itself a salutary dose of what Jesus, accoring to an earlier parable, had given his enemies: "If they will not listen to Moses and the prophets, they will not be convinced even if someone were to rise from death" (Luke 16:31).

We might get the opposite impression from the first reading about the danger of looking for signs: "Many miracles and wonders were being performed among the people by the apostles" (Acts 5:12). There, signs and miracles seem to be a desirable thing. They swell the numbers of the believers. It is important to recall, however, that this section of Acts describes the honeymoon for the church rather than the marriage itself. As Acts develops, many more hard-nosed issues surface. The church discovers that the Spirit brings not only signs and wonders but also doctrinal headaches and arguments, cultural impasses, political embroilments, personality clashes at high levels, and the stunned realization that not everybody is going to believe. In other words, believers learn that complexity, suffering, and the need for conversion are part and parcel of life in the Spirit.

The search for signs crops up again and again in the life of believers. Is Jesus working in us? Where are signs of Jesus' risen presence in the world around us? Some people are inevitably interested in signs of a more garish quality. They would like to bring back signs such as those performed in the afterglow of Pentecost by Peter and the other apostles: "Sick people were carried out into the streets and placed on beds and mats so that at least Peter's shadow might fall on some of them as he passed by" (Acts 5:15). While some might call this desire nostalgia, others are convinced that such signs are the normal fruits of the Spirit. This is particularly so in what is called the charismatic renewal.

Charismatics do not demand to see signs as a condition of their believing. They want instead to be signs for others and for themselves that the Spirit in whom they believe is at work in the world. So they try to show forth the Spirit in healings, in the prayer of praise, in joy, in speaking in tongues, in informal exorcisms, and so on. It would be hard to complain about such a goal. All other things being equal, a smile is a surer sign of the Spirit than a sour puss. On the other hand, the lesson of Thomas stands: The desire for signs can be a dangerous and deceiving business.

Third Sunday of Easter—A

Acts 2:14, 22–28
1 Peter 1:17–21
Luke 24:13–35

Telling Tales

"And so your faith and hope are fixed on God" (1 Peter 1:21).

Most of us have friends who embarrass us to death on occasion. (We might even be such friends to others.) Not just the foot in the mouth, Lord, but the knee and hip, too. In the midst of describing some scene or event, they suddenly unveil some massive prejudice, ignorance, insensibility, or other gaucherie. You want to crawl under any nearby cover, but your loyalty to them makes you stay there to interpret benignly their *faux pas*. "What my friend means...," you say; or perhaps you suddenly notice something nearby that demands everyone's immediate and total attention, so the topic shifts and the situation is saved.

The first reading has Peter getting off such a lulu to the crowds on the day of Pentecost: "In accordance with his own plan God had already decided that Jesus would be handed over to you" (Acts 2:23). A statement like that could be taken in a benign sense, maybe. It could mean that, though the Jewish leaders thought they were masters of the event, there is no master but God. Not only do the so-called masters have to use a hated occupation force to do their work for them, but God undoes it anyway by raising Jesus from the dead. But in the course of saying this, Peter gives the unfortunate impression that God goes around planning his own Son's death and planning to use people to bring it about. That's just awful.

It also gave rise, in the course of time, to theologies of the redemption that would curl your hair. In a standard version, Jesus is the price exacted for our salvation. In some theologies, the price would supposedly be handed over to the slaveowner, Satan, despite the fact that this theory puts the Father in the weird position of having to deal with some second-rate subangel in long, red underwear. In other theologies, the price would be paid directly to the Father. This picture of things doesn't help very much, either, since it makes the Father some strange kind of Shylock, exacting pounds of flesh from himself (his Son) for himself. Today's second reading, therefore, which pushes us into this business of payments, must be read with caution: "For you know what was paid to set you free from the worthless manner of life handed down by your ancestors. It was not something that can be destroyed, such as silver or gold; it was the costly sacrifice of Christ, who was like a lamb without defect or flaw" (1 Peter 1:18– 19).

Jesus gives a lot better explanation of his suffering in today's gospel, the Emmaus story. The interplay between the stranger and the disciples is delicious. The disciples are frankly disappointed in God. They are full of the events that recently dashed their hopes. They also may well be taking it on the lam from Jerusalem. The stranger at first plays dumb. But when he talks, a different picture of God emerges than the one Peter gave above. Jesus, too, speaks of a certain fixed pattern in the events that were supervised by God from the beginning: "How foolish you are. . . . Was it not necessary for the Messiah to suffer these things and then to enter into his glory?" (Luke 24:25– 26). But the necessity for this suffering is not attributed to any machinations on God's part. It is explained in terms of what usually happens when sin and love and freedom clash. The record of this clash is found in the Scripture: "And Jesus explained to them what was said about himself in all the Scriptures, beginning with the books of Moses and the writings of all the prophets" (27).

His point is not simply to justify to them his own fate. Their own humanity is touched. So much so that they invite the stranger to stay along with them. It is the kind of gesture you make when you meet people who communicate to you that they have been there, that they have seen the depths of humanity and can still be loving. It excludes the intent to sit around and gripe about the way God runs the world or "plans" things. The disciples learn that, if anything, God has such great compassion for humanity that he becomes its patient servant. God doesn't indulge in false heroics, first tripping us up and then rushing in to pick us up and brush us off. God treats us as adults, and that means a certain necessity is upon us to learn, from our own stupidities and those of others, the real price of freely giving ourselves in love.

We can still stumble, however, over the language. In a day when you have to watch your step with chauvinist slips and ethnic jokes, it should not be too much of a burden to watch what we say about God, too. Perhaps it would even be better to speak without words, in the silent and significant breaking of the bread.

Third Sunday of Easter—B

Acts 3:13 – 15, 17 – 19
1 John 2:1 – 5
Luke 24:35 – 48

The Light That Failed

"Was it not necessary for the Messiah to suffer these things and then to enter his glory?" (Luke 24:26).

Some of us spend vast amounts of mental energy justifying our personal failures. It is a familiar pastime. We look for external villains to whom we can attribute some malicious mood or purpose. "They had it in for me all along," we say. Or we lament brutal developments in society that supposedly brought about our failure: how the new generation has gotten so greedy, how nobody cares any more, how a different product or a different city or a different team might have led to success. We gloss over a lot of our own behavior that contributed to our downfall: the hours we failed to put in, the phone calls we didn't make, the diversions we preferred, the alliances we let slip because of neglect. Caught in the meshes of such regret, we rehearse every pain and poke over every circumstance of our collapse. We can't think straight about the next move because we are retracing every previous move so fixedly. Exhortations to us to put the matter out of our minds are unheeded. It would take a lot of counseling for us to find some sense of present solace or future possibility.

We can't really say whether the disciples on the road to Emmaus were reliving some personal scenario like the one just described. They certainly seem to have a keen sense of failure. More pertinent here, however, is the manner of Jesus' counseling. We'll be brave and say that he almost gives an argument in favor of failure: "Was it not necessary for the Messiah to suffer these things and then to enter his glory?"

Jesus' point is that God's kind of Messiah is not one who goes from glory to glory all along the way. Rather, God's kind of Messiah has to be determined to share much more realistically in the process that ensnares those who need to be saved. For the latter, there is a necessity for the props to be removed, for plans to be interrupted, for superficialities to be stripped away. Why? In order that they learn to place their reliance on God and on God alone.

Failure is being measured by some new kind of standard here, which humankind has trouble grasping. The only failue worth the name in God's new world is trying to go it alone without a real place for God in one's heart. We do this often enough and in such subtle ways; even being religious can be a nice way to put God off. Only some hard knocks or failures in life can bring us to the point of honesty. Jesus describes to the disciples on the road to Emmaus the hard knocks that messiahs endure. His description was all the more compelling because he had experienced what it was to be with the Father in life and death.

Third Sunday of Easter — C

Acts 5:27–32, 40–41
Revelation 5:11–14
John 21:1–19

Pick of the Pack

"The disciple whom Jesus loved said to Peter, 'It is the Lord!'" (John 21:7).

It would be interesting to ask people whether they disliked certain parts of the Scripture, and why. Even more intriguing would be to ask them whether they feel free to be so discriminating. We're not talking here about disliking central teachings about sin, about God's unstoppable love, about the tasks of Christians, and so on. We are talking rather about the language and style with which those teachings are clothed. The language and style are often the products of the individual temperament, peculiar talent, and personality of the scriptural writer.

A case in point is today's second reading from Revelation. "To him who sits on the throne and to the Lamb, be praise and honor, glory and might. . . . The four living creatures answered, 'Amen!' And the elders fell down and worshiped" (Revelation 5:13 – 14). One Christian might say: Look, John's praise of Christ is wonderful. I fervently want to join in it as much as the next person. But the imagery of Revelation is something else. Maybe a Stanley Kubrick could bring it to life. And I'm well aware that apocalyptic writing was a form of underground communication that enabled the church to do business under the nose of its persecutors. Even so, any scene dominated by a big lamb is—well, there I draw the line. In fact, I don't like the whole finale to life dreamed up by John in the rest of Revelation. It seems like a boring skating party, with gloating Wagnerian virgins in severe albs gliding around on invisible runners over a sea of glass. Give me the synoptic version of the eschaton any day, with the crooks and publicans, the bums and sinners crashing the never-ending banquet.

Another person might prefer the dramatic narrative of a Luke, as in today's second reading. It stirs sentiments of consolidated action, of dignified determination, with a little bit of we-told-*them*-off thrown in.

Or someone might like the way John captures individual character. In today's gospel, for example, it is the disciple whom Jesus loves who first spots the distant figure of Jesus. Or we watch a hard-charging man like Peter gently brought down to size in awkward, flushed stages—on the theory, perhaps, that the realism of people in authority should extend to themselves.

The fact that scriptural writers are inspired does not excuse them from conveying their own peculiar imagery and tone in their writings. Even if they in turn have borrowed imagery from Old Testament writers, the borrowings are selective. The Old Testament writers themselves form a massive pool of styles, expression, and flavor. So, whom you borrow from in the Old Testament tells a lot about you.

The question of scriptural styles runs deeper than simply the imagery the writers use. The style is the man. This seems to say that we will have as many likes and dislikes for Scripture as we have for people. All charity maintained, it would be a long day for some of us spent with John or Paul or Mark. And vice versa.

Accordingly, may we complain of John's Jesus for being too much in possession of himself, too serene, always one step ahead, slightly omnicient? May we fault Paul (as indeed some of his contemporaries did) for seeming to be blasé about sin, given the cavalier attitude toward forgiving that he attributes to God? May we be annoyed with his sheer intelligence and ranging imagination? May we bristle at the bellicosity of James? May we lament—wherever they crop up—the lashings given to the Pharisees and scribes, the ganging up on Judas, the untutored mixing of pious hearsay with solid tradition, the moralizing without motivating, and so on?

We are brought back to the question of how much preference is legitimate. In matters of religion, preference is often ruled out by higher authorites, lest the masses get too picky and choosy. But it is just as often denied by ourselves, so that we won't have to face the actual likes and dislikes within us.

Yet, when preference is denied, love itself becomes suspect. Is it love when everyone likes everyone so equally that we never have to be reminded of differences in taste, sensibility, talent, whim, and so forth? Without turning the whole thing into a matter of likes and dislikes, there does seem to be scope for our individual tastes. This is true not only in the matter of reading Scripture, but in spirituality in general. In the end, some disciples are more beloved than others, both by Jesus and by us. Yet, it is the same for us as it is for God: having favorites is not the same thing as playing favorites.

Fourth Sunday of Easter —A

Acts 2:14, 36– 41
1 Peter 2:20– 25
John 10:1– 10

No Stranger

"The sheep follow him, because they know his voice. They will not follow someone else ... because they do not know his voice" (John 10:4– 5).

The image of Jesus as a gate is one of the more fascinating and controversial images in the New Testament. Positively, a gate promises access; it welcomes. A gate hints at what might be within; it makes us curious. But negatively, a gate claims legitimacy in a way that makes those who ignore it fraudulent and suspect. A gate is a kind of checkpoint, where selectivity is exercised. When we are asked at many gates in our lives: "What is the purpose of your visit?", suppose we have no answer? And then we know, with Kierkegaard, that many gates in life do not swing inward, so that we can force them; they swing outward, and therefore we can do nothing.

To apply this image of gate to oneself seems the height of vanity. Yet the scandal of Jesus lies in the claim to uniqueness that he makes for himself. Learned societies struggle with this claim, not without much mumble and fog. They try to isolate what makes morality specifically Christian. They try to see how Christian community and identity differ from other traditional wisdoms. Sometimes there is a hint of an inferiority complex in these reflections, the fear of saying one's differences out loud.

The question we all must ask is whether Jesus is unique only because of *who* he is, God's own Son. To say that Jesus is important because of his connections, and to leave it at that, makes it look as though God operates on a who-you-know basis, apart from anything else. Notice today's first reading. We find that in support of his testimony, Peter used "many other words" (Acts 2:40). We do not know what these arguments were. But if they all touched only upon the divinity of Jesus, we might wonder how persuasive they would have been.

What is most striking in today's readings is that Jesus' uniqueness is to be found in his great humanity. The first thing we see about Jesus is that he carries many burdens that are not properly his own. This is a common human experience. Nowhere do feelings of unfairness well up more strongly than when we feel we are being dumped upon indiscriminately by others. Some people carry the weight of the world on them without knowing how it got there. They do not realize that it is other people who are sloughing off their own personal and moral garbage on them. So they feel like a walking slum, not knowing why. But Jesus knew why. He carries around the sins of others in his own person. He shoulders the emotional burden of strained or broken or nonexistent relationships. He takes it on as God's man. He gets the kind of flak that God gets—the accusations, curses, and indifference.

Second, Jesus does not vent his anger on others. "Christ himself suffered for you and left you an example, so that you would follow in his steps. He committed no sin, and no one ever heard a lie come from his lips. When he was insulted, he did not answer back with an insult; when he suffered, he did not threaten" (1 Peter 2:21–23). There is more to this behavior than meets the eye. We know how people carp at their fate, resenting this turn or that in their affairs. Some of the greatest sweats we get ourselves into are those in which our rightness, our sincerity, or our integrity are supposedly "at stake." Joan of Arc has nothing on us. We squirm over hurts that we have itemized and totaled up. We find ourselves reliving incidents, rehashing the sequence of a quarrel, checking the circumstances that surrounded one of our more notorious imbroglios. We are such lawyers! But the attitude of Jesus is free of such litigation. There is a resolute decision to be judged finally by the One he loves. That takes a big person, a person who is convinced that the truest and most solid thing about being human is that complexity is part of life. The rest is excuses. Trust has to be exercised in the midst of what actually happens in our lives, with all its actual limitations, excursions, and adventures.

To picture Jesus with this kind of faith might seem scandalous to some. Many would prefer to see Jesus being so much in charge of events that he never has to throw up his hands and turn the whole thing over to his Father. And yet the Scripture is clear: "He . . . placed his hopes in God, the righteous Judge" (1 Peter 2:24).

Thus, a picture emerges of someone who is unique by being so very, very human. If we return to the imagery of today's gospel, Jesus is the gate that defends us from thieves and marauders who *invite us to escapist expectations about our humanity*: the people who steal from us our hope of coping with the frailty within and around us. These people are strangers to our humanity. He is not.

Fourth Sunday of Easter — B

Acts 4:8 – 12
1 John 3:1 – 2
John 10:11 – 18

One Day

"They will become one flock with one shepherd" (John 10:16).

If you have had much contact with Christians of various persuasions, you probably noticed that the similarities between them are more striking than the differences. Protestant Christians soar and sink, gripe and grapple pretty much the same way Catholic Christians do. Complaints about the pastor or minister sound just about the same as complaints about the parish priest. The higher-ups come in for the same abuse, whether we talk about synod or convention or assembly. And while most churchgoers are happy when their leaders get headlines, authority figures in whatever the church seem to report to their doctors the same kind of nervous twitches and generalized anxiety. Quaker kids probably hate compulsory catechism as much as Lutheran kids or Baptist kids. Theologians divide up into the usual sides in Presbyterian schools as they do in Catholic seminaries. Money problems plague everyone without distinction. Everyone's closet has its share of skeletons (although in some churches even skeletons have trouble grinning). High-church types feel just as uncomfortable with low-church services, whether you are dealing with Catholic churches or with Methodist or Anglican ones. The great unwashed feel miserable in any church. On moral issues, Christians line up, at least unofficially, along the same mind-boggling spectrum. Some Christian denominations have sacraments without calling them such. Many have popes without admitting it. The same rote, the same fanaticism for what is peripheral or irrelevant affects all. You get the same impatience with caparisoned liturgies in the Eastern rites as in the Western rite. As many Pentecostals dislike fraternal overfamiliarity and slobbering kisses of peace as Catholics do.

At a deeper level, Christians across their divisions are moved by the power of the good news. They struggle to remain committed to a life of charity. They pour themselves into good causes in the name of Jesus. They pray and beat their breasts in unison. They suffer persecution and they suffer a lot of nonsense in their pursuit of the mystery.

Why, then, are we not all more "persuaded" about our unity? Why do we cling to our supposed divisions?

Several explanations could be put forth. First, many would respond that the several Christian denominations have tried to give expression to certain gospel values that they found lacking in other Christian traditions. If we do too much ecumenical tinkering, would not the values that denominations have built into their structure and esprit be lost?

Second, we are reluctant to give up our stereotypes of others. We live rather comfortably with them. Stereotypes give us a certain control, an assurance that we have properly pegged people in predictable ways. We *know* that Mormons are sober and solid. We *know* how quickly Catholics tend to obey. We *know* how emotional Pentecostals are, and so on. This habit of pigeonholing others is ingrained in us; our stereotypes, we think, at least make life more manageable.

Third, some would insist that differences must be worked out with proper research and documentation. Otherwise, they tell us, any unity we achieve will be superficial and unconvincing. They would find the picture of our similarities given above too slick, even sentimental. Authoritative channels—there, there's where the thing must be worked out, they say; there's where the hope lies!

It is difficult to know what to make of all this. We might wish for a more candid admission that a lot of self-serving and pompous poop also flows through authoritative channels. We wonder why "proper research" ends up telling us what we suspected all along—that divisions were more often historically based not on spiritual loyalty or discernment, but on personality issues, sheer misunderstandings, power struggles, and catty back-and-forths. The ecumenical movement might do better to include large doses of Social Psychology 101 and tone down the posturing about fidelity to divinely held truths, since many of its issues are organizational and managerial ones, and little more.

Today's second reading says: "My dear friends, we are now God's children, but it is not yet clear what we shall become. But we know that when Christ appears, we shall be like him, because we shall see him as he really is" (1 John 3:2). Perhaps we are having trouble getting into Jesus' vision of unity because we fail to see him as he really is. We don't seem to have a Jesus who is capable of dealing with our diversity in any other way than rallying the opposite sides. What we see is indeed what we get.

If we cannot see other Christians as being like us, all we will be offered is a vision of disunity. We won't be able to be with them in the same flock. Stressing our similarities, therefore, might be the best route to go—especially if similarities are the most obvious thing there in the first place.

Acts 13:14, 43 – 52
Revelation 7:9, 14 – 17
John 10:27 – 30

Sheepish Smiles

"My sheep listen to my voice; I know them, and they follow me" (John 10:27).

Many people are repelled when claims are made about who is saved and who isn't. The fanatical ways in which this kind of discrimination has been practiced over the years by different religious bodies is depressing.

When you meet people who give you the once-over spiritually, you are at once enraged and astounded by the gall and pretentiousness that go into their calculations. As an old Irish missionary sister (30 years in the Bombay slums), now thumbing her way on her rosary beads into reluctant retirement, once said in her slow brogue: "It's better to be around sinners. They don't put on airs, you know."

Yet we are stuck with the impression from todays' gospel that some sheep belong, while others don't. It is not clear from the passage whether Jesus, in his humanity, knew in advance which was which. (Perhaps John was more fortunate.) Who, then, is "in" and who is "out"?

The second reading puts one category of people decidedly "in," those suffering persecution for their faith. "He will guide them to springs of life-giving water. And God will wipe away every tear from their eyes" (Revelation 7:17). Divine approval in such cases is bold and clear. The difficulty is that, because John is dealing with do-or-die situations of fidelity in the face of persecution, his division of the good guys and the bad guys is not very helpful. We learn who are "in" only when they are on the way out. We seem no closer to a criterion that would help us choose the right set of sheep.

Nowadays we hear a lot about "choice of ministries": Where should we spend our time and energy evangelizing? Who are we to look on as sheep and who as goats in our apostolic efforts? The early church had the same problem: "Paul and Barnabas spoke out even more boldly: 'It was necessary that the word of God should be spoken first to you [Jews]. But since you reject it and do not consider yourselves worthy of eternal life, we will leave you and go to the Gentiles' " (Acts 13:46). Paul and Barnabas reject Antioch; they protest against the pressures and the bad will that force them to leave. "The apostles shook the dust off their feet in protest against them and went on to Iconium" (Acts 13:51). But note the grounds on which they made their decision. Their protest was directed against those who refused to be free. They were rejecting those who wanted to base their religiosity on their own correct performance rather than on the explosive, joyful realization that God loved them and others. Is this, then, how we are to recognize Jesus' sheep? Are we to seek out situations in which people are not wedded to controlled and correct performance but are open to the demands of love?

This is a frightening question for the churches today. So much energy is expended on trivial matters, on dramatic choices about such zingers as communion-in-the-hand, statues in the church, religious garb, and so on. Controlled performance seems to be the tone of much of our sacramental life. So much so that we might wonder: Would Paul and Barnabas shake the dust from their feet today if they saw the quality of life in some of our parishes and religious centers?

But before we shake too much dust from too many feet, we might take a look at the other point made in today's readings: "The believers in Antioch were full of joy and the Holy Spirit" (Acts 13:52). Perhaps we can tell Jesus' sheep from the rest by their cheerful smiles.

Fifth Sunday of Easter—A

Acts 6:1–7
1 Peter 2:4–9
John 14:1–12

Room Service

"It is not right for us to neglect the preaching of God's word in order to handle finances" (Acts 6:2).

Service is the big word these days. Everyone is knocking each other out to be the servant of everyone else. It can even be dangerous not to let someone serve you who really wants to. There is something exciting and appealing in all this. People are trying to get away from any high-handedness in religious matters, any pompous condescension and know-it-all triumphalism.

All the more surprising, then, to find in today's first reading that the apostles are having second thoughts about servanthood as a worthwhile pastime for themselves. They do not indulge in too many mental gymnastics about it, either. They do not argue that, after all, the ministry of the word is itself a form of servanthood. They don't argue that they can fulfill the formal definition of servanthood by their prayer and preaching. No, someone else is simply going to do the serving.

It is even more interesting to note the reason why the apostles handed over certain servantlike operations to the deacons: "As the number of disciples kept growing, there was a quarrel between the Greek-speaking Jews and the native Jews. The Greek-speaking Jews claimed that their widows were being neglected in the daily distribution of funds" (Acts 6:1). One might conclude that the apostles knew when to punt! In a more serious vein, we might ask how the apostles could abandon, or even give the appearance of abandoning, the example of Jesus, who often said he was in their midst as one who serves. Jesus must also have given his apostles a respect for practicality. The good news did not replace good sense.

It all goes to show that the imitation of Jesus is tricky business. It does not call for an exact paralleling of our actions with his. If it did, we'd all be crucified by now. Today's gospel contains the remarkable statement of Jesus: "I am telling you the truth: whoever believes in me will do what I do—yes, he will do even greater things" (John 14:12). That Jesus could predict such initiatives for his disciples is inspiring, even if a bit frightening. He seems to be gently hinting that, just as personalities and talents differ among his disiciples, so too there will be variety in the works they undertake. He uses the image of his Father's house, which has, he says, "many rooms" in it. The different arrangements fit different personalities: some want a view and morning light; some don't mind being next to the elevator; there is the carpet crowd versus the linoleum crowd; some prefer golden bathroom fixtures.

The problem is that as soon as we get into differences, people seem a lot more touchy than Jesus did about who is doing the greater or lesser work. How much energy is wasted in our churches on the question of whose work-role is higher or lower than the next person's!

Much of the envy could be avoided if lay people felt that they had defined work-roles in the community. Defining work-roles in any community or organization is always intricate. Filling those roles on the basis of talent rather than on the basis of pesonality is a higher art still. In the churches, lay people often feel that the *only* real work-roles belong to the priests, or, more recently, to the renewed office of deacon. A handful of laity find some role identity on committees: they prepare the liturgy, provide the cooking, count the money, or teach small urchins religion. Beyond this special group—and the complaint is that they are always the same people—few lay people could speak of their membership in the Christian community in terms of a clearly defined work task.

A work-role *can* be defined for the laity. Their membership in the church need not be thought of as a pick-up game, a catch-as-catch-can affair. A lay person picks up a job description at baptism that is just as definite as the one the priest picks up at ordination (maybe *that's* the problem!). We could call it a sacramental work-role: The lay person is to take responsibility to expand the community; to keep its maturity level high; to foster a critical attitude toward what gets said about love in the community, especially in regard to marriage; to care for the sick and dying; to forgive the needy sinner; to memorialize the Last Supper in which Jesus met his personal crisis successfully; to foster the organization and unity of the community. This is work. These are predictable tasks. Other issues will arise in the life of the church. These call for the nearest helping hand. But there does seem to be a common underlying work-role that every member has.

Because such a role is not very evident, we often end up crouching around trying to be more servantlike than the next person. We recognize people for their personalities, not for what they actually do around here. That's fine, but it still leaves us with the necessity of defining our work-roles in the church more clearly. Unfortunately, it is often at this point that people simply go back to their separate rooms in the Father's house and close the door behind them.

Acts 9:26 – 31
1 John 3:18 – 24
John 15:1 – 8

Actions Speak Louder

"Our love should not be just words and talk; it must be true love, which shows itself in action" (1 John 3:18).

Human life is geared to action. In centers of business and industry, in shopping malls and tourist strips, on the roads and at the airports, you get a sense of infinite energy. Go, go, go; be doing and moving. When one kind of action ends, another begins with renewed intensity. Offices and schools spill out people who scurry off on new rounds — play, chores, visits. And late in the night, sirens wail.

Yet, for many, a paralyzing sentinel stands on the threshold of action. Conscience is its name. At this checkpoint many draw back. For action is no longer treated as an end in itself. Instead, actions are specified and labeled. Questions are asked: "Why this action and not that? For how long? Have you talked this over with the parties involved? Where did you get your authorization for this action?" It gets more and more personal: "Why this particular course of action for *you?* Other people are not the issue. I was talking to you, sir. Perhaps we could go through the matter again. Now, what were *your* reasons for this course of action?"

The damnable thing about conscience is that we agree with our interrogator about the main issue: how to maintain our basic human dignity in our actions? If we could dismiss this issue, as many try to do, things would be simpler. However, we are haunted by the conviction that some actions are appropriate for us, for me, but others are not. The imperative quality to conscience's voice makes us sit up alertly. True, sometimes we do this in knee-jerk fashion. In those cases we suspect we are reacting to voices from our distant past, or to voices from our attic or our cellar. We may indeed at times misread the urgency of conscience. Sometimes it refers to nothing else than the fact that other people are shouting their opinions at us. Moral debate surrounds us; moral opinions flood over us. We are bombarded by a rabble of voices on every side.

Christian tradition, however, claims that we can come to some personal moral clarity despite the din. God does give us the light to sort out the various moral messages that cross our desk. Some, we know, are to be disregarded by us, at least for the moment. Others go into the circular file. We note those that are marked "personal" and require our immediate attention. The thought that God does not give people enough inspiration to maintain a basic moral identity and integrity in life is cruel. If anything, God acts like a good moral counselor, sometimes prodding, sometimes looking skeptical, mostly listening and remaining sympathetic, always tailoring his urgings to our individual situation.

Many people expect something different from this. Conscience seems to them hardly more highly developed than a system of jungle drums. Others have long ago subcontracted the operations of their conscience to some outside agency that specializes in that sort of thing. People can be so disappointed with their encounters with conscience that they need a renewal in faith concerning its workings.

Today's second reading makes two important points about conscience. First, it tells us that loving action is about the best criterion for a good conscience that we can get. This is not a perfectly satisfactory criterion, to be sure, since conscience can continue to bother us even in the midst of loving action. So Saint John says, "If our conscience condemns us, we know that God is greater than our conscience and that he knows everything" (1 John 3:20). This is at first confusing, since we wonder how we can be at peace with God when conscience, the voice of God in us, is still charging us with things.

That is why Saint John adds a further point. He announces an absolutely essential principle about the workings of conscience, namely, that everything depends on the kind of God we think we are dealing with in our conscience. If we think that the God of conscience is itchy, erratic, and hypertensive, if we think that God makes everything hinge on the consistently flawless functioning of the conscience mechanism, then no wonder we would be paralyzed and unable to act. Saint John puts his principle quite simply: "God is greater than our conscience" (3:20). God can handle all the foul-ups; God can work with what he is given and make arrangements accordingly; God knows that a person is more than his or her morality; God can cope with malfunctions in the system better than we can.

What Saint John's principle does is to reinforce the fact that God is more interested in our getting down to living, less interested in having us stay inside our own heads, than we might have thought. Conscience is not meant to make cowards of us all, but to lead us to energetic action in the world. It would be a shame for us to use the voice of God to drown out the sounds of life.

Fifth Sunday of Easter — C

Acts 14:21 – 27
Revelation 21:1 – 5
John 13:31 – 33, 34 – 35

Trying on Love

"Love one another. As I have loved you, so you must love one another" (John 13:34).

Alright, let's try to formulate how he loved us: "I will act as though I'm not God. I know I am who I am, but I'll drop that for a while. I'll go the acculturation route, wear native dress — they call it flesh and blood — live like them, be one of them. I will take on their full emotional range. I will let myself get angry, frustrated, anxious, annoyed, guilt-striken.

"I will learn their language. I will study what passes for politeness and direct speech among them. I will learn the art of small talk, and hope it's not too boring. I will get knots in my stomach before a sermon, like they do, and have to raise my voice to be heard.

"I'll learn to be religious. I'll read the Bible (if I can get hold of one!) with human eyes. I'll see what it is like for them to pray under distracting circumstances. I'll taste the silence and the waiting of prayer. I'll experience the fear that in prayer I just might be waiting for the echo of my own voice to return. I'll have to learn to relate to my Father from a new perspective. I won't capitalize on my connections. I will draw near to the Father in human form, and pray that I don't melt when I get too close. I will feel the deep human shudder before the mystery—the helplessness and incomprehension.

"If all this goes well, I will try to free up other people in their relationship to the Father. People seem so constipated in this regard; I don't know whether to laugh at them or cry. It will take a lot of convincing to get them to see that the Father is smarter, funnier, more sophisticated, more tender and knowing, more classy than they are. I will probably lose my poise at times and run on about fire and brimstone. But I can't be expected to take upon myself an inhuman kind of measured expression.

"Most of them are over twenty-one. So if I break a law here or there in order to make some point about my Father, they should be able to figure that out, too.

"I'll reject sin, not because I am God, but because I will have come to see sin as the enemy within my own humanity.

"Getting things across to people will be the hard thing. They seem so uptight, vicious, isolated, and selfish. Will that happen to me?

"In any case, there will be no shortcuts. I will be particularly conscious of people's history—where they have come from, with what resources, customs, and habits. I'll live with their legends and late-night storytelling. I'll work out how to deal differently with adults and with young people. I'll blush and wonder with the best of them when it comes to figuring out women.

"I'll forge my own values out of the disarray I see and the conflicting opinions I hear. When I share these values with others, I'll take the usual consequences—incomprehension, misquoting, suspicion of my motives and of my conviction (they really go after the weak spot, don't they?).

"But it won't be so bad. At least my friends will never abandon me. And who would want to hurt anyone who is in favor of love?"

Jesus is not talking about a divine put-on. The love he loved with is human in shape and form. We know that human shape and form from some primal memory or some primal hope that we have about love. The problem with Jesus is not that he is also God, but that he is relentlessly human. We continue to be suspicious that God is interested only in God's glory. So much so that at times we might wish he would take his "glory" (John 13:31–32) and go home. But we cannot escape an ancient truth here, one that holds for Jesus, too: the glory of God is a human being, fully alive.

Acts 8:5–8, 14–17
1 Peter 3:15–18
John 14:15–21

Recognition

"Be ready at all times to answer anyone who asks you to explain the hope you have in you" (1 Peter 3:15).

For old grads who haven't been making the reunions in a while, recognition can be a problem. Faint traces and contours are all that remain of former companions. You look in vain for the young lions.

Yet, if you drew a line about four inches in on either side; if you noted the way the feet turned slightly in; if you halved the thickness of the glasses, and especially if you got rid of the ridiculous ascot—that suburbanite over there might indeed be Harry Phelan, the terror of your Spanish class!

But this is due, of course, to physical changes. Life is subject to such physical changes that make recognition more difficult. But there are spiritual changes as well, and spiritual recognition becomes an issue for us. Today's gospel speaks about the Spirit of truth whom the world cannot accept "because it cannot see him or know him" (John 14:17). What does it mean when it says that the world cannot recognize truth?

The gospel is not talking about accidental diffculties people have in recognizing truth, the way you can pass an acquaintance on the street and miss him or her against the general blur. Nor is it talking about the problem people have when truth "changes." There are many people whose favorite tune is the collapse of truths they have known and loved, whether in politics, religion, or economics. Some of the lyrics of this tune go: "Didn't we hold that a man can keep what he earns? . . . Wasn't it true that you could walk the streets safely years ago? . . . Weren't we told that the church never changes?" These people cannot recognize the need for and value of a new stage of things. They just long for the good old days.

The gospel is talking about a reaction to truth that is more furtive and malicious than this. It involves the world's denial of the truly known shape of love. It accuses the world of putting on blinders to its own capacity for loving, of looking past the obvious evidence and urging for love that is all around us. The gospel tells us that there is a Holy Spirit within us that keeps reminding us of the shape of love. Like an art teacher, the Spirit often has to wave arms wildly, rant and storm at our handiworks of love in the world: "No, no, no, no, no. Not that way; *this* way, with a softer stroke but full, and daring— don't poke at the canvas of love; *wield* yourself."

Actually, in the gospel imagery the Spirit is more like a lawyer, making the case for love against those who would deny its presence. The Spirit insists that love is possible and presses the point that love has a shape and form in life. Not everything will pass for it.

Another gospel expression captures the drama that is involved here: "You will not be left all alone [orphaned]", says Jesus (John 14:18). An orphan literally loses the embodiment and shape of love that is most familiar to him or her. The amorphous state that follows can be devastating. But Jesus promises his Spirit, to convince the disciples that they will never lose the ability to recognize the silhouette of love.

The Spirit has to act like a lawyer at times. It is the world's way to fudge the picture of love that is written in our hearts. We know that we can talk ourselves into the greatest viciousness, infidelities, and distractions—all in the name of love. Sometimes the only way the Spirit can get our attention to debate these points is to sue us. Yet, paradoxically, the Spirit is also gift, since God comes again and again to the heart of humanity to do it the favor of reminding it about the true shape of love.

Sixth Sunday of Easter—B

Acts 10:25–26, 34–35, 44–48
1 John 4:7–10
John 15:9–17

Catching Up

"Whoever does not love does not know God, for God is love" (1 John 4:8).

Few words could strike more terror into human hearts than the above. We have had other experiences—at work, in school, in sports—when experts have brought us up short with the fact of our ignorance. "You know nothing about reading a book," they told us, and we saw in a flash the dimensions of our illiteracy. "Here is the way you talk to a customer," they said, and we were suffused with shame at having to take baby steps in learning our sales profession. "You have it completely backwards," we heard, and we wondered if we could ever learn how to hold a basketball or swing a racquet. But love of God, we thought, at least *that* comes naturally. Isn't everyone attuned to the basic rhythms that attach creatures to their creator? Apparently not. Thus the shock, the humiliation upon hearing that we might be all wet in this area, too.

The crux of the matter is the tie-in that Saint John makes between charity toward others and the knowledge of God. It seems to flay us with its simplicity: "Dear friend, let us love one another, because love comes from God. Whoever loves is a child of God and knows God" (1 John 4:7). There it is. A seemingly iron-clad sequence is indicated: If we love one another, we know what it is to love God. If we don't. . . .

This sequence disheartens us because love is not our strongest suit. Many screw up their faces in puzzlement when love is the topic. Others reduce love to such a narrow range (to *our* kind, to the family, to this or that person) that it looks too cozy and protected. The best of us, devoted wives and husbands, confess to the struggles we have in loving even one other person. The more we try, the more we feel our limitations. How can all these stops and starts, how can the relentless unfolding of new sensibilities and of surprising turns in the relationship, how can this constant necessity of renewing our resolve ever mirror and measure the love of God?

Saint John's point is not to discourage us. He shows how God breaks us down with flattery. Here in the world we know what it is to be wooed, to be pursued, even to be lusted after lovingly. When someone's preference and initiative light upon us, when someone takes the first step toward us, well, we just puff up and enjoy it while we can. Saint John wishes to overwhelm us with the sense that we are cherished when he says, "This is what love is: it is not that we have loved God, but that he loved us" (1 John 4:10); or, again, "You did not choose me; I chose you" (John 15:16). This feeling of being chosen will, we hope, touch us and soften us in turn toward others. In motivating us in this way to be sensitive to others, Saint John is hinting that we might do well to incorporate this first quality of divine love into our love of neighbor. Many of the problems we encounter in loving others stem precisely from the fact that our love never really went through such a crucible of choice. We bumbled into love, or we loved because it was the thing to do. We decorated our insecurity or our loneliness with love. We joined love as though it were an organization that needed members. We ambled over to love like it was the corner bar. We never really zeroed in on another person and said, "I am going to love this person to death." By reviewing our love of others in the light of God's kind of love for us, we will be helped to dig in for the duration of love. When our love is based on choice, the way God's is, its chances improve greatly. When love becomes our initiative instead of our reluctant duty, then possibilities stretch out like a spreading smile.

There is a second quality of divine love that we might profitably look at if we are to understand love of our neighbor. Jesus says: "I do not call you servants any longer, because a servant does not know what his master is doing. Instead, I call you friends, because I have told you everything I heard from my Father" (John 15:15).

How often have we heard lovers complain: "You keep so much from me. You never tell me what you're thinking about or how you feel. I seem so distant from the real you." Easy and open communication is a sign of love. If we can't say a word—our word—to those we are supposed to love, what likelihood is there that love will last? That is why God speaks his Word to us, a Word of union and solidarity with us. Jesus is the straight story, right out there for us to deal with. Unless, of course, we think God has been keeping secrets.

Choice and communicativeness—two qualities of God's love that might work wonders in our love life. They won't solve all our problems, but then they didn't solve God's, either.

Sixth Sunday of Easter—C

Acts 15:1–2, 22–29
Revelation 21:10–14, 22–23
John 14:23–29

Policy Changes

"The Holy Spirit and we have agreed not to put any other burden on you besides these necessary rules..." *(Acts 15:28).*

The first reading today is a bit of a jumble. It runs together what were two separate incidents. The first incident concerned an argument in the church at Antioch about whether converts to the faith from paganism (as opposed to converts from Judaism) ought to be circumcised. This issue was resolved at what has come to be called the Council of Jerusalem in A.D. 49 (see Acts 15:1–12).

The second incident took place shortly thereafter. It dealt with the question of whether the Gentile converts had to observe any special dietary laws. The decision taken on this question (Acts 15:13–33) was a prudential one, aimed at maintaining an uneasy peace between Gentile and Jewish Christians.

What is important about both decisions is that they indicate the role of policy making in the early church. Saint Paul was generally unimpressed by the repute of the Jerusalem church, although he had the good grace to explain his work to the people there. Yet he brought the first issue above to Jerusalem for a decision. This step was due in part to the fact that the troublemakers in Antioch had come from Jerusalem in the first place. But it was also out of respect for the policy-making role of the Jerusalem church. Above all, it was out of Paul's hardheaded realization that it is policy that keeps the body of Christ together and keeps its momentum going.

Picture the problems at Antioch more closely. The Gentiles had taken up the faith, with its explosive sense of freedom before God and man, its aura of joy, service, and devotion. Should they also have to take on the external trappings of Judaism? The Jews were all circumcised, *n'est-ce pas?* Shouldn't Gentile converts demonstrate their seriousness and good will by adapting themselves to their Jewish Christian forbears in the faith? Gulp. Clarification is sought from Jerusalem. Word comes back: no need to circumcise them. Sighs of relief are heard all over Asia Minor. Policy can be crucial at times.

But the bickering goes on. Even if the former pagans won't be circumcised, won't they make any concessions to the Jewish tradition of their Christian brothers? Are they free to act any way they like? Again Jerusalem speaks, this time to the issue of dietary laws. We won't lay any unnecessary burdens on you Gentiles. Just don't eat what you're used to eating! (Actually, the strictures mentioned in Acts 15:29 were similar to the normal ones placed in former days upon Gentiles who wished to live as guests in Israelite communities.) In other words, Jerusalem proposes a practical suggestion for keeping the peace with Jewish Christians. In principle, freedom from the Jewish law is the conviction of Christianity. But in practice, a policy of coexistence and compromise was advised.

Many today would argue that all this bickering seems foreign to what they would call "the Spirit of Jesus." They would not consider any policy to be "strictly necessary." They would feel that even large movements should be able, in the Spirit of Jesus, to get things done and to interact without policies coming down from Rome or from other such places. The policy squabbles of today's church, in short, would irk them. They would rather appeal to the simple words of today's gospel: "Whoever loves me will obey my teaching. My Father will love him, and my Father and I will come to him and live with him" (John 14:23).

The problem is that such oversimplification may well mask a flight from reality. To be sure, Jesus promises to send us his indwelling Spirit who will "make you remember all that I have told you" (John 14:26). But that Spirit comes as Paraclete, as lawyer. Only people in a pickle need a lawyer. Sides are drawn. Briefs are prepared. Argument is expected. Settling out of court is often the best option. There may not even be question of villains or heroes—just of people struggling to discover truth and to claim justice in a complex world.

Church policy is one of the ways the Spirit of Jesus acts. It will take the pressure off some; it will complicate life for others. It will shift and change from city to city. It will spring up out of events and be undercut by new developments. It will involve politicking and politicians. It is the church's way of trying to keep everyone pointed in the same general direction. Generally.

Seventh Sunday of Easter—A

Acts 1:12–14
1 Peter 4:13–16
John 17:1–11

Whose Amazin' Grace?

"I am no longer in the world, but they are in the world" (John 17:11).

A veteran spiritual campaigner often talks about what he calls an "individual's grace." What he means by the expression doesn't always leap out. He is not one of those people who pushes doing one's own thing all the time. There is something in his expression that relates to scriptural charisms, but he really doesn't mean by this "individual grace" a person's gifts or talents. What he seems to be trying to express is that God deals with people as individuals, taking them in their full actuality, sensitive to their present moment in the light of their past strengths and weaknesses.

There is certainly some creativity built into this grace, but it is hardly miraculous or exotic. It is almost banal. It takes into account so much that is ordinary in their lives: how they are treating their spouses, how much they're drinking, how they feel toward their jobs, whether they go to church much, and so on. But, as with many ordinary events, their present reaction can be crucial. If they blow this grace, they have missed a chance to take hold of their own concrete selves. They remain diffuse and, to use the classical phrase, dissipated.

These thoughts about individual grace come because of today's readings. The first reading pictures the disciples, in the period before Pentecost, gathered in the upstairs room: "They gathererd frequently to pray as a group" (Acts 1:14). The epistle is an exhortation to embrace suffering in the name of Jesus: "If you suffer because you are a Christian, don't be ashamed of it" (1 Peter 4:16). The gospel has the apostles at the Last Supper listening to a long speech from Jesus about his glory. When you think of the millions of individuals who will hear these passages read on Sunday you sometimes wonder what goes on in their heads and hearts. Are they to understand that frequent prayer is *their* individual grace? Are they to consider ways in which *they* can suffer with Jesus during the coming week? Will hearing at length about Jesus' glory advance *them* spiritually?

Many Christians don't even have this question. They approach the Scriptures like a grab bag. Anything they get is better than nothing. They poke about the readings with a buyer's eye, trying to get something that fits their taste and need. They can live for days or weeks off some tidbit that particularly strikes them. In these ways, they do adapt the Scriputres to their individual lives. Even if they do so more out of diffidence than anything else, they succeed in leaving room for their individual grace.

But some Christians don't. They take the Scriptures literally. They consider it their task to ape everything they read in the Scriptures that sounds like a principle or a rule of conduct. If frequent prayer is the topic, then that's for them. If Jesus' suffering and glory are mentioned, then they want to do both simultaneously. They are nervous that they are constantly falling behind in performance.

They fail to see that because their individual grace has not been consulted, frequent prayer might be the worst thing in the world for them; any reference to sharing suffering with Jesus might be deceiving; and thoughts of Jesus' glory might be disastrous. But even though the Scriptures give them indigestion, they plug bravely on.

Such people do not seem to realize that the Scriptures are primarily describing *other* people's individual graces. They are talking about another world. Our world might coincide with theirs in many ways, but we will always have to cope with the differences that our own individual world creates. Reading the Scripture is like having a conversation with strange people. It takes time to see where and in what respects our own lives might be like theirs. We can approach these strangers with the boorish presupposition that they have nothing to teach us. Or we can pretend that everything they do or say is the best in some absolute sense. And we can go ahead and imitate it literally. But this way we can end up looking like a tourist from Texas who wears lederhosen in Italy.

Where does this leave the vaunted power and inspiration of Scripture? What the Scripture does, and does with the effectiveness of God's own Word, is to jar us into personal questions that lead us then to discover our individual grace. But that grace may take us down far different paths than the people in the Scripture took. In fact, if we read the Scripture with this business of individual grace in mind, we might gain more appreciation for how the Holy Spirit dealt so individually and realistically with the scriptural characters themselves. We might see that, in its individual context, the frequent prayer of the disciples in the upstairs room was not like your annual retreat. We might pick up the special nuances of Saint Peter's epistle, in which exhortation to suffer in the name of Jesus in time of persecution sometimes comes out: They're going to kill you anyway, so you might as well go out for a good cause. We might, in the gospel, catch a certain nervousness in all the talk about glory.

Who knows? We might even find that our individual grace and their individual grace aren't so far apart after all.

Acts 1:15– 17, 20– 26
1 John 4:11– 16
John 17:11– 19

Shaky Foundations

"Not one of them was lost, except the man who was bound to be lost —so that the scripture might come true" (John 17:12).

In the early church, much energy was spent trying to show how the life, death, and resurrection of Jesus, even the development of the Christian community itself, took place in fulfillment of Scripture. We have been seeing many instances of this effort in the post-Easter liturgical readings. Speeches by Jesus, by Peter, and by other disciples all drive in the same direction, namely, that what was happening to them was in some way foreshadowed in the Old Testament. Today's first reading makes the same point: "The scripture had to come true in which the Holy Spirit, speaking through David, made a prediction about Judas, who was the guide for those who arrested Jesus" (Acts 1:16).

Most commentators agree that the aim of such passages is not to attribute prophetic powers to individuals from earlier times. It is not to claim, in the above instance, that David knew something about Judas. Rather, what is being described is the growing realization of the first disciples that "it all figured." They looked at the events taking place in their lives and searched around for ways to make sense of them.

The event that gave them the most trouble, of course, was the death of Jesus. So they took another look at their own sacred writings. They began to see passages they once missed. They noted events that previously their eye had skimmed over, either out of habit or because of a lack of interest. Words suddenly leapt out that until then held no great significance. They began to see how things now "figured." This made antecedents in their Scripture "pre-figure." Earlier events, people, and fates gave credence and almost inevitable direction to the way things were moving now. The idea that *the scripture had to come true* captures this eye-opening and liberating review of their religious and historical past, a review that enabled them finally to make more sense of their present experiences.

Something like this happens to many of us. We experience a peak joy; we accept this job or form this new relationship. At the same time, we find ourselves reviewing our past, fixing on a conversation here, a month spent there, dredging up a key encounter, recalling a book read or a skill learned. We begin to see how some invisible thread stretches from our past to our present position. We find our present situation in many ways prefigured in our personal history.

But more than reinforcement is implied by the idea that *the scripture had to come true*. Reading Scripture was not always simply this kind of leisurely confirmation of present experience. There was also an element of anxiousness in their recourse to the past. We sense that scriptural writers are under some urge to prove, to be sure, to argue and illustrate. It is as though their present experience could not stand on its own feet without props from the hoary past. The Old Testament is searched, but seemingly with the hope that credentials be found, that pedigree be established. No doubt, this procedure is partly explained by the fact that a polemical situation existed between the first Christians and their former co-religionists. But more is involved. There is also the pressure on faith, on God, to give a more nailed-down, cohesive accounting of things.

We should not be so hard on God. If God knits together threads of our lives to lead us to joyful experiences now, we should not keep such a close eye out, lest the knitting needle slip. To the extent that the first disciples looked diligently to the past in order to justify God's ways to themselves, they risked overlooking how chaotic and haphazard God's ways can be. In today's same reading, the disciples choose a successor to Judas. How do they do it? A little prayer, and then roll the dice! Not far from it: "They drew lots to choose between the two men, and the one chosen was Matthias, who was added to the group of eleven apostles" (Acts 1:26). This vignette, showing Christian history advancing by the toss of a coin, is in delicious contrast to the massive effort these same disciples were making to show how their faith stood on firmly traced antecedents.

The moral is to dig deeper into the experience we do have, to trust it and not to deny it. If we get reinforcement for it from the past, fine. But we should realize at the same time that we better keep the dice handy.

Acts 7:55 – 60
Revelation 22:12 – 14, 16 – 17, 20
John 17:20 – 26

"God Is Great" — Pass It On

"I pray not only for them, but also for those who believe in me because of their message" (John 17:20).

Early in his gospel (John 1:13), John gives the impression that believing is so much a gift of God that no one else has anything to do with its genesis. In today's passage from his gospel, that impression is corrected. At least, John explains more fully *how* God draws us to faith. We find that he draws Christians to faith through the faith of other Christians. Faith has a horizontal life in history and is not simply something that descends vertically from on high. It is handed on to us by others, by the people of God, in either workmanlike or slipshod ways. We carry it gingerly from one generation to the next, careful and anxious that we do not spill it along the way. A terrifying thought. For it means that the faith of others is somewhat in our hands.

Communicating our faith to others can be a dangerous business for us, too. Look at today's second reading, in which Stephen gets paid for his efforts in preaching the faith: "Then they all rushed at him at once, threw him out of the city, and stoned him" (Acts 7:57 – 58). Although we do not usually meet the fate of a Stephen in communicating our faith to others, we are put to the test in many ways. Just ask parents or religious educators how much they are subjected to the third degree when they open their mouths to others about the faith. As believers, *our* integrity, *our* liveliness, *our* ability to conceptualize, *our* structures, performance, and social utility all come under the scrutiny of those who are called to believe through our faith.

Much of this testing of us stems from a legitimate curiosity on the part of the next generation. It comes from an understandable desire to get a readout on our seriousness. Those who talk of trust in God ought to give some signs in their other relationships that they know what trust is all about.

On the other hand, some of the testing is mischievous. There are those who would be distraught and angry if faith proved authentic. Faith would then be perceived as a rebuke to them. Some of the testing is cowardly. We cannot but wonder whether those present at the stoning of Stephen were crudely "examining" his faith out of their own indecision: "Let's stone him and see how he holds up. Then we might get into this faith thing ourselves."

In all of this testing, we experience the pain of handing on the faith. How turn this pain into joy? One problem is that we sometimes settle for handing on the externals of faith, without offering anything exciting to potential believers. We tell them to go to church, to receive sacraments. We urge that they contribute financially to good causes. We invite them to cooperate with us on church committees. We ourselves try to maintain ethical standards in business and in our personal lives to give testimony to the faith we want to pass on.

What is missing here is any testimony about the kind of person we think Jesus is. Do we ever indicate to others how friendly, sane, sophisticated, or tender we think God is? Is it clear to others how we think God deals with our initiative, idiosyncracy, or talent? Or how adult God allows us to be? These are the kinds of things that the next generation wants to know from their Christian forebears. It would find testimony about these more cogent than much of what we tell them about faith. To be open to such questions from others requires that we first face them in ourselves.

As if to compound this problem, there is the disunity among Christian believers themselves. Our ecumenical track record seems to belie the prayer of Jesus in today's gospel: "I gave them the same glory you gave me, so that they may be one, just as you and I are one" (John 17:22). Whether we are talking about passing on the faith to the next generation or about sharing it with our contemporaries, every communication of faith we engage in seems to entail misunderstanding, selective hearing, and schism. As a result, people settle for less. They trot off with faith to their private worlds, keeping faith with themselves but nervous about mentioning it to others.

Jesus' prayer challenges all this. It calls for greater efforts on our part to present a consistent, glorious image of our faith to others. A lot of people are waiting for our good news.

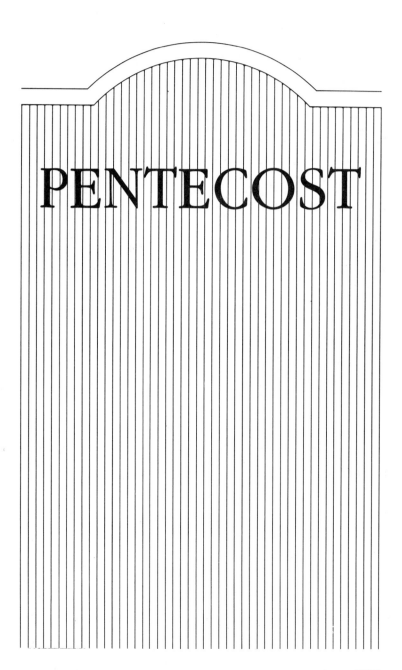

PENTECOST

Acts 2:1– 11
1 Corinthians 12:3– 7, 12– 13
John 20:19– 23

A Rush of Spirit

"Each one of them heard the believers talking in his own language (Acts 2:6).

We've often heard people say with enthusiasm or with relief: "Now you're speaking my language!" A channel suddenly opens up between people. A bridge is thrown across, firm and inviting. Communication sparks. The usual dissembling and marking time is dropped. The pretense that things are being said and heard is no longer necessary.

Something like this is reported to have been the remarkable outcome of Pentecost, when the Spirit of the risen Jesus rushed upon his followers at Jerusalem. "These people who are talking like this are Galileans! How is it, then, that all of us hear them speaking in our own native languages?" (Acts 2:7– 8). That scene must have stirred feelings like the ones we get watching a silent film of some great orator such as Teddy Roosevelt or Lenin: the hammering desire to reach out to the audience, the dogged jabbing, the alert craning, the eyes locking here and there, the calculated pause, the renewed pursuit, the victorious flow of energy from speaker to listener.

And yet, there is something pushy and egocentric about wanting to hear things said in "my language." Very often it is a cover-up for not wanting to hear certain things said at all. We often distrust the protestation of those who say they would be interested in this or that, "if it spoke my language a little more." To put the whole world at the mercy of catching the least nuance of one's own private idiom is a bit too much. On that very principle, teachers have heard everyone from Plato to Shakespeare to Dickens written off by dull students.

On the other hand, there *is* a deeper capacity for language in all of us that seldom comes to utterance. It is what Saint Paul calls inarticulate groaning, or what others perhaps call a primal scream. Its voice is ageless, croaking and puling. It is an inebriated chant. It is a straining moan as we lurch upward from guilt or squirm against invisible spiritual bonds. It may also be a bubbling chuckle deep within us, a joke that wants to be shared across all language barriers. It is a music looking for a melody, in troubled harmony with distant spheres.

The Spirit of Jesus at Pentecost reached this deeper level of our language through the Apostles. We do not want to give the impression that garble is good when it comes to religious expression. The apostles' spirited words were not free from argument, persuasion, pleading, flattery, and so on.

It does seem, however, that the success of the apostles' preaching stemmed from their communication of Jesus' love. They could communicate because the gift of the Spirit—as today's gospel indicates—made them convincing. True to Jesus' word, they could offer the promise of reconciliation to strangers.

Many years after Pentecost, the church was struggling to keep the fire of the Spirit alive. Today's epistle finds Saint Paul belaboring the principles by which the

Spirit acts in the church: "There are different kinds of spiritual gifts, but the same Spirit gives them. There are different ways of serving, but the same Lord is served. There are different abilities to perform service, but the same God gives ability to everyone for their particular service. The Spirit's presence is shown in some way in each person for the good of all" (1 Corinthians 12:3–7). Even at that early date, the church seems plagued by the same tiredness, the same carping divisions, the same lack of communication that is sometimes prevalent today. But there was a moment and a memory that inspired the early church, the incredible force of Pentecost that was to transform and enliven it as it had done to Jesus. It is this same moment and memory that we celebrate this Pentecost, when from our deep selves we cry out: Come, Holy Spirit.

A Gathering of Spirit

"All of us, whether Jews or Gentiles, whether slaves or free, have been baptized into the one body by the same spirit" (1 Corinthians 12:13).

We live at a time when the Spirit of God is felt to be especially active. Many Christians attest that they are caught up in the Spirit in ways that are clearly faithful to the New Testament picture of the Spirit. One person heals, laying on hands that will not yield to the raging power of sickness. Another person utters prophecies, spearing current events with faith-ful insight, reading God back into them, watching God toss restlessly beneath the most ordinary happenings. Still others speak in tongues, inarticulately giving expression to the comprehensiveness and strangeness of God, whose determination to communicate with humanity brooks no restraints of literacy or language. All testify to the welling joy within them. All announce that they are more inside themselves, that they are enthusiastic about the image taking shape in them. All tell us that they know well what the breath of the Spirit is like when it sweeps creatively over former wastelands. Their prayer, they find, moves beyond a staring, sullen silence, beyond veiled debate, to something more loose and energetic—all to the growing beat of hymns and hosannas. Like the Christians of Acts, modern Pentecostals and charismatics are also aware of a corporate force, a communitarian swell expressed in larger and larger numbers: thousands at Steubenville, more thousands at Notre Dame and Atlantic City. A gathering of Spirit that sweetly steamrollers everything before it.

All this activity forms part of the Christian celebration of Pentecost today. It feeds like a freshet into the mainstream of acclaim and praise that is directed to the Spirit of God on this feast. It is quite appropriate.

Or, should we say, appropriated. The small print—if we recall correctly from the theology books— says that much of what we attribute to this or that person of the Trinity really pertains to all the persons. We talk at Pentecost of the Spirit as the principle of healing, joy, prayer, solidarity, and so forth. But in talking this way we are not expressing things that the Spirit really does on his own, as it were, because of some prior internal division of labor agreed upon by the Trinity. Saint Thomas said that what we are trying to do by this way of assigning things to various persons of the Trinity is to help us make sense of our experience. It is as though we were saying, "We know that we're doing these good things for a change, and we'd like to thank *somebody*. So we pick out this or that divine person to get credit for our new experience." Even Jesus' remarks about the Spirit were made under the same constraints of human language that we have!

In the theological tradition, the qualities assigned to the Father were power, eternity, oneness, and creation. Anyone can see that these qualities are true of the other divine persons as well. The Son was identified with truth and exemplarity (as a kind of model for everything else). The Spirit got as a special province things like action, love, fruition, and so on. These descriptions were often thought to derive directly from scriptural descriptions of the divine persons. But things are not so simple. Each generation comes to this business of appropriating things to the divine persons with its own agenda in mind.

It would not be surprising if we were to deceive ourselves a bit in these efforts. To play with Saint Thomas' expression, we not only use certain language of this or that person of God to explain our faith, but we also give away our lack of faith by that same language. We could probably learn something about our general attitudes toward God from the way we say who does what.

Today, what seems particularly lacking in our own language about the Spirit is, if you will, the pragmatic and businesslike side of the Spirit. Today's liturgical readings stress the fact that the Spirit's "job" is to build unity amid a disruptive diversity. It is to get people to face their real divisions and differences and to forge some unity out of them. How much does our current Pentecostalism really face that?

Social, educational, racial, and economic differences may lend themselves less spontaneously to hosannas, but they are truly the arena of the Spirit. Sometimes it seems that those who are struggling for unity and diversity in the Middle East, in Northern Ireland, in Africa and Asia are the real heroes of the Spirit. They tell us in some obscure, eucharistic utterance that we are one body. Let their sufferings be added to the praise of the Spirit that we speak today.

SEASON IN ORDINARY TIME

Exodus 34:4– 6, 8– 9
2 Corinthians 13:11– 13
John 3:16– 18

Three Cheers for Love

"Strive for perfection; listen to my appeals; agree with one another; live in grace. And the God of love and peace will be with you" (2 Corinthians 13:11).

When Trinity Sunday rolls around, theologians shudder. You just can't start off: "Now, you see, this is the way it is with God. What happens is. . . ." In an earlier age, fundamental issues about the Godhead were debated vigorously and confidently by the populace at large. Whole cities took sides in the trinitarian controversies. One crusty Father of the Church grumbled that he couldn't even go down to the public baths on a Saturday night without some attendant asking him conspiratorially: "Are you on the side of those who think the Son is divine, or of those who think he is just another creature?" No wonder Frank Sheed used to say that, when other topics like finance, politics, and the church would get a big yawn from his street audiences, they would argue to the death about the mechanics of the Trinity.

But we all cannot come to the topic with the faith and ingenuity of a Frank Sheed. Our great temptation is to oversimplify. To get a handle on God is enticing. Expertise in the matter is a sure-fire plume in the cap. Yet the awesome mystery of God puts us off; it makes us chuckle at our own pretensions. We are reminded of a travelogue recently read, T.H. White's *America at Last*.

The British author is in a strange land. Not even his great goodwill and sensitivity can save the book from a certain oddness. When he speaks of things we Americans know and experience from the inside, it all sounds a little off-key. He either gives too much praise or not enough. Or the right thing gets mentioned for the wrong reason. For example, he gives long speeches about American posteriors that make you uncomfortable. He is impressed by the clear, bright air of Las Vegas. He thinks taxi drivers are charming and friendly. You begin to wonder.

Does this mean that in talking about God we can only point and poke thus at different things we think are representative of the Trinity, risking at the same time the raised eyebrows of others who are more familiar with the territory?

We have been—we admit it—circling. There seems little else to do once you have exhausted the traditional analogies that were used to "explain" the Trinity. Most of these borrowed from the instance of diversity-amid-unity that is found in the psychological processes of one conscious person's thinking and feeling about himself: The self-knower is not the self-knowing, nor the forceful reaction to what is known, but all three are simultaneously one and related. Come to think of it, perhaps we aren't the only ones who are circling.

The first reading today is more cautious. It tries to relate what the triune God does for others, without getting too much into the inner workings, so to speak, of God. Even this presents problems: "I, the Lord, am a God who is full of compassion and pity, who is not easily angered and who shows great love and faithfulness," says the text (Exodus 34:6). The liturgical compiler, also apparently merciful and gracious, leaves out the part of this text that has God threatening to make people pay for their sins to the third and fouth generation!

The New Testament directs us to examine our own experience of love in community in order to learn what God is like. "Live in peace. And the God of love and peace will be with you." To live in harmony and peace, we have to identify ourselves with others. Love presupposes a vision of oneself in the other and of the other in oneself. Love reproduces one's own features in another and another's in oneself, the way old married couples sometimes are said to end up physically resembling one another. It is no doubt difficult for us to see ourselves in some of our fellow Christians. No one wants to identify with people they consider too distant for comfort: the parish candlelighter; the professional joiner; the draped liturgist; the ponderous catechist; the scrupulous, haunted type who pesters the rectory; the railing activist. And yet, our capacity to take all these people within us is an indication of the similarity between our love and God's. The Father is not the Son is not the Holy Spirit. But imagine if they started excluding one another.

Trinity Sunday—B

Deuteronomy 4:32–34, 39–40
Romans 8:14–17
Matthew 28:16–20

Mirror, Mirror

"Those who are led by God's Spirit are God's sons" (Romans 8:14).

Preachers tremble, kids fidget, many simply shrug; a few usually quiet types suddenly won't shut up; finer points are debated later at Brennan's Bar after a little lift. It probably is good for us that we are hit with Trinity Sunday once a year, but it is backbreaking to talk at all about the mystery of God celebrated in this feast.

We say that it probably is good for us. First, it's nice to be reminded from time to time how little we can comprehend the mystery of God. It fits with what we suspected in the first place. A lot of people are quite ready to give us the inside story on God, little realizing that they are just reporting their experience of God. In their enthusiasm, they can frighten others off from ways of experiencing God and of expressing that experience, which is quite legitimate.

Second, there is a marvelous opportunity to learn something about our own mysteriousness when we reflect on the mystery of God, in whose image we are made. However much the comparison might limp doctrinally, it's nice to reflect without embarrassment on the three (or four or five) persons that each one of us seems to be at times. There's mystery for you! We could have a field day applying to ourselves all the woolly technical talk about divinely subsisting relations, extrinsic missions, circumincessions, inseparable presences, and so on. It might even explain how we feel some mornings after a particularly hard day. There is a certain relief in being reminded that the mystery of God isn't necessarily clarified in us, who are God's image. *We* might be equally mysterious.

Third, we are forced to approach the mystery of God the way we do other mysterious persons, by politely waiting for them to reveal to us something about themselves. According to the Christian tradition, the waiting has certainly paid off. God is revealed as prompt to love and to give. The Book of Deuteronomy (today's first reading) captures with generous strokes this divine initiative: "Search the past, the time before you were born, all the way back to the time when God created man on the earth. Search the entire earth. Has anything as great as this ever happened before? Has anyone ever heard of anything like this? . . . Has any god ever dared to go and take a people from another nation and make them his own?" (Deuteronomy 4:32, 34). God wants to be known, it seems, for this kind of spontaneous, almost violent predilection. God wants attention, not for narcissistic purposes but precisely to convince humanity that God is there for us.

God also wants to be known as Father, as we find in today's second reading. When we really catch God's Spirit, we go around as if we *owned* the place. We have the sureness and sense of belonging that children in a happy family have.

Today's gospel takes the picture of God's activity further. God not only loves us but he makes us loving. God drives us to believe in community. God propels us to be less timid and to extend the circle of those we care for. God makes us reach out: "Go, then, to all peoples everywhere and make them my disciples" (Matthew 23:19).

God is revealed, then, as a doer, but one around whom even children feel comfortable. That's not a bad reputation for anyone to have. But if God is as God does, a lot of people are ready to argue about why God doesn't do more. Why the war, the suffering, the hunger, the moral and social ills? Anyone is welcome to that argument. Some of us prefer to be a little more reserved around the mystery. We try to believe, despite it all.

But, as we saw, this works to our own benefit. When our own mystery is questioned, when what we do does not measure up to people's expectations of us, when our giving and loving seem to flag, when our self-revelations come out garbled, we hope that others keep trying to espy the real us and to believe in us. Or, at least, that the children do.

Proverbs 8:22–31
Romans 5:1–5
John 16:12–15

Imagine God

"All that my Father has is mine; that is why I said that the Spirit will take what I give him and tell it to you" (John 16:15).

It is difficult to know where to begin. We are talking about the Trinity, and that's no easy subject. We are even officially put on notice that, in mysterious matters like these, we are limited to feeble comparisons between what we already know (and this gets shakier every day!) and the mystery we are trying to unravel.

Gregory of Nyssa, a great saint and one of the Fathers of the Church, offered the following assessment of our efforts to describe the triune Godhead: our language—even our scriptural and dogmatic language—reminds him of the inarticulate mumbo-jumbo of a mother trying to communicate to her baby in its imagined idiom. (A hard one to capture, but: oohzhooga-gadadawoowoo!) Or again, it reminds him of the pathetic obscurity of hog-calling language. (One more stab: sookeesookeesookeeheeawh.) Or, finally, it reminds him of someone rolling home drunk, whose wobbly language and shlurred speech hardly seem to communicate at all.

Does this mean that we go back to the triangle or the shamrock? It certainly smacks of a theological defeatism we are unused to. But we are rightly cautioned against thinking we can sum up the mystery of God very accurately. Perhaps what matters more is that babies realize they are loved, and that hogs and drunks get home safe. But as far as finding helpful words to express our Christian faith in the Trinity, were are we?

The first reading today offers us one avenue of understanding. Obviously it is not talking directly about a Trinity, as though full faith in that mystery existed when Proverbs was written. It does, however, picture the wisdom of God as operating somewhat dependently upon God, and yet somewhat in its own right. "I was there when he set the sky in place. . . .I was beside him like an architect, I was his daily source of joy" (Proverbs 8:27, 30). If you extended this imagery a bit and saw God so delighting in his wisdom that "delighting" would also have an independence of its own, you would be focusing more on God's "spirit" or mood. God would be thinking, imagining, being expressive; God would also be reacting naturally within himself to what is thought, imagined, and expressed.

Attempts at understanding the Trinity are built up in this fashion. We might be tempted to say that they are more ingenious than convincing. We might wonder why other aspects of God—his power, justice, eternity—don't each have a "person" assigned to them, so that we would end up with a quaternity, or a. . .quintinity. The conviction seems to be that all the key aspects of being a person or of having person-traits come back sooner or later to how persons *think* and *feel*. So, as with Proverbs, you can go round on this same theme: God, in his wisdom, thinks up human beings. God gets a playful kick (the Spirit) out of them. God is wise to be playful. God delights in being wise. And like that.

All this is hardly foreign to our way of talking about ourselves as persons. (At least if we don't have too poor a self-image or are not too dispirited about ourselves.) Imagine the best within yourself or about yourself: not the dross or triviality, not the hang-back insecurity, but the beautiful you, the best you in terms of your talent and savvy—you in all your glory. Then let yourself react to that best in yourself with every sentiment of love, joy, peace, patience (should the image get blurred), benignity, and kindness you can muster.

Look on your neighbor this same way (as the Golden Rule directs). Imagine the best in him or her and react to it accordingly.

Imagine God, too, and then react.

In all these cases, there's you, your imagining and your reacting. Welcome to the club.

Some have concluded that we have indeed imagined God, in the sense of having invented God and having projected our own triune image "out there" to make up for our tattered and diffident self-image. Christians believe otherwise. They believe that God saw us first and liked what he saw.

Corpus Christi

Deuteronomy 8:2–3, 14–16
1 Corinthians 10:16–17
John 6:51–58

Our Bread

"The bread we break: when we eat it, we are sharing in the body of Christ" (1 Corinthians 10:16).

Scholars tell us that even the simple words of the Our Father, "Give us this day our daily bread," are not as simple as they seem.

First, *bread* has a wider meaning than just food. In the light of Old Testament tradition, bread also means a kind of life-giving *wisdom*, a sense of purpose and direction in life that sustains us.

Second, the word *daily* is a fitful translation of ancient words that meant more than the delivery by God, one day at a time, of just enough wisdom for us to get by on. It meant, rather, a *continuous* tie between God and ourselves. We would be buying into an ongoing relationship. We would be admitting that a relationship with God is not the nodding politeness that goes on with our friendly milkman or storekeeper. It is a relationship that will last and have implications forever.

Third, our daily bread is precisely that; it is *ours*. We envision a body of people who take their wisdom from Jesus, from his way of acting and reacting, from his insights into life. By praying for "our" daily bread, then, we are opting again into the whole reality of our life *together* in Jesus.

All this is leading to the point that it takes nerve to say the Lord's Prayer! For whether we speak of our bread as the message of Jesus or whether we speak of it, as we do in the eucharist, as Jesus' own person and presence, we are led in any case to see bread as a sign of struggling love. Jesus, that wise person, relentlessly makes the connection between love and suffering. To give oneself to the Father in trust, to share oneself with others, to promote one's neighbor to the status of important person—and to keep doing this again and again—this is the strenuous program that our eucharistic bread stands for.

Saint Paul makes this point in today's epistle. He urges the Corinthian community, which had been engaged in various kinds of infighting, to discover the paradox of the eucharistic bread: It is broken, but no matter; something is being shared, and that is what counts. The goal, however, is not to break other people's bodies or hearts but to let oneself be vulnerable first.

Underpinning this vision of things is Jesus' own Last Supper experience, in which he takes full measure of the prices to be paid in loving. There he gives himself to his followers in the vivid gesture of the bread. He demonstrates that not every instance of being torn, pulled, divided up, passed off, or devoured need be the violating of love that it seems to be. It can also be the expression of love and the pledge of solidarity.

Today's gospel is loaded with references to the primitive church's practice of the eucharist. While ostensibly narrating an event early in Jesus' career when he miraculously feeds the multitudes, it casts that event in what is probably a much later eucharistic language. The points it makes reinforce the picture given above of the eucharistic bread as a sign of suffering love. It does this a bit awkwardly, since the cannibalistic overtones seem excessive and unnecessary. But it is eloquent in maintaining the tie between bread (Jesus) and life. Lifelessness is trying to love without passion. Trying to love without sharing is a dead end.

Can we honestly say that this picture of struggling love is an attractive prospect? Many people want to love at a distance. Or they believe that love happens just like that. They want love to be unruffled, free from the things that usually dry up love: when people use you and play you off against others; when they are vain and out for themselves at your expense; when they take without giving and give only after taking careful measure. As a result, much of our energy goes into not getting hurt. Or sharing ourselves with others becomes such an arch and stilted process that we feel like slow-moving laborers under a draining sun.

The eucharist doesn't solve this problem automatically. We can receive communion after communion and miss the message of it. We will not be force-fed, either. The eucharist is an invitation to us to focus on the secret the world knows in its heart but has trouble admitting: To love is to suffer. But this is the kind of thing you can't just say to people right off. You have to reach out to them first and break bread with them.

Isaiah 49:3, 5 – 6
1 Corinthians 1:1 – 3
John 1:29 – 34

Shooting Stars

"You will see the Spirit come down and stay on a man; he is the one who baptizes with the Holy Spirit" (John 1:33).

There was an ancient Jewish tradition which held that the Messiah, when he came, would remain something of a hidden figure. This tradition probably stands behind John the Baptist's statement in today's gospel: "I did not know who he would be" (John 1:31). The Baptist had to be told that the Spirit of God rested on Jesus.

Traditionally, the Messiah was also supposed to be the effective agent of God's work in the world, and certainly John the Baptist expected such a powerful figure. His expression *Lamb of God* indicated not the Mary-had type of lamb we usually think of, but a gigantic lamb-figure who would crush out sin in the world.

So we have a paradoxical picture: on the one hand, someone unrecognized and inconspicuous; on the other hand, someone effectively bearing God's powerful spirit. How fit these paradoxical qualities together?

We admit to a prejudice against hidden effectiveness. Where it looks so hidden, might it not be because it is not there? There was a time not long ago when Christian piety made much of a hidden life. But sometimes it seemed more like a convenient argument for maintaining an unhealthy isolation from reality. Keep straining novices down, prolong self-defeating and vicious marriages, don't broadcast disturbing intellecutal discoveries—that sort of thing. Many people were told in the name of God to stay within the boundaries of their own desperations, or worse, to keep their surging talents under check. Hiddenness sometimes became a cover-up for the misuse of talent, the fear of confrontation, the dissipation of enthusiasm, and many other things. Yet obscurity was supposed to serve some spirited purpose of God.

But perhaps the issue is not one of hiddenness at all. Perhaps what the Scripture is getting at is the human problem of working without recognition for what we in fact do accomplish. This is something we all feel, and you have to get in line these days to make your complaints in this department. Priests, nuns, and laity (yes, laity) all report a great sense of thanklessness for their work in the kingdom. For at times the sharpest suffering comes from this lack of recognition, which tends to put a taunting question mark around our effectiveness.

In this sense, today's gospel reminds us that Jesus, too, must work at times without recognition. It is his faith in his Father that keeps him going. So, when the Spirit of God lands on us (as, thank God, it does with such wonderful variety), we have to console ourselves with the same thought. It is no small comfort to think that at least God is saying with conviction and applause: "Ah, that's fine work, wonderful. . . you and you and you. . . ."

Second Sunday of the Year — B

1 Samuel 3:3 – 10, 19
1 Corinthians 6:13 – 15, 17 – 20
John 1:35 – 42

Chance Meeting

"Jesus turned, saw them following him, and asked, 'What are you looking for?' " (John 1:38).

It is commonly said these days that people are searching. Some are searching for the right job, others for security, many for identity and respect. Still others are looking for reasons even to care.

Sometimes this searching has the aura of an "in" thing. It is fashionable to be searching. But in large part the search is an honest one. People are fed up with the rat race, with bureaucratic establishments, with the tinsel and incessant bickering, the lies and the massive boredom. They want an experience of worth; they want some spiritual excitement.

Today's gospel pictures the future disciples of Jesus as men on the lookout. They have only vaguely formulated for themselves what it is they are seeking, but their expectations are high: They want a messiah. They want someone to galvanize their talents and enthusiasms and to bring them to a focus of dedication and action. They are lucky they ran into Jesus.

This business of searching and finding does seem to be a matter of sheer luck after a while. Many people find the search frustrating, because they lack the kind of initial contact to rivet them that Jesus' disciples had. Or when they follow someone home, nothing happens.

At one time or another we are all stumbling blocks to others who are searching. It is not simply that we fail to go out to people with our full energies at the first meeting. It is that we have the bad habit of revealing our deeper, richer selves to others only as a last resort! Most of all, we can hardly see ourselves as capable of being the answer to other people's agitated searching. No wonder, then, that a sense of haphazard chance dominates all the searching.

This is not always the case. Our Christian tradition stresses the fact that searching is a two-way street. As the case of the young Samuel shows, God is busily searching for ways to put himself in our paths. The hunters, it turns out, are the hunted.

Second Sunday of the Year — C

Isaiah 62:1 – 5
1 Corinthians 12:4 – 11
John 2:1 – 12

Name Calling

"You will be called by a new name, a name given by the Lord himself" (Isaiah 62:2).

We live in an age of packaging. The outside of the cup has to be just right. Whether the cup leaks, cracks, or is coated with poisonous paint, it has to look right. And the name on the label has to fit. Shrewsbury's Frankfurthers just won't make it; neither will Jones' Best Diamonds. Max's Sables is less felicitous than Roundfield's Convertible (the bedpan, not the car). All the manipulation has made us slightly mad; we tune out quickly as slogans, nicknames, brand names, altered brand names, the original or the new old names are shouted at us by announcers, billboards, and television screens.

Even without this aggravation from the hucksters, names and labels can be touchy things among people. A person's job description can indicate status or a supposed lack thereof. A misplaced Ms. or a missed Miss can get you in trouble. A Reverend may not be Right. Harold has offended many a Harry. Caricature and typing are the worst enemies, those killing adjectives that lock one person into being an "intellectual," and another into being "dedicated." We are transfixed by names, and nicknames can be our undoing.

In today's first reading we have the case of God changing Israel's name. "No longer will you be called 'Forsaken,' or your land be called 'The Deserted Wife.' Your new name will be 'God Is Pleased with Her.' Your land will be called 'Happily Married' " (Isaiah 62:4). We approach the text cautiously. It is more of the same? No, the obvious difference is in the way God calls names. The names God gives carry compassion. They contain insight and vision. They promise power. They smooth over history. They cement relationship.

Sometimes we wonder whether anyone really knows our name. Not the name we carry in our wallets or our purses; not the name on the mailbox or in the phone book, but our inner name, the one that captures our talents and our aspirations, the one that gives us definition. The bride and groom in today's gospel are never mentioned by name. We don't know who they were or how they fared. Everyone else—Mary, Jesus, the waiters—no doubt were busy saving the occasion. The bride and groom were speaking each other's inner name in love.

Third Sunday of the Year—A

Isaiah 8:23—9:3
1 Corinthians 1:10–13, 17
Matthew 4:12–23

A Fishing Expedition

"One says, 'I follow Paul'; another, 'I follow Apollos'; another, 'I follow Peter'; and another, 'I follow Christ.' Christ has been divided into groups!" (1 Corinthians 1:12–13).

Group psychologists speak of a process called differentiation, which occurs in the life of groups. It sounds like a big word, but it means something familiar to all of us. Differentiation is the process of dealing with the presence in groups of potentially clashing individual traits, talents, genders, styles, limitations, mannerisms, and so forth.

At early stages of this process, there is an unspoken demand for conformity in the group. This leveling of differences offers cold comfort in the long run, because it denies the reality of the differences present. It pleases no one and frustrates everyone, very democratically.

At a later stage, differences are allowed to emerge, but timidly and in a specious way. They are located, with much caricature, in this or that faction of the group. There is a lot of taking sides. The factions *seem* to be truly opposed. But much has been going on in unconscious stratagems. The factions are, in fact, the way the group expresses some aspect of itself that *all* the members find hard to handle. Everyone might be having a problem with organizational or sexual issues or confidence, but separate factions act as if they and they alone carried these problems. The group can cope with its common issue only by having faction-leaders defend or attack one another in exaggerated fashion. The factions thus mirror the ambivalence everyone feels about the issue in question. What the group cannot yet do is work with differences creatively. So it clings to the factions with premature righteousness.

Something like this seems to have been true of the Corinthian community Saint Paul speaks about in today's epistle. Factions in the community were rife. When Saint Paul rebukes the community, then, is he calling them to return to conformity? Is that what he means when he says they should be "completely united, with only one thought and one purpose?" Hardly. We have only to consult his letter to the Romans (chapters 14–15) to see that this is not so. There, we find him defending diversity and justifying it on the grounds that

God deals differently with different consciences. We would be mistaken to hope to achieve unity by wiping out every visible differrence. And it would be doubly mistaken to try to do so in the name of the gospel.

Saint Paul seems to be seeking a basis for unity that takes into account the actual differences of people. He hopes that devotion to Jesus will get people over their hastily embraced factions. He is convinced that Jesus lets individuals be what they individually are. So he sees no need to seek support for one's individuality by creating divisive large-scale factions.

Today's gospel offers another example of working together in a group. A team of disciples is formed. Their tasks are clear: The disciples will work with Jesus by announcing the good news of the kingdom, by calling others to a change of heart, and by curing people of every illness and disease. They are going to go fishing for human lives, to use Jesus' vivid image (Matthew 4:19).

But soon they will have to face the problem of differentiation in their own ranks. The tradition has certainly etched in sharply their different traits: Peter the hard charger, brusque and inquisitive; James, strict and cutting; John, the sweet guy; Andrew (and this can be a devastating difference), who was also there. These differences affected their work throughout, and even the presence of Jesus could not save them or him from this aspect of the human condition. To the bitter end, they will be struggling with differences in their ranks.

Jesus' absence will make the problem of differentiation even more acute. People fear that other people's differences constitute an edge, that they mean power. So, dealing with differences is often a matter of competing for leadership. While Jesus was around, the leadership question was solved. But when it's a question of mere apostles, relatives of Jesus, evangelists, saints, and preachers, that's when the factions start to develop. And the adherents of each faction make it clear that leadership will be trusted only if it comes from people who are different the way they are different!

What is so pathetic about the way we deal with our differences is that it cuts us off from cooperative efforts in the service of others. It's such a stupid waste. We refuse to cooperate to alleviate real needs in the world, because of a partisan allegiance to a Lefebvre or a DePauw, to liberationists of various decibel ranges, to charismatic enthusiasts, to this church or that. This is not the best we can do.

Instead, we must contact and cooperate with people who differ from us, inside of and outside of the Christian community. This means taking the plunge. We must test the waters of those who look strange to us, not with bias but with the openness of real fishermen. We must seek common cause with them as allies of peace and justice, which after all were Jesus' causes. They may not know his name. They may not see him exactly the way we do, with our own peculiar bents and convictions. But what fish knows the fisherman's name?

Jonah 3:1–5, 10
1 Corinthians 7:29–31
Mark 1:14–20

The Compleat Angle

"Come with me, and I will teach you to catch men"
(Mark 1:17).

The old theology books described faith as being simultaneously most certain and quite obscure. By the time you finished bending your mind around that one, you weren't sure whether faith was certainly iffy or definitely vague, or both, or either.

Pity the poor theologian. Faith is not the easiest thing to describe. Yet anyone can find, even within his or her profane experience, instances in which trust does seem to be made up of equal parts of certainty and obscurity: I trust you implicitly, but I'm not sure of some of the things you do. Or, I'm not sure whether it's you I trust or some version of you that I conveniently project upon you. In the midst of our trust, I cannot see where you're going, so I see blurred edges around the future of our relationship. My trust in you ends up jerky and off-balance. I even say things like "I trust you implicitly," when the more proper language would be, "I trust you explicitly."

A similar pattern appears when we talk about faith in God. The certainty is there, but so is the obscurity—only everything is upped several million degrees.

These thoughts are mainly prompted by today's second reading. There, Saint Paul is offering advice to the Corinthian church on certain practical matters they have asked him about. He tries to get them to look at these practical matters in the light of faith. "From now on married men should live as though they were not married; those who weep, as though they were not sad; those who laugh, as though they were not happy; those who buy, as though they did not own what they bought; those who deal in material goods, as though they were not fully occupied with them. For this world, as it is now, will not last much longer" (1 Corinthians 7:29–31). Things like marriage, weeping, rejoicing, and buying have a certain solidity and density to them. They are tangible. By contrast, faith seems unsubstantial and vague. So Saint Paul suggests a kind of counterweight to their this-worldly quality. He says that if faith invariably seems intangible by comparison with other things, we must then treat those other things with a kind of artificial reserve. We must play them down by a pious pretense that gives our faith a chance to compete.

This muting of one reality in favor of another is risky. We could end up with too much pretense, using faith to escape the brisk reality of the world. But this need not happen. Saint Paul's "as though" is not ideology; it is technique, a way of checking, so that faith has a chance to root and flower in oneself. Anyone who has tried out trust knows that we must distract ourselves from dealing with some things in another person in order to concentrate on the legitimate reasons we have for trusting. When someone like Saint Paul suggests that we play down marriage, business, and other such emotional stimulants, we get some idea of how real he thinks the faith in God that is in us should be!

But faith need not always appear in threatened and fragile contrast to our more concrete and normal experiences. Sometimes it can be seen in continuity with them. This is the case in today's gospel, in which Jesus is shown calling his disciples together. Notice how he doesn't run down what his disciples-to-be are already doing. Fishermen are invited by him not to give up their profession entirely, but to be fishermen of sorts. Their knowledge of the lure, the wait, the measured guess, the movements and the currents, the kill—all these will be taken up into some more exciting pastime: "Come with me, and I will teach you to catch men." Faith in this instance will be more of the same thing, only better. What the disciples will need to practice is something they already know a lot about.

It remains a delicate matter whether we as individuals are to look on faith in the one way or the other: as something close to our natural instincts, or as something so foreign to us that it needs to be fanned and fostered. Cardinal Newman once said, "Belief engenders belief," by which he meant that we have a far greater experience of faith in our lives, even before it comes to religious faith, than we might suspect. If we fail to recognize our given capacities for faith, it may well mean that we will have to go around a lot "as though" things were not what they really are. In any case, if you end up with something that isn't certainly murky or murkily certain, it probably isn't faith.

Nehemiah 8:2– 6, 8– 10
1 Corinthians 12:12– 30
Luke 1:1– 4; 4:14– 21

Body Language

"All of you are Christ's body, and each one of you is a part of it" (1 Corinthians 12:27).

There are moments when we feel we don't belong. It might be at the office, when everyone's opinion on a project is asked—except ours. Or at a family gathering, when plans are made around us and we are not consulted. Or at a liturgy, when we feel like the only sinner in the place. It might be at a heated committee meeting, when we see a vote gradually slipping away from us. Or at a party, when our contribution gets a big ho hum from everybody.

Our problems with belonging are experienced at two levels. At one level we may not feel part of the fabric of personal relationships (ties, sentiments, trust, sexual ease, age, and so forth) that are present in a group. At another level we may feel that our work does not fit in with the work others in a group are doing. Whether we are talking about our person or our work, belonging is important. The alternative to fitting in, to having roots in a circle or organization, is a sense of isolation and exclusion.

All this can be put placidly enough, in theory. It is less pleasant when we experience a lack or loss of belonging in practice. This is especially true when it is a case of church membership. Reports multiply about church membership being off. Many admit that they do not go to church. Others straddle the boundary between in-and-out of church. Faith without membership is the ideal for still others; they defend one kind of belonging (by which they seem to mean maintaining a relation to God) and reject more formal kinds of belonging. It is difficult to assess what feelings, guilts, contentments, or resentments lie behind these various stances toward membership in the church. Whatever the rationalizations and realizations involved, we should not be surprised at the fluctuations. Establishing and maintaining conditions of membership in a church numbering more than 500 million members is a giddy prospect to begin with. What could belonging possibly mean in that circumstance? So most of us end up like the Israelites described in today's first reading (Nehemiah 8:9): the law of our faith is read at us and we break into tears!

Saint Paul was an intellectual. When faced with tears, he explained things. In today's epistle, he tries to cope with the complexity of Christian community by using his image of the body of Christ: "God put every different part in the body just as he wanted it to be. There would not be a body if it were all only one part! As it is, there are many parts but one body. So, then, the eye cannot say to the hand, 'I don't need you!' Nor can the head say to the feet, 'Well, I don't need you!' " (1 Corinthians 12:18–21). Saint Paul invites us to break new ground in our thinking about belonging to this church. He tells us in advance that belonging is not something that happens automatically through baptism. We have to struggle with real issues of pluralism in the church; in that context we have to claim our place in the church by a deliberate effort. We will constantly be running into people with interests different from ours: different talents, different degrees of commitment, different status, and so forth. Often it is such variety with the church that scares us away and makes us feel that do not belong. But the image of Christ's body continues to challenge us; if we don't belong to each other, we don't belong to him.

Fourth Sunday of the Year—A

Zephaniah 2:3; 3:12–13
1 Corinthians 1:26–31
Matthew 5:1–12

High Times

"He chose what the world looks down on and despises and thinks is nothing, in order to destroy what the world thinks is important" (1 Corinthians 1:28).

In the Gospel of Saint Matthew, the Sermon on the Mount is the high point of Jesus' teaching. It begins with the beatitudes, the subject of today's gospel reading. The Sermon on the Mount brings us into contact with a Jesus who could be, depending on how we interpret the sermon, frightening or uplifting. At least four major interpretations have traditionally been put forth about the sermon.

The first interpretation leaves us with a severe Jesus, indeed. Every sentence of the beatitudes, for example, comes across as stern law. You *must* be poor in spirit, you *must* make peace, you *must*, and so forth.

A second interpretation has a less demanding Jesus, but a preachy one all the same. Knowing full well that no one can live up to the ideals he presents, Jesus nonetheless presents them in order to show how hapless we would all be were it not for the favor of God. This interpretation has God in the business of toning down our human boasting. It stresses our utter dependency on God to avert retribution for our sin!

A third interpretation makes the beatitudes an interim ethical policy established by Jesus, because he supposedly expected the immediate end of the world and was calling for rather drastic measures to prepare people for that event.

A fourth interpretation, made by the German scholar Joachim Jeremias, sees the matter differently. He says that what Jesus teaches in the sayings collected in the Sermon on the Mount is not a complete regulation of the life of the disciples, and it is not intended to be. Rather, what is here taught are symptoms, signs, and examples of what it means when the kingdom of God breaks into the world. The beatitudes thus describe the kinds of things people do as they are gradually being gripped by the kingdom. They say, in effect, that when the kingdom takes over a person, that person is new, is changed.

One way to see this would be to divide the beatitudes right down the middle into two columns. The concluding phrases in the right-hand column describe God's kingdom in traditional terms taken from Old Testament prophecy and faith. (Perhaps "God's kingdom" is itself too trite an expression to be helpful; it really means "where God is running things.") Where God is running things, there is (as in the concluding phrases) care for people; there is consolation; there is a sense in people that they own the place like true sons and daughters who are heirs; there is satiety and mercy; there is recognition by God and recognition and comprehension of God.

The opening phrases of the beatitudes, in the left-hand column, would describe those whose lives are imperceptibly drawn to God's service. A variety of stations and conditions are mentioned: the lowly, the poor in spirit, the sorrowing, those who are trying and those who are trying more single-mindedly, the persecuted, and those who work with the persecutors to make peace. These categories of people are often considered to be losers. Change is thought to be difficult or impossible for them. We never expect their lot to be transformed or successful.

Yet, Jesus actually *makes* the two columns go together. He takes the people listed in the left-hand column (the opening phrases) and has them suddenly demonstrating in themselves the signs of the kingdom's presence. The lowly actually feel blessed. The poor in spirit actually feel as if they own the place. Once again, Jesus demonstrates the power of God to transform the world into the kingdom.

Because of Jesus' example, Christians through the ages have signed themselves up in the left-hand column with the hope of furthering in themselves the signs of the kingdom that appear in the right-hand column. It's a strategy that makes a lot of sense; it certainly shows goodwill. It is a hope based on Jesus' own example.

This hope cannot be betrayed. It will be, if the churches are never seen to be lowly and poor and to be at work among the poor and lowly. All of us can use Saint Paul's admonition in today's epistle: "From the human point of view few of you were wise or powerful or of high social standing" (1 Corinthians 1:26). A cozy, complacent church cannot convince people that God wants to transform them regardless of their station. So if we can't make it into the right-hand column, the left-hand column might not be a bad place to start.

Fourth Sunday of the Year—B

Deuteronomy 18:15– 20
1 Corinthians 7:32– 35
Mark 1:21– 28

Indirect Discourse

"Then Moses said, '. . . God . . . will send you a prophet like me from among your own people, and you are to obey him' " (Deuteronomy 18:14– 15).

In today's reading from Deuteronomy, people are told that they have a choice: either they can get God's word straight from the horse's mouth, or they can get it secondhand. But one thing is certain: They will know God's word when they hear it and therefore they will be held responsible for their reaction to it.

The Israelites, for example, did not like their dealings with Yahweh to be too direct: they "begged not to hear the Lord speak again or to see his fiery presence any more" (Deuteronomy 18:16). God obliged them. He said he would speak to them through intermediaries like Moses and other prophets whom he would raise up. But a warning was added: "I will punish anyone who refuses to obey him" (18:19).

Why the warning? Simply because dealing with intermediaries gives us so many excuses to miss the message. Their truth appears to us at times no firmer than rumor, hint, or hearsay. We can accuse them of being untidy or incomplete in their reporting. We are influenced by a look, an inflection, a shrug. We can easily turn them off.

Many modern-day prophets parade before us on the Sunday morning media. "Whose word is really being spoken there?" we ask. Is that preacher staring too hard and too often at the teleprompter? Why is he dressed that way? Why the flawless molars? Whom does he talk to off camera? The producer? The IRS man? We have similar reactions to live presentations from the pulpit on Sunday mornings. The slightest sign in the preacher of lack of preparation, of doubt, or insecurity is picked up and magnified.

People hear what they want to hear from prophets and preachers. Everyone busily filters, erases, spins dials, develops hearing problems, and so on. Listening is never very neutral. Even those who normally can read faces will misread a prophet's face when this serves their purpose. If they don't like what the preacher says, people will run back to their special revelations and their direct line to God. The fact that a prophet is not heard in his own country is no guarantee that he will be heard in another country.

But perhaps this is not entirely bad. Perhaps Deuteronomy put the case too strongly in favor of the prophet. Perhaps preaching should set up a dialectic between the prophet and the people, rather than a one-way communication. Today's epistle, for example, contains Saint Paul's controversial preaching on celibacy in relation to marriage. "An unmarried man concerns himself with the Lord's work, because be is trying to please the Lord. But a married man concerns himself with worldly matters, because he wants to please his wife" (1 Corinthians 7:32– 33). Most commentators agree that Saint Paul's point is not to downgrade marriage. On the contrary, much of his letter defends marriage against certain tendencies toward angelism in the Corinthian community. But Saint Paul did not hesitate to express his own personal opinion that if we really took the service of the Lord seriously, people would forego marriage. Imagine how that little piece of prophecy went down! Later, in Ephesians, marriage is seen as more intimately connected with God's plans than was thought earlier. Evidently, Paul had learned something from the people he preached to. Despite God's use of preachers and prophets, God does continue to speak to individuals in their hearts. So the prophet must be open to people's feedback and input.

Today's gospel could give the impression that Jesus was free from the dialectic of which we are speaking. As preacher, Jesus is described as meeting with total success: "The people who heard him were amazed at the way he taught, for he wasn't like the teachers of the Law; instead, he taught with authority" (Mark 1:22). But recall that Saint Mark is describing the early stages of Jesus' ministry. People haven't had a chance yet to pick at his phrases, to fix on his mannerisms and detract from his content, to supply shady motivations for his words. They will.

But Jesus would not have wanted to be excused from the normal risks that intermediaries of the Father have to take. What he preached he no doubt learned in part from the people he was preaching to. Taking on our human condition involves taking on the rhythms that usually attend the interaction between preacher and preached-at. It would be good if more preachers did the same.

Fourth Sunday of the Year — C

Jeremiah 1:4– 5, 17– 19
1 Corinthians 12:31 — 13:13
Luke 4:21 – 30

Odd Men Out

"Set your hearts, then, on the more important gifts. Best of all, however, is the following way" (1 Corinthians 12:31).

Is it only the odd man who can believe in love? Reading Saint Paul's rhapsodic, hypnotizing description of love in today's second reading, it is tempting to finally write the whole thing off as visionary ecstasy. In a Carol Reed film on the Irish troubles, *Odd Man Out*, James

Mason once delivered Saint Paul's lines in feverish delirium to an addled company of listeners. Is this the only way they can be delivered, with a protective aura of fantasy around them? Is it that Saint Paul is too far from the grinding realities of everyday living? Or is it that he is getting too close to home?

Saint Paul's description of love may be accused of being a composite of many isolated outbreaks of human altruism: a patient father we have seen; an act of kindness we observed in a crowded train; a bigwig we know who does not put on airs; someone who bounces back from personal affront without brooding. But to aim at *all* these qualities in oneself seems illusory. Are we, by some naive logic, elevating into a noble thesis what are in fact pieces of a puzzle?

Saint Paul freely admits that we are as bumbling at love as a child is at grown-up pursuits. In our hands love is as unwieldy as a child's building blocks. Yet, though we may sweep them away in our frustration, we always come back to them for another curious try. People find it hard to commit themselves in life to something so provisional as love. Those who have been disappointed in love will line up to din into our ears how their best efforts at loving crashed on the rocks. Unless we are swept away by some flawless, romantic passion or enthusiasm that we call love, love can be a steep path indeed.

Sigrid Undset once said that love is almost invisible since it has no well-documented history. Either our attention wanders away from love or, more often, the history of hate and sin seems more engrossing. So the detailed workings of love are lost in history or relegated to edifying footnotes.

Another anxiety: Can the supply of love meet the demand? The demand cries out in places like Northern Ireland or South Africa. It is high in marriage and in friendship. It affects us as we get old, or get stung, or just try to get by. We feel a twinge of guilt for even thinking that love leads ultimately to dead ends. But as our energy to love is sapped, what else can we conclude? To this, Saint Paul says bluntly: "Love is eternal" (1 Corinthians 13:8).

The most shocking thing about love is the fact that, at times, it must put on a hard face. This is illustrated in the first reading, in which Yahweh tells Jeremiah: "You will be like a fortified city, an iron pillar, and a bronze wall" (Jeremiah 1:18). In today's gospel, Jesus seems no less frosty. He confronts his townspeople for their prejudice and small-mindedness. He accuses them of distracting themselves from love by raising such minor issues as his pedigree, his academic credentials, his forceful and imaginative way of making a point, and so forth. He faces them down in the interest of love. "When the people in the synagogue heard this, they were filled with anger. They rose up, dragged Jesus out of town, and took him to the top of the hill on which their town was built. They meant to throw him over the cliff, but he walked through the middle of the crowd and went his way" (Luke 4:28– 30). The compatibility of divine love with such rugged confrontations is one of the great mysteries of love. Even granting that Luke's Gospel, for its own special purposes, highlights such confrontations, we know this same problematic side of love from our own experiences of it.

Well, that's what we get when we talk about love. For the believer, however, it is clear that the vast, humming resource of God's love is there for all to draw upon. May we prefer to look slightly odd in the pursuit of love than to take the other way.

Fifth Sunday of the Year—A

Isaiah 58:7–10
1 Corinthians 2:1–5
Matthew 5:13–16

Flaunting It

"Your light must shine before people, so that they will see the good things you do and praise your Father in heaven" (Matthew 5:16).

A contemporary cartoonist, Ashleigh Brilliant, has a cartoon with two luminous eyes, rounded in terror, peering out from the darkness of a stone enclosure. The caption reads, "If you're careful enough, nothing bad or good will ever happen to you." In a similar vein, today's gospel speaks of not hiding our light under a bushel. We are urged to shine it, if not in the eyes of people, at least before them.

When we read the small print, however, this becomes a frightening prospect. For what is meant concretely by this kind of religious visibility? The first reading supplies us with a readout: "Share your food with the hungry and open your homes to the homeless poor. Give clothes to those who have nothing to wear, and do not refuse to help your own relatives. Then my favor will shine on you like the morning sun, and your wounds will be quickly healed" (Isaiah 58:7–8).

This is a tall order. Broadcasting such achievements seems beyond our reach when achievement itself escapes us. The very things for which Christians are to become conspicuous take a high emotional toll on those who would do them. For example, sharing bread with the hungry—if we look at the actual figures on world hunger—reminds us of the possibility of our own supplies running out. Sheltering the oppressed requires that we enter the tense domain of landlords, lawyers, building unions, slum clearance, utilities, and so forth. And to look beyond our own prejudice, mutual suspicion, and egoism to see others as our own kind—that seems the greatest achievement of all. What, then, do we have to broadcast?

Saint Paul felt the same diffidence. He said to the Corinthians: "When I came to you, I was weak and trembled all over with fear" (1 Corinthians 2:3). The picture of the glib, brilliant apostle arriving in Corinth with knee-knocking modesty seems a bit farfetched. Yet, he was goint to be telling the people there things that were emotionally jolting. They would not only have to change their ways; once changed, they would have to flaunt them. Where does he think they will get the inspiration for such preaching?

The gospel indicates that the only people who can do such things are those who are inspired by a desire to praise God. That seems to be the point of the last phrase of our opening text. Strong emotions are replaced only by stronger ones. We will not be willing to expose ourselves to doing good, nor to expose the good that we do, unless we become more emotional about God, more enthusiastic, even exhibitionist. A generation of religious rule-keepers might find it strange to hear that God is exciting. It is not always our way to strut and boast about God. If people feel they have been haunted by a bullying God, they are not about to parade him and show him off. But that sentiment is precisely what unblocks many a spiritual logjam.

Fifth Sunday of the Year — B

Job 7:1 – 4, 6 – 7
1 Corinthians 9:16 – 19, 22 – 23
Mark 1:29 – 39

At Evening

"After the sun had set and evening had come, people brought to Jesus all the sick and those who had demons. All the people of the town gathered in front of the house. Jesus healed many who were sick with all kinds of diseases and drove out many demons" (Mark 1:32 – 34).

Care of the sick and infirm is perhaps the most explicit embodiment of Christian charity that there is. This statement might offend those whose personal expression of Christian faith takes them in other, more positive directions: the Christian parent who fosters growth and ambition in a healthy child; the Christian educator who harnesses leisure to learning and boldly explores the world; the civil servant who plans and organizes a portion of the kingdom; the entertainer who unbends us; the artist who makes us soar. All these Christians would naturally say that their creative and rec-reative efforts are equally vital embodiments of Christian faith. Why, then, picture Christian faith as more ideally allied to the care of the sick and infirm? Why identify as the real heroes nurses, doctors, aides, psychological personnel, trainers, hospital chaplains, relatives of the sick, therapists, custodians, live-in helpers, auxiliaries, and so on? Does it not give the impression of a God who relishes weakness and decline and almost seems to capitalize on them?

Yet, the case of the sick and infirm reminds us most visibly of how God deals with us graciously in our weakness. There is a tendency in all of us to glory in our strength: the wide shoulders, the attractiveness that melts others, the sheen of health and glow of talent. We tend to rely on these things or at least to think them central to our relationships with others, including God.

We are less sure that God or others can relate to us when these glistening endowments are absent. We need some kind of forcible reminder that God does not finally glory in our accomplishments. God loves us for who we are, fragile and failing human beings, bent for another kind of glory where the accomplishment is God's, and ours is the gratitude. This is not to say that the brightness and smart wit of the beautiful people are not pleasing to God. Surely God enjoys matching them. Nor do we want to say that the gloomy Job of today's first reading best represents the mood of Christian life. But

God does see the end of things and the passion—and God cares.

This giving, sensitive God is mirrored in the actions of those who care for the sick. Glory is far away from those they help. They brook the smell. They clean and reclean. They remember the times and the schedules of caring. They make daring decisions to act or not to act, and these decisions are critical. They are exposed to the emotional disarray of the sick. They listen patiently as fear and pain transform the sick into arrogant, unreasonable, and mischievous children. They deal with the anxious presence or with the loud absence of relatives.

And what does all this do to them? How do they endure the constant reminder of their own mortality that they get from sick people? There is a romantic view of caring for the sick that requires the healer to catch the sickness in order to be credible. Damien the leper leaps to mind. There's also a stoic view of caring for the sick that requires the healer to be hard and unfeeling if he or she is to be of any help to the sick. The truth probably lies between these extremes. The healer is surely touched by the misery, weakness, despair, and decay that are dealt with on a daily basis. In today's epistle, Saint Paul says: "I make myself everybody's slave in order to win as many people as possible. . . . Among the weak in faith I become weak like one of them, in order to win them" (1 Corinthians 9:19, 22). Saint Paul is not speaking about pragmatic pretense. He resolves to let the actual condition of others touch him personally, so that he might deal with them realistically. But that means that he himself must feel weak, scrupulous, dirty, traitorous, anxious, and resentful at times. A similar challenge awaits those who care for the sick. They will not be shown much mercy in return. Like Saint Paul, they will find their real recompense in the freedom with which they love the sick.

Was it any different with Jesus? Today's gospel pictures him literally surrounded by the sick. What does this demanding, draining, depressing vision of the sick do to him? Does he ask, with healers everywhere, "Why me? When will the rot stop? When will the torture let up, the tears, the hopelessness, quackery, amulets, heartsickness, the attacks, onsets, and inevitabilities? Who can ever cure this great aching mass of flesh and spirit that is humanity?" The gospel pictures Jesus, after his day of healing, going off alone to pray. If the sick haunt his prayer, we would not be surprised. And yet, when his disciples come looking for him, he promptly sets off on another round of caring: "We must go to the other villages around here. I have to preach in them also, because that is why I came" (Mark 1:38). The message that sustains the healers of this world is quite simple: God cares.

Isaiah 6:1–2, 3–8
1 Corinthians 15:1–11
Luke 5:1–11

Keeping Track

"Christ died for our sins, as written in the Scriptures" (1 *Corinthians 15:3).*

How do we feel about being Christians? Do we toss and turn at night with the excited sense that in the morning we will have something important to do because of our faith? Is our faith an itch that must be scratched? Do we wear faith like a charm bracelet? Do we use it like a club on others? Is faith an ethnic prop for our act? Does it rouse us more than bowl games or nights on the town? Is it more real to us than our financial ambitions? Than our physical fitness kicks? Do we stare at our faith like a string around our finger that vaguely is supposed to remind us of something?

Questions like these are somewhat unfair. They should be asked at the beginning of a long and pleasant evening of conversation. They come to mind here only because today's readings all describe people who pursue the life of faith with a vengeance. And they do this *despite* the fact that they have been sinners in the past.

How do they sustain faith as something so real and at the same time remain fully conscious of their sin? Many people, it seems, cannot. The literal sense of the introductory quotation above simply escapes them: that God can see past the sin to the sinner whom he respects.

Hence their life of faith becomes many other things to them—unreal, punitive, arbitrary, gnawing.

In contrast, the main characters in today's readings avoid these negative attitudes. Isaiah could have used the fact of his sinfulness to forego any mission from Yahweh. Instead he says: "I will go! Send me" (Isaiah 6:8). Saint Paul has to face the realization that he actually persecuted his fellow Christians at one time. He admits that he, too, is a sinner. But this does not paralyze him. "I have worked harder than any of the other apostles" (1 Corinthians 15:10). Saint Peter, again, is an example of someone heavily aware of his own sinfulness. "Go away from me, Lord. I am a sinful man!" (Luke 5:8). But he surmounts his personal sense of sinfulness to become the Fisherman.

Past sinfulness is the source of depression for many. It seems to ruin everything. Energies sapped by this preoccupation with former sins are enormous. Behind this feeling—and it is more a feeling than a conclusion rationally reached—is the suspicion that God has absolutely no truck with sinners before, during, or after their sin.

The first work of faith is to know how to handle this feeling. It is a giant step in itself to accept that the Lord works with sinners. This is a kind of acid test, which must be passed before anything else can become a solid issue. The memory of sin is strong. The fantasies tying sin to retribution are vivid. The distancing that sin causes between God and humankind is underscored with such vehemence by highly placed religious personages that many people throw up their hands in futility. It becomes incredible to them that God would choose sinners to be dynamic apostles of faith. Where can we get the enthusiasm for faith that leads to works of praise and service if we are grounded by a fog of diffidence and gloom? How can we see ourselves as agents of God's good news in the world, if we think this is automatically ruled out by something accurately filed in our past records.

What we are on the track of here is some explanation of why so many people approach faith with a gingerliness, even a pall, that makes faith finally unbelievable. God and the church seem very drab to them. Religion is an irksome proposition. Jesus, saints, and clergy form a stiff, imposing pantheon stationed round about their minds. Some statues are more important than others, but all seem to lack flesh and blood. Moral taskmasters abound, but even when you do what they say, you are never sure you are pleasing anybody. Sacraments are performed, but it doesn't seem to matter even to ask anybody why. Perhaps some hostile presence will be placated. In sum, religion seems the same sullen business it was when we were fifteen.

Is it unreasonable to suggest that our sullenness stems from our lack of faith in God's generosity and broad-mindedness in the matter of our past sins? Do we really think that God is thwarted by our sinfulness? Do we believe that in his general nervousness God marks us down as "unreliable" or "high risk" when it comes to making us instruments of his good news? It almost looks as though we are the ones who are using our own unworthiness to keep God at a distance. But thank God, this does not stop the great expectations he has for us. At least his record on working with sinners is clear.

240

Sirach 15:15–20
1 Corinthians 2:6–10
Matthew 5:17–37

Cold Reckoning

"You can decide whether you will be loyal to him or not" (sirach 15:15).

Today's gospel is truly frightening. We refer to the longer version, in which Matthew's Jesus hammers out another chunk of his inaugural program, the Sermon on the Mount: We'll insist on performance as the bottom line of authenticity, attacking the scribe and Pharisee within ourselves who teach one thing and do another (Matthew 5:17–20). We'll resist in ourselves the slightest anger against our brethern, and we'll never let argument or incident pass that we don't confront, address, and work through with them (21–26). We'll act as though lustful attraction between sexes simply does not exist for us, and we'll call certain forms of marriage nothing better than adultery (27–32). We'll never blurt out the least curse or oath or swear word or casual mention of God's name. We'll restrict ourselves to stolid one-line answers to everything.

The bald, relentless, stoical and exacting picture of humanity that emerges from this passage cannot be missed by anyone. It does not help to point out, as scholars do, that Matthew's main point is to contrast the program and authority of Jesus with that practised by Matthew's contemporaries in the Jewish camp. For there are legitimate grounds for wondering whether, as the passage stands, it promotes an inhuman evacuation of emotion and presupposes in people a kind of disembodied capacity for choice. The first reading supports in its own way such an image: "If you want to, you can keep the Lord's commands. . . . He has placed fire and water before you; reach out and take whatever you want. You have a choice between life and death; you will get whichever you choose" (Sirach 15:15– 17).

Our point is hardly to deny the existence of responsibility in us for the choices we must make. Nor are we ignorant of the fact that responsible choices, when they run counter to our own self-gratification and general whim, do seem to be made with blood cold and eye blank and colorless. But to set up this style and manner of acting as the ideal is suspicious. The suppression of emotion in the name of religion has a long-standing appeal for those who wish to suppress emotion in the first place and who only seek legitimation from religion to do so. They might attempt to read today's gospel as some kind of justification for turning life into a series of phlegmatic choices, but they are wrong. For this would betray the general spirit of the New Testament picture of Jesus. Behind the energetic program, he sets forth an equally energetic, even passionate loyalty to God. "You can decide whether you will be loyal to him or not." The life of Jesus on earth demonstrates that God deals in emotion, complexity, and struggle. Our choices, too, are made in such a context. Let's not read Matthew in a way that obscures that fact.

Leviticus 13:1 – 2, 44 – 46
1 Corinthians 10:31 — 11:1
Mark 1:40 – 45

Sound Off

"Indeed . . . Jesus could not go into a town publicly. Instead, he stayed out in lonely places, and people came to him from everywhere" (Mark 1:45).

Today's selection from the Gospel of Saint Mark illustrates a common theme in Mark, that of the "messianic secret." Don't go away. It really is an interesting topic and not all that difficult to follow. Notice how Jesus tells the leper he has just cured: "Listen, don't tell anyone about this" (Mark 1:44). Saint Mark has Jesus saying things like this frequently. Jesus forbids demons, for example, to say out loud who he really is, namely, God's Holy One, the Messiah, the Son of God (Mark 1:25; 1:34; 3:12). He puts similar strictures on his disicples (8:30; 9:9). Besides the leper in today's gospel, he also warns a deaf-mute (7:36), a blind man (8:26), and the family of a dead girl he has raised (5:43) not to make the cures public. While the demons and disciples seem to obey, others spill the beans very quickly, like our leper today: "The man went away and began to spread the news everywhere" (1:44).

Now, what is Jesus up to with all the secrecy? When we remember that Saint Mark is an earlier witness to the tradition than the other evangelists, the question becomes all the more important. We are really asking what kind of Jesus Jesus was. And for this we have to ask

243

what sort of person would go around hushing others up the way Saint Mark describes.

We have all met the type who invites you to the parousia. He alone knows the exact time and place, but he asks you to keep it to yourself, since no one else knows yet that he holds all the tickets for it. Even as you begin to inch away from him, you realize that his greater sickness is in the secretiveness. We don't improve matters by saying that Jesus, at least, has the right to act this way because he is God. The behavior would remain just as weird.

Nor would it help us to interpret Saint Mark's messianic secret as a kind of aw-shucks modesty on the part of Jesus, as if Jesus were teaching us to be humble about our accomplishments. This interpretation appeals most to those who would enjoy playing Superman in the first place.

So strange does Saint Mark's secretive Jesus appear that some have finally said that the secretiveness was not Jesus' at all, but is attributable to Mark. By this they mean that Saint Mark, writing as he did only after consciousness about Jesus' messiahship had gradually taken root in the faith of the primitive church, read back this gradual consciousness into Jesus' own times and had Jesus responsible for it. This, they think, would explain the anomolous accounts in which Jesus doles out little hints of his messiahship along the way.

It is not necessary to lay such pious inventiveness at Saint Mark's door. Other scholars think that there are indications right in the gospel text that better explain Jesus' behavior and preserve its historicity. For example, in today's selection from Saint Mark there are two expressions that are noteworthy. First, Jesus is said to be "filled with pity" at the sight of the leper (1:41). An earlier Greek reading has Jesus being filled with anger, not pity. The picture of anger would go hand in hand with the second notable expression, when Jesus speaks "sternly" to the leper (1:43) and sends him on his way. This translation is tame for the Greek word, which is closer to "fume" or "storm." Taken together, the two expressions present Jesus as an angry, even livid person. Why?

The reason Jesus seems to be upset is because his healing is being misinterpreted by people. Some take his healing ministry as a rejection of formal religion, which he in no way intends ("Go straight to the priest and let him examine you; then in order to prove to everyone that you are cured, offer the sacrifice that Moses offered"). Others fasten on the wonder-working aspects of his ministry, or on their own momentary joy. Jesus is angry because by such sentiments people fool themselves about the ultimate place and nature of suffering in human life, about what Saint Mark often calls "the mystery." No amount of healing or holiness is going to exempt people from passing through human pain and suffering. Jesus is calling people to exercise faith in a loving Father in the midst of *that*. He is, by Saint Mark's description, saying in effect: "Better to say nothing at all about me than to misrepresent me." And he is not all that polite and unruffled in saying it.

That Jesus came down thus on the side of hard reality is comforting. Yet, he still attracted bent and broken people in greater and greater numbers. Even in their shortsightedness, their disobedience about the silence and their private purposes, people were saying in turn to Jesus: "Listen, Jesus, we know all about the mystery of suffering. We are the sufferers, from long ago. What we're saying is that a little or small part of the faith you preach is such a gain for us that we want to grab it and shout about it. So don't be angry at us. Be glad."

Sixth Sunday of the Year—C

Jeremiah 17:5–8
1 Corinthians 15:12, 16–20
Luke 6:17, 20–26

In Memoriam

"If our hope in Christ is good for this life only and no more, then we deserve more pity than anyone else in all the world" (1 Corinthians 15:19).

Saint Paul has a fairly straightforward understanding of the resurrection. Jesus died, Jesus rose. We die, we rise. He was dead, now he's not. We're going to die, but that isn't the end of it for us. Get it? What comes as a shock in today's second reading is that his argument about the resurrection was not with outsiders. It was with some of his fellow Christians. The shock becomes numbing confusion when we find significant amounts of theological literature today tending in the same direction as Saint Paul's Corinthian opponents. Why on earth (sorry) would anyone bother being a Christian if Christianity were gutted of its central doctrine? Why would theologians argue, as they have, that our desire for personal resurrection is a greedy, idolatrous tendency in us that runs counter to the principle of "glory to God *alone*"? Does such an opinion take too literally a remark like the one in the first reading: "I will condemn the person who . . . puts his trust . . . in the strength of mortal man" (Jeremiah 17:5)? In any case, theologians are not the only ones who demur. The little old Irish lady has her version of it when she looks away and says with firm lips: "Well, no one has ever come back to tell us about it."

Skepticism about the doctrine of the resurrection seems to stem from several sources. First, some socially oriented people see it as providing an easy excuse for others not to get involved here and now. They are frustrated in their efforts to galvanize the population around pressing social causes, because everyone is looking forward to some future, more comprehensive reorganization of things in the resurrection. "Why apply Band-Aids" they hear, "when major surgery is in store?" They end up resenting the fact that pie-in-the-sky has more appeal than bread-for-the-world. They feel that the only way to break this appeal is to tell people it's now or never.

Second, some people have trouble with reconstructed risen bodies: Where do the old atoms go, how retrieve lost limbs—that sort of thing. Frankly, this kind of question always savors of the mentality of a nervous stock clerk. More likely we should ask such people what they think of their bodies *now* and whether that influences their interest in getting them back!

Third, resurrection stikes others as a kind of showboating or tricksterism. Now you don't see it, now you do. This marvelous sleight-of-hand seems to go too far when people are involved rather than rabbits, cards, coins, or handkerchiefs.

Fourth, there is a kind of theological domino-theory connected with belief in the resurrection. The chain reaction set off might lead to other challenging beliefs such as creation, incarnation, real presence, inspiration, and so on. One must see down the road on these matters and not take any step that commits one to a confining course of thought or action.

Fifth, a not-so-subtle argument runs: "If they can't raise you from the dead, they can't do anything bad to you after you die." This is really covering one's bets! But the fear is there. The blessings promised in today's gospel (Luke 6:20–22) seem to be offset by the curses (24–26).

What emerges from all these objections is not, finally, a problem with resurrection: It is a problem with God. God comes out of it all a hideous *potpourri*: Frankenstein, major surgeon, magician, mind-bender, potential redestroyer, general distraction from pressing problems.

Perhaps this is what happens to us when we lose sight of the connection between Jesus' resurrection and the kind of life he lived. The resurrection is not simply a statement about the power of God. It speaks, rather, of the ultimate potential for integrity *in* man. When the Father raises Jesus from the dead, it is to show what he thought of the human life Jesus had lived. All Jesus' striving, all his quiet reflection, the speaking engagements, the explosive encounters, the personal struggle to do something worthwhile and valuable in his life, the shy notoriety, the stiffening determination at the end—next to these, the Father places a final Yes. He undoes Jesus' own undoing by those who hate or fear a life of love.

Hence, there is a logic, an argument, in the resurrection. The resurrection is a statement that the Father himself was moved to applause by the human drama of Jesus. The *yes* was also a *bravo*. This is the kind of God who raised Jesus from the dead. The same God, by a marvelous condescension, has thought to extend his applause to our human dramas, by raising us together with Jesus.

Now that surely beats a statue in the park with birds sitting on your head!

Seventh Sunday of the Year—A

Leviticus 19:1–2, 17–18
1 Corinthians 3:16–23
Matthew 5:38–48

On the Way

"You must be perfect—just as your Father in heaven is perfect" (Matthew 5:48).

If anyone remembers, that text used to be translated, "Be perfect as your heavenly Father is perfect." Now, it is sometimes translated "be perfected" rather than "be perfect." The difference is in the pace. The early version of it hit you like a ton of bricks. Perfection was something you were supposed to have achieved yesterday. That being impossible, many people simply retired to a make-do position, their self-image permanently wounded and their hope-levels low. The current version conveys some sense of process. Perfection is seen as something we are working toward. Religion is more candidly a project, an undertaking, and adventure.

Ironically, the direction in which religion takes us is one that we often travel anyway. Many of us learn the hard way that "he makes his sun to shine on bad and good people alike, and gives rain to those who do good and to those who do evil" (Matthew 5:45). A growing compassion is often the result of the shocks and embarrassments, the strivings and failures we experience in life. In the early days, when we were trying to carve out the contours of our individual identities, we were harsh and categorical. "Good" and "bad," "just" and "unjust" were weapons in our arsenal, used defensively or aggressively as we felt our fragile self-definition threatened. Later, things changed. A sensitive philosopher, Maurice Nédoncelle, put it this way: "When a man reaches the age of fifty, he has often come to the conclusion that the laws commonly held to be the expression of an eternal system of morality have continued to evolve in the course of his own life. He notes that this is due to the fact that a considerable number of individuals have emancipated themselves from them, and so have 'done wrong'. He is forced to recognize that, while sometimes the law has recorded a lowering of the standard of morality, yet changes due to the increase of sin have their good side and even, in certain cases, register moral progress."

Some might view this statement as maudlin reverie, as a sloppy capitulation to the *status quo*. But there is enough force to it to support the point we are making, namely, that life drives us to a wider compassion, in which we are not so quick to throw around terms such as "good" and "bad," "just" and "unjust." We contemplate one another now with a gentler eye. We sympathize with one another's differences. We note the diverse fortunes and irregular outcomes of people with more reticence and even acceptance. We learn to hope for one another, to foster one another's inner peace and outer comfort, knowing that death will soon be the issue for all of us.

We get to the point where we would not withhold the sun or the rain from anybody.

Jesus teaches us to do all this with greater elan and conviction. He wants us to accept now what we must anticipate later, and to see this acceptance as a godlike quality in us. He wants us to be able to bless life as his Father does.

Perhaps because his time was running out, Jesus got old young.

Isaiah 43:18 – 19, 21 – 22, 24 – 25
2 Corinthians 1:18 – 22
Mark 2:1 – 12

That Masked Man

"As surely as God speaks the truth, my promise to you was not a 'Yes' and a 'No'" (2 Corinthians 1:18).

Sometimes the urge comes to place an antechamber before every voting booth in the country. In the antechamber we would play those old Wesern movies, in which a clear-cut portrayal is given of hero and villain. The hero is the wholesome-looking fellow with the wholesome-looking horse. The hero has a huge white hat on and pearl-handled revolvers. Both hero and horse have good teeth and exude sincerity. Sometimes the horse looks more intelligent than the hero. The villain, on the other hand, is dressed to his spurs in black. His moustache and even his teeth are black. Both he and his horse tend to slouch and snarl a lot. They are innately mean. Well, when the voters pass through the antechamber, if they cannot tell the villain from the hero, that would be it. We would disqualify them from voting, and the body politic would be better off.

These deranged thoughts only arise out of a certain pique. Why do people fail to identify or to follow the consistency of a character created by authors or filmwriters? They seem to latch on to a word here or there, but they're not sure what they heard. They miss a hundred intervening words and gestures that complete the intended characterization. It is depressing, too, to find this kind of inattention in those who read the Scriptures.

In today's gospel, we have heroes and villains displayed in full panoply. The heroes are Jesus and the believing friends of the paralytic, who let the man down on a stretcher through the roof into the crowded room where Jesus is preaching. The villains are some of the scribes, whom the evangelists, with consistent prejudice and overgeneralization, present as the bad guys. In this scene, it is the bad guys who say, "How does he dare talk like this? This is blasphemy! God is the only one who can forgive sins!" (Mark 2:7). Now normally we would hiss and boo at their words, since this is the expected thing when villains speak. By some curious route, however, we merely conclude that Jesus is God. Even though this is perfectly so, it would be a mistake to base that conclusion on *this* passage. It would be wrong to see Saint Mark's characters as making the point about Jesus' divinity despite themselves. It would be a mistake to look for the deep irony in Saint Mark that we find in Saint John. Although Jesus' ultimate identity (as Son of Man, Son of God, and so on) is an issue for Mark, the evangelist also teaches us to look straightforwardly at the human quality of Jesus' behavior. In this light, today's passage seems rather to have Jesus *reject the very principle* stated by the scribes.

This is borne out by the rest of the scene. Jesus poses a comparison to his enemies: "Is it easier to say to this paralyzed man, 'Your sins are forgiven,' or to say, 'Get up . . . and walk'?" (2:9). Notice that Jesus sets the argument in terms of easy– difficult. He thereby takes direct issue with their claim that forgiving sin is impossible, far above him as a mere man, too much, and so on.

To make his point, he does the harder thing (curing the paralytic) in order to demonstrate that the *easier* thing (forgiving another person's sin) is indeed within his grasp *and anyone's grasp*. Only if the latter is implied does the villainy of the unforgiving scribes get its full comeuppance in the story. Jesus clearly wanted to get the bad guys to be more forgiving, just as he set forgiving others as the task of anyone who would follow him. So he had to attack their very principle: that God alone forgives sin. He is hardly saying by that fact that God has nothing to do with forgiving sins. What he refuses to collude in is the pretense that God's forgiving is so closely guarded that we can never imitate or embody it in ourselves.

In many ways, this is all just another tiresome instance of how things get jumbled when the topic is God's forgiving or our own forgiving of others. People get stuck somewhere between their fantasies about God's forgiving (Will he or won't he? Does he or doesn't he?) and their own forgiving (Could we even, or ever? Why should we or would we?), and the whole thing finally comes out a muddle.

Jesus is more clear than that. He knows his Isaiah (today's first reading, 43:24–25): "You burdened me with your sins; you wore me out with the wrongs you have committed. And yet, I am the God who forgives your sins. . . . I will not hold your sins against you." Jesus tried to make this attitude of his Father his own in the flesh. As Saint Paul says in today's epistle: "Jesus Christ. . . is not one who is 'Yes' and 'No.' On the contrary, he is God's 'Yes' " (2 Corinthians 1:19). The problem of forgiving is manifestly our problem, our hesitation, our reluctance to let God empower us to be forgivers. That is why we hurry back to the old game of whether God alone forgives sin.

What will trigger in us a forgiving spirit, and probably the only thing that will do so, is to reflect on Saint Paul's words and to apply them to our personal lives and to our relationships with others: Jesus Christ was never anything but Yes. And—to keep things straight—in the story Jesus is the good guy.

Seventh Sunday of the Year—C

1 Samuel 26:2, 7– 9, 12– 13, 22– 23
1 Corinthians 15:45– 49
Luke 6:27– 38

Transformations

"Love your enemies and do good to them; lend and expect nothing back" (Luke 6:35).

Hearing today's gospel is a raw, grueling confrontation with goodness. It isn't talking about an isolated case of altrusim, such as is described in the first reading. (Gee, did you notice how David didn't spear Saul when he had the chance?) The demands of love in it are relentless: ungrudging restraint of all our favorite hatreds, a readiness to act kindly, the refusal even to see someone as an enemy.

A lot of ink has been spilled deciding whether Jesus' vision of mutual love and forgiveness is to be taken literally. Is it something our race must aim at if we are to avoid falling further back? Is it a practical possibility for us as a race? Can Jesus really shift the balance of moral history?

Today's epistle says that he already has. Saint Paul speaks there about a first transformation of humanity from dust into living soul. He is describing in his own way the awesome passage of man and woman into history, where before the crust of earth had welcomed only witless birds and things that crawl. Whatever hulking thing it was that first took on the attributes of a living soul, it would scarcely recognize itself in the subsequent explosion of science, learning, art, and speculation attributed to it. Sophocles' *Antigone* puts it better: "Wonders are many on earth, and the greatest of these is man, who rides the ocean and takes his way through the deep. . . . He is master of ageless Earth, to his own will bending the immortal mother of gods by the sweat of his brow. . . . The use of language, the wind-swift motion of the brain he learned. . . . There is nothing beyond his power. For every ill he found its remedy, save only death."

And there was a lot of death. This first transformation of humankind met with mixed success. For man and woman also learned to hate, to rob, to kill, and to justify themselves in boring speeches. A second transformation was greatly needed. Saint Paul's point is that in Jesus a second transformation *is* under way. Living soul is moving into Spirit.

We find it hard to think these days about "new ages" or "new societies." Turning things around on a global scale seems beyond our reach. We are too aware of the myriad determinisms that attach us to our old ways, like some straining Gulliver. Psychological hangovers, biological inevitabilities, economic pressures, ethnic and racial traditions—all seem to forge strands that strangle our hopes for change. True, we have scattered instances in our individual lives of a swing in events that transforms us as persons. We know roughly what it is to move from "before" to "after" with awakening and elation: it was when we were captured by honest ambition in our job; it was after we escaped a dangerous situation by the skin of our teeth; it was when we broke with a certain crowd, or picked up with a key person; it happened when we were bitten by a cause, or when we decided finally to make ourselves into a cause. In these instances, we could recognize the change in ourselves and hope in it.

But Saint Paul is talking about a larger shift. "Just as we wear the likeness of the man made of earth, so we will wear the likeness of the Man from heaven" (1 Corinthians 15:49). In the Spirit of Jesus, humankind will bear the stamp of mutual charity and forbearance. This most massive transformation is God's promise to us. But when?

Elsewhere, Saint Paul admits that the new transformation seems to be moving at about the same agonizing pace as the first one (Romans 8:18–30). We are still rising from the dust with tortured groanings. He invites us, however, to hear the loving groaning of the Spirit beneath our own voices of human pain and straining. Transformations are not serene or bloodless. But whoever said that the Man from heaven did not himself have to groan and strain in order to be charitable?

Now is the time for transformations. We go back to the drawing board to trace the passage from dust to glory that is our past and our future. There is still a lot of dust in us to shake. There is still a lot of our own humanity to be claimed. Above all, there are still many enemies to be loved.

Eighth Sunday of the Year—A

Isaiah 49:14–15
1 Corinthians 4:1–5
Matthew 6:24–34

Business as Usual

"You should think of us as Christ's servants, who have been put in charge of God's secret truths" (1 Corinthians 4:1).

A public servant is supposed to be trustworthy: know the job, check the inventory, pace the budget, be at the desk, keep the correspondence moving, set aside think-time, remember what has to be remembered, anticipate and plan, handle the personnel, set the constructive mood, grind it out, put in the hours, delegate, pick up the pieces, move it, move it. Most of us have some idea of the demands and rewards of good administration. But we are surprised to hear that we have that kind of job when it comes to the mysteries of God! The priests, yes, they seem to be some kind of administrators; or the religious education coordinator or this or that official. But all of us? What, we ask, could we possibly be administering?

A modest answer can be attempted. What we are in charge of is a very simple message: that God loves us with an eternal love. Today's gospel says this in a roundabout, though effective way, making the point that we are *more* than our possessions and achievements, our time-schedules and arrangements. We are even more than our neediness. We are loved by God in the old-fashioned way, just because we are who we are. So we can be ourselves and bask in that love. The first reading puts it even more strongly: "Can a woman forget her own baby and not love the child she bore? Even if a mother should forget her child, I will never forget you" (Isaiah 49:15). The preposterous image of a mother losing conscious memory of having been linked to, having borne, having known and nursed her own child serves as a forceful contrast to the kind of love God has for us.

It is this mystery of love that we are to administrate, and we begin to get a sense of the size of the job. We leave this task to others at our own risk and at the cost of reliquishing our baptismal prerogative. First, we have to keep reminding ourselves about the business we are in: others might want to push creepy, vindictive, arbitrary, or devouring gods, but that's their problem. That's not our God. Second, we have to keep accurate files on God, not mixing in complaints with successful experiences of God's love. Third, we have to do a lot of public relations work for our product. We must track down rumors to the contrary, and set people straight when we can. Fourth, we have to try to maintain an environment in which our trust in God's love for us can be seen openly in the decor and lifestyle.

One thing in our favor, though: The budget is endless.

Eighth Sunday of the Year — B

Hosea 2:16– 17, 21– 22
2 Corinthians 3:1– 6
Mark 2:18– 22

A Matter of the Heart

"We say this because we have confidence in God through Christ" (2 Corinthians 3:4).

Out of today's readings tumble images of stolid, deadened, entrenched people who are in need of heart. In each case some remedy is applied.

Hosea pictures the Lord leading Israel off to some out-of-the-way place, there to speak to Israel's heart (Hosea 2:16). Israel is like some tired and embittered wife who has forgotten how love once was; she is dirtied and numbed by life and cannot feel the old things. The Lord will teach Israel how to recover the old resolve for social justice, mercy, and human rights. All this is put in the language of espousals. Israel will regain a sense of intimacy and frank response. Dead silences will be filled and the heart touched.

In the second reading, Saint Paul suffers at the hands of the Corinthian church. They ask him in a heartless and formal manner for his credentials, for letters of recommendation. He is convinced they are hiding behind such formalities rather than facing the more embarrassing and sensitive aspects of his relationship with them: "Could it be that, like some other people, we need letters of recommendation to you or from you? You yourselves are the letter we have, written on our hearts for everyone to know and read. It is clear that Christ himself wrote this letter and sent it by us. It is written, not with ink but with the Spirit of the living God, and not on stone tablets but on human hearts" (2 Corinthians 3:1–3). Saint Paul simply says that they are kidding themselves with all the formalities, or are doing other business through them. The reality is that he has talked Jesus to them, seriously. This is the deep-down stuff. Whatever complaints they have with him, let them deal with on that deep level. Letters of recommendation, credentials, and references—it's all too legalistic for him. So he says right out: "The written law brings death, but the Spirit gives life" (3:6).

The gospel gives still another picture of cautious, heartless people worrying about the formalities. "The followers of John the Baptist and the Pharisees were fasting. Some people came to Jesus and asked him, 'Why is it that the disciples of John the Baptist and the disciples of the Pharisees fast, but yours do not?'" (Mark 2:18). We are familiar with this kind of objection in our own day. People who make it are usually sharp-eyed, and they use questions like sandbags. They hover near religious personages, watching. Priests and ministers, especially, receive their ministrations. The slightest sign of humanity, affection, emotion, or weakness of spirit in a religious figure, and they are ready to pounce, if only from a safe distance. Heaven knows what notion of "religion" they are working with!

Jesus gets their full attention in today's gospel. His answer to them is consistent with his own view of religion. He has nothing against fasting, but the important thing for him is to be clear about God. If fasting gives the impression of a denying, restrictive, and closed God, then that impression must be corrected. Jesus prefers to live with the religious image of a wedding feast. It has warmth and hope to it, and it includes a rather cheery God as host of the party.

His point will be lost on people who are so rigid in their ways that they cannot accept such an intimate and affective portrait of God. Jesus even seems to sense a certain futility in making his point. "No one uses a piece of new cloth to patch up an old coat. . . . Nor does anyone pour new wine into used wineskins" (Mark 2:21 – 22). His vision of things will be no more than a Band-Aid, unless people literally take it to heart.

A lack of heart and of spirit dooms religious people to the dullest kinds of formalism. It is beyond our competence to apply this thought in any detail to the pastoral and social scene in which we live. People have to ask themselves where the dead, dry, heartless areas exist in them or in the social structures around them. Some people find it a major accomplishment to get beyond stumbling stiffly over a handshake, in or out of church. For others, it is a breakthrough just to feel something—anything—about God. Some people need to stop putting job efficiency above growth in personal relationships. Others have to come to terms with the rote and the entrenched protectiveness of their labor union or of their sales policy.

What cuts through all these situations is the fact that God will not keep a refined distance from our hearts. The Spirit of God will continue to speak to us there, in pain and anger, in tenderness and hope, in enthusiasm and the glow of new wine.

Eighth Sunday of the Year — C

Sirach 24:4 – 7
1 Corinthians 15:54 – 58
Luke 6:39 – 45

Acid Test

"Never praise anyone before you hear him talk; that is the real test" (Sirach 27:7).

The text from Sirach seems to imply that peole are measured squarely and objectively by the things they say: their speech discloses the bent of their minds, their faults appear, and so on. This probably is the depressing truth. After you've dined on your own words often enough in life, you realize that the menu was of your own choosing. What we say shows us to the world as shallow or devious, joyful or muddled. There is a thread that leads from our speech to our secret selves. There are many windings and detours along the way. But one iron law remains in effect: it's easier to see into a person who has his mouth open. Freudian slips, bloopers, gaffes, giveaways—all line the route that leads from heart to tongue. Sirach is so right, and so is today's gospel: "The mouth speaks what the heart is full of" (Luke 6:45).

But there are marauders along the route, too. Of his months of interrogation in the dreaded Lubianka prison in Moscow, Fr. Walter Ciszek, S.J., wrote: "After I had been over the same questions and the same answers a number of times with a number of interrogators, I simply gave up arguing. I concentrated instead on trying always to give the same answer, for the least little variation on my part would be treated as a slip. And yet if I repeated exactly the same story time after time, the interrogator would get furious. He would take the sameness of the answers as proof that they must be part of some carefully memorized lie." We have here an example of how people are perversely tested in their speech. The reason for much of our muteness is not the fear of compromising self-revelations. It is because we suspect that our speech will be waylayed. We stammer and stutter until we see that the way is clear and friendly. We button up when people sit back along the route and snipe at our exaggerations or halting confusions, at our misshapen verbal productions.

Students in school feel particularly vulnerable in this regard. An expression they use about authors is quite revealing. They do not say, "The author said . . . ," but they say, "The author *came out and* said. . . ." Students seem to be vividly aware of a distance yawning between thought and expression. The good teacher is the one who can entice them from those deep recesses in which they see their thoughts detained.

There is no such reticence about God. God speaks a Word full of flesh and Spirit. True, that Word is in its own way halting and garbled by the same pitfalls of communication that pester the rest of us. It is hard to hear that Word aright when Jesus is going to his death like any ordinary loser. But the Word of God is precisely a statement about what losing and winning are all about. In that respect it is a Word uttered with a firm voice. And woe to us if we try to trip God up with his own Word.

Ninth Sunday of the Year—A

Deuteronomy 11:18, 26 – 28
Romans 3:21 – 25, 28
Matthew 7:21 – 27

The Real Goods

"Not everyone who calls me 'Lord, Lord' will enter the Kingdom of heaven, but only those who do what my Father in heaven wants them to do" (Matthew 7:21).

In the liturgical readings, we're suddenly back to the Sermon on the Mount. Recall that Saint Matthew's version of the Sermon stresses observance of the new law. Mere membership counts for little. The ability to prophesy, to exorcise demons, to cure people miraculously, means nothing.

To get a sense of how disturbing such teaching could be, imagine if the list continued: regular church attendance, contributions to good causes, devotional fer-

265

vor, dedication to the religious life, papal awards, holy water, subscriptions to religious magazines, and so on.

The gospel imagery is powerful enough to make any of us panic lest we be caught in such artificial religiosity. First, there is the image of the collapsing house. We are invited to picture our own effort, having gone into the cost and construction of a house. We are to imagine that our own talents and planning are at stake. When the house crashes down, this outcome is a personal statement about us. We can expect the hee-haw and the shaking heads to be directed at us. To compare our spiritual endeavors to such a fiasco is frightening. Imagine the dismay as our spiritual edifice—supposedly build out of solid loyalty and integrity, peace, devotion, and virtue—suddenly comes apart like clapboard.

Second, there is the image of God's reaction to the artificially religious person: "I never knew you" (Matthew 7:23). To build our hopes on a personal association and then be told that we have totally misread the relationship can be traumatic. It's like rushing up enthusiastically to someone we thought of as our best friend, only to get an uncomfortable look of embarrassment in return. What, then, if our entire religious orientation gets nothing but puzzled or annoyed looks from God?

How useful is a general warning that we might be fooling ourselves in religious matters? Today's gospel does not in fact give very elaborate criteria that help us distinguish authentic religious behavior from the spurious kind. We are urged simply to do the will of our Father in heaven and to carry out Jesus' commands. Even though the latter have been spelled out to some extent in the Sermon on the Mount, the problem still remains of discerning what religious practices and structures today embody the principles of the Sermon: the storefront church or the dignified basilica, the parish motley or the *intime* prayer group, the bishop-executive or the priest-revolutionary, the prison guard sodality or the prisoners on the inside, the learned scholar or the community organizer, the specialist on world hunger, or the good family man who sells exotic loungewear?

And then there is the troublesome Saint Paul. In today's epistle, he cements the impression that observance of law is an inauthentic basis for any true religiosity.

So we are left to worry whether our religious practice is helping or hindering doing God's will. Maybe it's good for us to worry from time to time about the forms our religious dedication takes. Our uncertainty forces us back to the more central question: What kind of God is the God we are dealing with? And that is a question that pushes us to prayer.

Prayer forges a situation of mutual caring between God and ourselves. In prayer we might discover that God has collapsing houses on his mind because he's trying to build a house, too, and doesn't want to look foolish for his effort, any more than we would. In prayer we might learn that God, like ourselves, wants to be known for what he is, without being misrepresented or having his identity diddled with. Prayer is an attempt to become sensitive to God; it is an opportunity to learn of the incredible degree of God's sensitivity to us. Prayer produces an atmosphere in which we (God and ourselves) are looking out for each other's best interests so much, that labels like "religious practices and structures" begin to look stuffy. Prayer fosters religious authenticity but does not always measure it by clear lists of things-to-perform. Prayer gets personal. But if we pray often enough and hard enough, at least God won't be able to pretend that he never heard of us before.

Ninth Sunday of the Year—B

Deuteronomy 5:12–15
2 Corinthians 4:6–11
Mark 2:23–28

All That Glory

"We are often troubled, but not crushed; sometimes in doubt, but never in despair; there are many enemies, but we are never without a friend; and though badly hurt at times, we are not destroyed" (2 Corinthians 4:8–9).

Saint Paul uses the above example to show that appearances can be deceptive; despite the otherwise shoddy look of things, glory shines on the face of the church and therefore on the face of all humanity. It is the same glory that shone on the face of Jesus who, though doomed to death, bore the *kabod* (glory) of God in himself—that heavy brightness that shows forth the vivifying presence and power of God.

Though Christians are afflicted, full of doubts, persecuted, and struck down, these conditions are not incompatible with the glorious presence of God. Saint Paul adds a twist, as he usually does: not only are these sufferings compatible with glory, but they also help to reinforce and underline the fact that it is God who gives us his glory and not we who earn it by our efforts. "We who have this spiritual treasure are like common clay pots, in order to show that the supreme power belongs to God, not to us" (2 Corinthians 4:7). The glory of God seems to be so tied to these sufferings that we become positively proud of *them* as well. Thus, the Scripture scholar John L. McKenzie can say, "The glory (*kabod*) which is proper to Jesus Christ as redeemer is obtained through sufferings."

Some sufferings that Christians endure do, in fact, seem glorious. Witness the heroic martyrs of El Salvador and Argentina, the dedicated servants of our inner-city jungles, those who go to prison for their religious conscience, and many others. These people seem to go Saint Paul one better; even when they are crushed, even in despair, even when abandoned and destroyed, they believe gratefully that the glory of God will shine through them.

There are other sufferings that Christains endure which look less glorious by any standard. To be caught in the mesh of ecclesiastic bureaucracy; to be insulted intellectually by sermons and policies of caution; to be waltzed with ponderous strides around the same old dance floor by theologians; to have to play the nervous, bug-eyed game of orthodoxy when more obvious truths abound—in these cases one wonders about the glory.

Note that these are all cases of suffering at the hands of those more highly placed than we are. It would be silly to attribute bad will to them, but power sometimes makes those who hold it less sensitive to the needs of those who lack it as their personal prop and support. Humanity needs to eat the holy bread that only the "priests" of our culture have been permitted to eat (Mark 2:26). Our institutions, programs, and procedures have to yield to the real needs of people. That's where the glory is.

Ninth Sunday of the Year — C

1 Kings 8:41 – 43
Galatians 1:1 – 2, 6 – 10
Luke 7:1 – 10

A Matter of Style

"When a foreigner who lives in a distant land . . . comes to worship you and to pray at this Temple, listen to his prayer . . . so that all the peoples of the world may know you" (1 Kings 8:41 – 43).

There is something attractive about the centurion in today's gospel. Though a Roman, he builds a synagogue for the local Jews; though of high rank, he is especially attached to a lowly servant. He is obviously sensitive and affectionate. Yet when it comes to religion and religious faith, he reverts at once to a military model. If he could have healed his servant himself, we could almost see the scenario: "Now hear this and hear it well. There's one C-in-C around here and that's God. He's giving the orders, so when he says jump, we jump. Sickness is hereby and heretofore contrary to his regulations, gone, dismiss. Got it?" Perhaps we are reading too much into his dialogue with Jesus: "Just give the order, and my servant will get well. I, too, am a man placed under the authority of superior officers, and I have solders under me" (Luke 7:7–8). The same lines could, after all, have been delivered with much fumbling self-deprecation and apology; but no other language than that of soldiering was available.

But the phenomenon is common enough. People associate this or that benign style of acting with themselves. They think it proper and fitting for them to be polite, suave, concerned, and delicate in their dealings with others. Yet rarely do they affirm such qualities in God. God often comes across as the hard-nosed drill sergeant, hard to please and even harder to get close to.

The style people associate with God is not always that flattering to God. All-knowing becomes know-it-all. Omnipotent becomes annoyingly competent. Invisible becomes elusive, if not cat-and-mouse. All-seeing becomes prying and judgmental. Eternal becomes stale and cynical. All this adds up to a formidable style indeed, one that puts people off.

For the most part we have to have patience with these versions of God and not jump all over those whose language makes God less stylish. In the gospel, Jesus is full of praise for the centurion despite the gung-ho images the centurion employs: "I tell you, I have never found faith like this, not even in Israel" (Luke 7:9). At other times, however, language about God must be challenged. In today's second reading, for example, Saint Paul complains that the good news was being twisted by some preachers. They were dampening the very goodness of the good news! They wanted to base people's relationship with God on the successful observance of elements of the Jewish Law.

This lugubrious standard seems to have been proposed with stylish persuasion by the preachers in question. Saint Paul is reminded of angels from heaven. And it is true, some of the sweetest, most exquisitely sollicitous and engaging preachers imaginable have promoted drab, controlled, and really mean world-views. When confronted with such angels of the law, Saint Paul is not above abandoning style in favor of a gross and argumentative directness. Sometimes we all have to do something like that to make it clear that the news is good.

Tenth Sunday of the Year—A

Hosea 6:3–6
Romans 4:18–25
Matthew 9:9–13

Believe It or Not

"Abraham believed and hoped, even when there was no reason for hoping" (Romans 4:18).

The character of Abraham is so central to understanding Christian faith that it cannot be overstressed. One of our eucharistic canons calls him "our father in faith." Jesus himself is called a lot of things in the New Testament: the new Moses, the new Elias, the new Adam, the new David—but he is never called the new Abraham. Abraham set the model for faith in such a way that even Jesus does not seem to have added to the shape faith would take as it is repeated again and again in human life. Faith would always be a way of seeing life possibilities where others see only death. Faith would always include a moment of pain before creative results. Faith would always involve submission to demanding claims upon us; it would always look a little like frantic groping for some purchase on life. Jesus' faith, like Abraham's, would take him through this same kind of adventurous clinging to God.

Saint Paul uses one expression for Abraham's faith that calls for comment. He says that Abraham's faith "was accepted as righteous by God" (Romans 4:22). The image of accepting is that of placing a mark next to somebody's name indicating some achievement or asset. Thus, God would be assigning a saving value to Abraham's faith. One commentator asks why faith would have to be accepted, as though faith were not appealing to God in and for itself. The truth of the matter is that God probably has trouble being impressed by the quality of our religious efforts generally, and by the quality of our faith in particular—the way a professional athlete has to look twice, squirm, and finally settle for less while watching the efforts of an amateur. We have to suppose that in reviewing our faith, God is always adding beneath his breath: "Well, it's kind of funny looking and not all that smooth, but it will have to do since it's too complicated to explain. So mark it down as faith."

The point is that faith can be authentic and pleasing to God even when it looks somewhat rinky-dink. It can be terribly meaningful even when it is being pursued through humdrum incidents in our lives. Saint Paul describes the scenario in which Abraham works out his faith in terms that are almost pure soap: Will Abraham overcome the cackling skepticism of Sarah, his aged wife, and have the child? Never mind. For God the scene is pure drama, because the personal relationship of faith is at stake.

The two other readings today expand our insight into what faith looks like. In the first reading, Hosea the prophet is dealing with the sectional rivalries that existed between the northern and southern kingdoms of Israel. He criticizes their unstable piety and the superficiality of their religious practices. What he faults them most for is that they do not really trust the God they are supposedly revering. Having avoided the intimacy that faith requires, they think that God is as unreliable as they are. Having firmly put God at a distance, they then proceed to bargain with him. Their lack of trust at this fundamental level naturally carries over into their mutual dealings with each other.

Hosea himself had been burned in a marriage relationship. He tried to learn from that experience, and he applied it to what our relationship with God should be. The struggles of married people to know one another deeply, their complaints and their expertise in this matter, can teach us all a great deal about how faith in God works. The first rule here seems to be: don't expect to be able to deal with me without giving me a chance to let you know me as I am.

As if to demonstrate this principle in action, today's gospel shows Jesus establishing a trust relationship with others by first getting close to them and letting them get close to him. He calls Matthew the tax collector to discipleship. Jesus and his disciples party at the home of Matthew along with other social outcasts and so-called sinners. The Pharisees complain. They ask, in effect: "How can Jesus be trusted if he consorts wtih sinners?" Jesus' response seems at first blush insulting to his dinner companions: "People who are well do not need a doctor, but only those who are sick" (Matthew 9:12). But the remark is loaded with sarcasm and directed rather at the Pharisees. This is borne out when Jesus cites a line from Hosea: "It is kindness that I want, not animal sacrifices" (Matthew 9:13). In this case, kindness means that he gives sinners a chance to discover that there is more to them than their sins. How can the sinner hope against hope that he might be acceptable to God if he never gets near enough to God to find out? Faith requires access, so Jesus flies in the face of convention to give sinners access to himself. He doesn't seem to worry that the sin might rub off onto him. Or perhaps he gains people's confidence precisely by letting this happen. After all, he died a disgraced public sinner. Now that's getting close to us!

Genesis 3:9 – 15
2 Corinthians 4:13 – 5:1
Mark 3:20 – 35

The Big Lie

"I assure you that people can be forgiven all their sins and all the evil things they may say. But whoever says evil things against the Holy Spirit will never be forgiven" (Mark 3:28).

The Greek historian Thucydides, describing how revolution and civil war ravaged the cities of his day, wrote: "To fit in with developing events, words, too, had to change their usual meanings. What used to be described as a thoughtless act of aggression was now regarded as courage. Making provision for the future was merely another way of saying one was a coward. The ability to understand a question from many different sides indicated that one was unfit for action." This perversion of public language reappears in human life with dreadful regularity. It is a kind of cultural vandalism that violates the normal patterns in which we give one another our word, with the confidence that it will be understood and accepted. Some people will go to any lengths when their own interest is at stake; in such circumstances the normal and accepted meanings of language and behavior suffer a strange fate.

In today's gospel Jesus accuses the scribes of the same violation of language and logic. His complaint is that while he performs acts of kindness, healing, and restoration, his enemies call them diabolic. What burns him is the ease with which his enemies interpret his good works in such a twisted way. His actions are read by them in such a bizarre fashion that even Jesus' family begins to look on him suspiciously: "He's gone mad!" they say (Mark 3:21).

This deliberate misreading of reality is what the sin against the Holy Spirit consists of. Many people upon hearing this expression expect some devious, malformed, preternatural form of spiritual perversion. But blasphemy against the Spirit is much more banal than that. It is not some sort of arcane and exotic spiritual adventurism. It consists of the most straightforward and recognizably cold-blooded lie about what is perfectly obvious to everyone. The one who sins against the Holy Spirit just wishes that the truth would go away. Words get twisted around so that their patent meaning is conveniently forgotten. Bad spirits are suddenly supposed to be at the root of good actions; good spirits at the root of bad actions. What a joke!

The origins of humanity were, it seems, less complicated. Eve, in today's first reading, is honestly fooled by the serpent, caught up and twisted around in a logic she cannot follow. She is merely hoodwinked, and thus is cast in the image of Dumb Dora. It is the serpent who abuses the facts the way the scribes do in the gospel. The serpent attributes a grasping, selfish, witholding attitude to God and accuses God of not sharing the fruit of the tree of life with humanity for that reason. All contrary evidence to such an accusation is conveniently neglected by the serpent—the paradise, the vaulted beauty of heaven, the mate, and the mating. The serpent maliciously proposes that something evil comes from the good God. And humanity falls for the big lie. It violates the Spirit of God and says finally that God is mean. No wonder Jesus gets angry. Not only do they not take him at his word, but they twist its meaning around.

Tenth Sunday of the Year—C

1 Kings 17:17–24
Galatians 1:11–19
Luke 7:11–17

School's Out

"The gospel I preach is not of human origin. I did not receive it from any man, nor did anyone teach it to me" (Galatians 1:11–12).

It was impossible not to be impressed with a recent television film, *Peter and Paul*. No bathrobe drama here, no stagey miracles or pleading violins. No one stared endlessly into the middle distance, a posture one English critic lamented as the bane of "religious" films. Peter was presented as a man with limited authority, harried, cautious, constrained by the old crowd, living off a fragile association with Jesus that was honored in theory but challenged in practise. Ah, and Anthony Hopkins' Paul! Volatile and serene, belligerent and full of doubts, eloquent even as he directed people's attention away from highblown talk to action, fatalistic and yet an earnest organizer. Every line one might have heard delivered ponderously and fatuously in other media contexts, Hopkins put normalcy and depth into. When Paul

278

grieved that he could not come with the spiritual deed to fit the spiritual goal, Hopkins had him say it like a beaten down Chicago Cub fan!

This kind of convincing realism is refreshing. By realism we mean that religious behavior is neither quirky nor utterly constricted. The fact of the matter is that Paul was torn. Between the lines of today's epistle, we read the tension he feels in doing what he thinks God wants him to do and in fitting into the prior scheme of things: "I did not go to anyone for advice, nor did I go to Jerusalem to see those who were apostles before me. Instead, I went at once to Arabia, and then I returned to Damascus. It was three years later that I went to Jerusalem to obtain information from Peter, and I stayed with him for two weeks" (Galatians 1:16–18).

The issue is one of independence, isn't it? That is a word that makes many religious people nervous. It smacks of aloofness and uncontrolled initiatives. It is viewed as freedom-without-responsibility, even where the hum of responsible activity is deafening. The independent person is seen as doing his or her own thing. More often there is some jealousy mixed in: "We have knuckled under (which we regret!). Why don't they?"

Religion is not for all that the private domain of mavericks. The number of people running around licensed by their private revelations is lamentable. Coordinated activity has a greater impact on society, no doubt about it. That's why Paul contacted Peter, to give his own work the integration and clout that it could never otherwise have had without Peter. But it is more a matter here of the mood set by religion: Does it foster initiatives that are not its own by habit and routine? Does it really look for the ways in which God initiates things by inspiring this or that individual—such as Paul—to follow a vision and act on it? Or does it feed all the creativity of its individual members through its own bland and crusted machinery before it trusts it?

In *Peter and Paul*, Peter finally follows Paul, leaving his own entrenched and self-satisfied associates to go to Rome, dying there amidst the Gentiles as Paul did before him. There's a lesson in there somewhere.

Eleventh Sunday of the Year—A

Exodus 19:2–6
Romans 5:6–11
Matthew 9:36—10:8

Head Count

"Jesus called his twelve disciples together and gave them authority to drive out evil spirits and to heal every disease and every sickness" (Matthew 10:1).

We are familiar with how symbolic numbers are used to announce the existence and cohesiveness of groups dedicated to this or that purpose. Think of the Chicago Seven or the Big Three or the Committee of Ten or, for that matter, the Four Hundred. Jesus' Twelve fall into such a category. Like the Seventy, they seem to have been a temporary configuration of Jesus' followers, since they do not figure much beyond the earliest days of the church's life. Yet the Twelve had a special role in the work of Jesus. The obvious reference of the number is to the twelve tribes of the old Israel. When Jesus tells his Twelve to cure the sick, raise the dead, and so on, he is recapitulating the language of Israel's program, in which Yahweh had these same kinds of things in mind.

But Jesus also seems to have been rejecting something about the twelve tribes when he stole the number and applied it to his apostles. Perhaps it was the very tribalism that he was attacking, affiliations based on blood and custom and stale traditions, living off myths and outworn formulas that had lost any relation to people's lives. Jesus was moved by the real needs of people around him: "As he saw the crowds, his heart was filled with pity for them" (Matthew 9:36). He was going to change things; he was going to act. His disciples would have to have the sense that they could do something about healing the world. When he authorized them, he was not giving them permission to do things. The gift he himself had received (Matthew 10:8) he gave to them as a gift.

We are reminded, by the season of the year, of ordinations, past and present. What do priests think they are being authorized to do when they are ordained? Who is doing the authorization? How is authorization seen? As a tightly controlled distribution of permissions or as a resounding impetus to act? What sense of camaraderie and mutual accountability exists among modern priests?

Like the Twelve, priests are caught up by the character of Jesus. They discover in him that great strength can be manifested in gentle giving. They find him less boring than many who clamor for their attention in life. But priests aren't the only ones with such a vision. Others in the church can be as highly *motivated* as priests. This is most likely the sense of today's first reading, where it is said of the whole people: "You will serve me as priests" (Exodus 19:6). Everyone can share in a basic kind of dedication to God's work.

The priest's *job* is another matter. It is basically a community-making function. By ordination, priests become the focus of the community. Like community officials everywhere, they can lay claim to the moral right to get people's attention. This is not in order to be able to tell people what to do (people already know this), nor to display their own personal dedication as Christians (laity will rightly turn this into an exhausting, competitive game), but in order to get people to look at each other to see how they are doing things *together*.

The problem is that when priests exercise this function, things get uncomfortable. For priests remind people not only of the great things they are doing, but also of the things that aren't being done in the community, the futilities, the heated moral debates, the strained mutual relations, the skeletons in the common closet.

No doubt, because of their focal position in a large-scale operation, the personal witness of priests can also be dramatically impressive on a large scale. But that is not the point. Priests have to fight off any tendency to make ordination some kind of personal enthronement or enshrining. Many people are only too happy to let priests pretend that they—the priests—are the only ones doing anything dramatic in the community. But where priests are doing their job, the drama will shift to the community itself.

Jesus' mathematics is behind all this and it is irrefutable: Twelve times something is a lot more than twelve.

Eleventh Sunday of the Year—B

Exekiel 17:22–24
2 Corinthians 5:6–10
Mark 4:26–34

Daring Images

"What shall we say the Kingdom of God is like?" asked Jesus. 'What parable shall we use to explain it?' " (Mark 4:30).

Metaphor has been described by some as a kind of verbal audacity. We have the nerve to interpret one reality by means of terms borrowed from another, different reality. We nudge the image of one thing up against the image of another and proclaim broadly, "See!" The funny thing is that people do see, that metaphor stirs their attention and grasp of reality. Wallflower, top banana, wet blanket, cold fish, high hat, straightjacket—all have become by now domesticated and convenient images. But there was a moment in someone's mind when they sparked forth with the pure, fresh insight that all metaphor supplies.

The use of comparison and parable characterizes Jesus' preaching. Perhaps he had heard the saying, "He who masters the metaphor, masters the world." Like any good public speaker, he knew the value of the audacious image to activate an audience. Yet, the experience he was attempting to elucidate with the help of comparisons was itself so new to people that it was hard to come upon the right image for it: "What shall we say the Kingdom of God is like? . . . What parable shall we use to explain it?" Jesus saw that reign (kingdom) of God variously as a hope, a goal, a beginning, a hidden force, a claim upon people's lives, a set of tasks, a boast, a gift. No wonder he had trouble finding images for it.

This makes the last statement in today's gospel more understandable: "When he was alone with his disciples, he would explain everything to them" (Mark 4:34). The text does not mean that Jesus was giving out one message to the crowd in parables and a different message to his disciples in private. There is but one and the same message: Jesus' experience of and conviction about the reign of God. But this message can be expressed in images and comparisons only up to a point. After that, there must be a living community in which experience is shared, sifted, explored, tested, and celebrated. The experience in community finally dictates this or that image of the reign of God is to survive.

Often, people try to decipher the church's images and metaphors in their own heads, without an experience of Christian community to back up their reflections. This impoverishes them. Take the image of the reign of God in today's gospel: "A man scatters seed in his field. He sleeps at night, is up and about during the day, and all the while the seeds are sprouting and growing. Yet he does not know how it happens. The soil itself makes the plants grow and bear fruit; first the tender stalk appears, then the head, and finally the head full of grain" (Matthew 4:26–28). We might try a little experiment with this image. First, try reflecting on it by yourself. Then, get together with a small group of people and have them share their experience of the text. See where the greatest insight comes.

Perhaps it may well turn out that the really daring image is that of community itself.

Eleventh Sunday of the Year — C

2 Samuel 12:7–10, 13
Galatians 2:16, 19–21
Luke 7:36—8:3

Taking the Cure

"Some time later Jesus traveled through towns and villages, preaching the Good News about the Kingdom of God. The twelve disciples went with him, and so did some women who had been healed of evil spirits and diseases" (Luke 8:1–2).

Evil spirits and sickness inhabit the women of today's gospel—or at least they did before being driven out. No such comment is made about the men who accompany Jesus on his missionary journey. Even granting the ambiguity about what healings and exorcisms meant to the people of that time, we can hear the modern feminist wonder out loud about the selectivity of Luke's reporting: "Weren't any of the twelve (men) cured of sickness? Didn't any of them have evil spirits cast out of them? Is all the weakness being stuffed once again into women?"

Such a judgment would be unfair to Luke. True, in his gospel it doesn't hurt to be a widow (2:36– 38; 7:11– 16; 21:1– 4), and women are said to have various fevers, hemmorages, and sickness, if they aren't already dead! (4:38– 39; 8:40– 56; 13:11– 13). Women are presented in homey roles (10:38– 42; 13:21; 15:8– 9; 17:35); there are also the effusive ones (11:27– 28), and they receive special consideration in time of trouble (23:27– 31). On the other hand there is the formidable faith of Elizabeth and Mary (1:24– 58; 2:5– 7, 48); there is a classy nameless sinner, also noted for her faith in action (7:36– 50); there is the Mary who has more on her mind than housework (10:36– 42); there is competence in the presence of death (23:55—24:11). And in Luke the case is made most vigorously that women are not the possessions of men (16:18; 20:28– 33).

More striking is the fact that the women accompanying the Twelve are mentioned at all. Today, on many an apostolic outing they might not even make the list. We seem to have gone to the opposite extreme: the women are indeed credited for their faith—for their tenacious personal dedication and heartfelt giving—but are not expected to have much contact with the decision-making power in the life of the church.

Society associates "power" with men. From this conviction stem all other attitudes towards women that are part of the present problem. Women have to be denied power, even protected against having it, if men are to be spared the frightening fantasies they have of powerful women: taking power from a woman seems a brutalizing act; submitting to a woman's power seems a capitulation to infantilism; envying a woman's power seems lustful; ignoring it seems ungrateful; comparing one's own with it seems something between grotesque and intimate. Women have to stay "weak" if men are to be relieved of these fantasies.

The situation will no doubt continue, since it is unlikely that either men or women will ever come to look on things like decision making not as "power" but as responsibility and service. Until then, women will have to go on being cured of their "weakness" before they can start traveling with the powers-that-be.

Twelfth Sunday of the Year—A

Jeremiah 20:10–13
Romans 5:12–15
Matthew 10:26–33

Imagine That

"If anyone declares publicly that he belongs to me, I will do the same for him before my Father in heaven" (Matthew 10:32).

Several years ago an experiment was conducted with today's gospel selection at the center of it. The experiment consisted in having the passage read interpretatively in five different styles. The point of the exercise was to show how different views of Jesus are conveyed by the very way we read the gospel aloud. It was also to get people's reactions to the various kinds of Jesus that emerged. Appropriate background music was assigned each interpretation. The five styles consisted of the following:

A tub-thumping, convinced, threatening, sweaty, haranguing Jesus. Strictly country, up and down the emotional scale, part display and part no-questions-asked dogma. Music, bluegrass.

A glib, cocksure, lucid, buttoned-down, reasoning Jesus. Never sweats. One of those people very confident about his own voice. Definitely a pre-Watergate, antiseptic quality to the argument: You have to agree because it's all so competent. No music here.

An introverted, searching, diffident Jesus. Half talking to himself, looking for some truth in his own utterings, angry that his own uncertainty is undercutting him as he speaks. Tentative, seeking reinforcement from his listeners for his own vision. Resentful if they believe him and if they don't. Music, wierd.

Your friendly Jesus, condescending, saccharine, uplifting. Flawless teeth. The voice reverberating nasally out of deep dishpans. American all the way. Soporific organ scales in the background.

A weather-worn, don't-kid-yourself Jesus. Been around. You think about it, you'll agree with me. You don't, that's your problem. But don't expect me to tickle your fantasies. It all figures, finally. Thank Peter Gunn for the music.

The striking result of the experiment was that most people said it didn't matter which interpretation was closer to the truth! Perhaps we should say shocking rather than striking. When you see people who in their normal dealings with one another are normally so very demanding about personality styles suddenly drop all interest in them, something seems amiss. Neither was their reason for disinterest the one we might expect, namely that the personality of Jesus is so refracted throught the personalities of the evangelists that it is difficult to get an uncluttered view of it. Rather, people were indifferent to the comparison of personality styles for one of two reasons: either they considered it enough that Jesus was God—that realization overshadowed the question of style to the point that it became improper; or, they assumed one style to be characteristic of Jesus, a loving one. No further nuances on that love were needed or desired.

It seems strange. For other scriptural characters, we seem quicker to seek out these nuances of style. In today's first reading, for example, the figure of Jeremiah emerges with personality traits firmly in place: cautious, harassed, vengeful, excessive, and a bit maudlin, yet with a simple integrity and deep faith. Again, in the second reading, the personality of Saint Paul is fairly palpable: the intricate intellect, the system builder laying out history as a prop for his ideas, the generous heart who somewhat naively tells people that God's goodness is in inverse proportion to their wickedness and thinks that this will cheer them up. But when we press to do analyzing like this with the person of Jesus, people seem not to want the same kind of drama to enter into their image of Jesus.

Saint Ignatius of Loyola encouraged people, in their prayerful reading of the Scriptures, to catch as much pictorial and psychological detail in the events and characters as possible. His point was not to give the imagination free subjective rein. But by the play of the imagination over the scene, people would increase in themselves sentiments and feelings in reaction to the scene. These sentiments and feelings could then in turn be used as a check on whether or not they were really letting the scriptural picture emerge.

Perhaps the opposite occurs as well: If we want to keep the scriptural characters, Jesus included, as bland as possible, then we would avoid getting in touch with our feelings about them and we would not ask too many imaginative personal questions about them, either.

We are left with today's gospel. Its Jesus tells us not to be intimidated. He mocks attempts to bury truth. He does not leave silence unchallenged; he will not have his followers bullied by mute pressures to shut up about the good news. He says that being scared is beneath our dignity. Above all, he insists on allegiance, so that if our souls depended on it, we would not give out compromising stories about him. What sort of person would say things like that?

Job 38:1, 8– 11
2 Corinthinas 5:14– 17
Mark 4:35– 41

Bigger Than Life

"No longer, then, do we judge anyone by human standards" (2 Corinthians 5:16).

Mere human judgment can be impressive at times. We are good at spotting every telling detail in other people. We can pick out their ambitions and weaknesses. We can figure out their probable income and accurately estimate their expenditures. We can guess what they read, where they come from, their politics and social involvement. We can trace ethnic influences and predict leisure pastimes. We take a lot in with cold and measuring eye.

Saint Paul does not pursue this route. It's not that he's not good at it. He can spear his Corinthian readers with a phrase here, an adjective there, as well as anyone can. But he has taken on himself a more difficult, more insightful task. He has assumed the responsibility to try and see in others what Christ saw in them. This is an awesome project. It requires us to search out in other people why Jesus might have died for them. What makes them loveable to the death? What in them makes them worth the constant effort of rekindling their faith and their hope?

Saint Paul does not settle for the easy way out; he does not accept people *just* because Jesus did. He drives forward expecting to find *in* them something attractive and appealing, something that commands his caution and sensitivity. Saint Paul was burned once; he had totally misread Jesus, whom he viewed as the founder of a dissident Jewish sect. How wrong, he thought, could I have been?

He became committed, therefore, to the idea of bringing imagination to the way he read other people. Imagination lets us get a new angle on what is tired and familiar. We see this in the first reading, in the poetic vision of the author of the book of Job: the sea leaps forth from the womb of nothingness; it is a torrential mass threatening to engulf everything before it. But the Lord treats it like a little baby; he compresses its force, sets natural bounds to it, throws a quilt blanket of clouds over it, and makes swaddling clothes for it out of darkness. A playful, mighty, caring Lord suddenly is espied behind the awesome force of nature.

This kind of imagination is to be invoked when we are dealing with others. We are to see others as the momentous works they are, full of brain and blood, pain and heartbeat, energy and drive. But we also have to envision them as children, vulnerable and growing, raw and seeking. God is passionately engaged in the process of their development. There is a beckoning, a distant music, a far journey, another version of their story. All we need to see this is a little imagination.

Zechariah 12:10 – 11
Galatians 3:26 – 29
Luke 9:18 – 24

Words Fail

" 'Who do the crowds say that I am?' he asked them"
(Luke 9:18).

How do we recognize prophets and messiahs? They line up to compete for attention: strident ones, gaunt ones, some with shaved heads or obvious orange wigs, starers and striders with flashing armbands, button-holers with ivory grins, glib satyrs, ponderous nodders, political agitators, bead-rattlers with pained brows, folk-heroes and astrologers. How can we tell who comes in the name of God? How do we deal with this exasperating shuttle-system of divine messages?

Jesus was challenged on the grounds of his parentage, his place of origin, his lack of eduction, his overseriousness, his frivolity, his friends, his manner, his statements, his silence and seductive leadership. The crowds that followed him were not only naive, they were often grossly superstitious. Some actually thought he was some old hero-saint-prophet come back from the dead. As though someone were to say that a contemporary president was Franklin Delano Roosevelt come back to us — and mean it literally! How do you get such superstitious people to face reality?

Jesus' apostles are not as gross as the crowds. They cast him in the role of Messiah, anoited by Yahweh for the reconstruction of Israel. But they seem to have given this role triumphalistic overtones. Jesus had to be careful about this image of him; he had to turn the conversation to the topic of suffering: "The Son of Man must suffer much and be rejected by the elders, the chief priests, and the teachers of the Law. He will be put to death, but three days later he will be raised to life" (Luke 9:22). This, then, seems to be the sign of an authentic message from God: If nobody mentions suffering, they're probably kidding you.

Now, although Jesus predicts suffering, he does not plan it. You cannot argue from the gospel that he enjoys it. He probably despises it as much as the rest of us. He probably is angered by the lie-down-and-die attitude of many in the face of those forces in life that further suffering: ignorance, hatred, self-centeredness, clumsiness, comfortable tradition, convenient forgetting of the harsher realities, and so on. Jesus never embraces suffering as an end in itself.

For many, on the other hand, suffering looms as a ghoulish goal, dear somehow to God and included all along in the Great Blueprint. Deep down they probably resent bitterly God's nonintervention policy in the matter of human suffering, but are afraid to say so. They are less than impressed that God should share suffering with humankind in his Son. They want a clean sweep of suffering, here and now.

But if God is not keen on suffering, what is he up to? How are we finally to understand Jesus' prediction of his own suffering and projection of ours? At that point Jesus gets vague. He goes on about losing one's life to save it. Perhaps here is the point where words fail.

2 Kings 4:8– 11, 14– 16
Romans 6:3– 4, 8– 11
Matthew 10:37– 42

Lifelines

"Whoever tries to gain his own life will lose it; but whoever loses his life for my sake will gain it" (Matthew 10:39).

If you've ever wondered why people give priests and religious money so freely, then you're probably a little late. Priests and religious wonder themselves. Getting the benefit of other people's charity can be adventurous. The lord of the manor drops by with a batch of rabbits he shot over the weekend, and the monks spend the rest of the week picking pellets out of their stew. The rabbits never had a chance. Or the nuns get enough surplus pastry to cut the heart out of any diet. Or the visiting missionary leaves the Holy Name party with fivers stuck in his pockets and cuffs, if not in his ear.

It's not so much the fact of a donation that can be puzzling. The generosity of people to apostolic causes and to individual apostles has always been a humbling tradition in the church. It becomes problematic only when people seem to be trying to trade off on the "holiness" priests and religious supposedly have. (You will have to accept the questionable premise here that priests and religious are holier than anyone else; we're talking about stereotypes.) When pressed, people can only say that they hope something rubs off on them through their act of generosity to the "holy" priests and religious.

Today's gospel seems to give some justification for this thinking. "Whoever welcomes God's messenger because he is God's messenger, will share in his reward. And whoever welcomes a good man because he is good, will share in his reward" (Matthew 10:41). If you help a person, you not only get rewarded for the help you give, but somehow that person's goodness becomes the measure of your goodness. It sounds at first as though this arrangement has been made arbitrarily, with no consideration of any inner logic to the process. But in fact people who try to help the holy person out are showing that they want to make the holy person's values their own. It is this latter effort that is being blessed, not simply the act of generosity in itself. The sad thing is that many people see themselves so removed from holy values that they feel they have to give money instead!

Today's gospel describes the real prices to be paid for discipleship in Matthew's day. First, family ties were challenged and strained as options were made to abandon the traditional practice of Judaism. Abandoning that great heritage or embracing Jesus' version of it would cause Matthew's contemporaries much pain. Second, the issue of Jesus was put to people squarely: "Whoever loses his life for my sake will gain it" (Matthew 10:39). Family squabbles are one thing. But Matthew promises that squabbles will arise within one and the same person over Jesus. This inner argument will rage — it should rage — because of the testimony of so many Christians who themselves have embraced the new faith.. Third, Christians are going to affect the people with whom they come into contact. Their values will enter every area of life. People will bridle at this; they will recoil. But Jesus' disciples will have to go through the pain of confronting people on these issues.

The same prices must be payed by us today. How do family ties affect our Christian discipleship? How do we relate our own personal growth potential to the gospel? How willing are we Christians to have our values become sources of conflict in social arenas? However difficult these questions, it would be nice if our response to them was more than: Support your local holy people.

Thirteenth Sunday of the Year — B

Wisdom 1:13 – 15, 2:23 – 24
2 Corinthians 8:7, 9, 13 – 15
Mark 5:21 – 43

No Hell on Earth

"God did not invent death, and when living creatures die, it gives him no pleasure. He created everything so that it might continue to exist, and everything he created is wholesome and good. There is no deadly poison in them. No, death does not rule this world, for God's justice does not die" (Wisdom 1:13 – 15).

Try standing in the middle of some hard-core slum and giving that speech. Or in some vicious political prison where truth is carefully locked away. Or in one of our modern bedlams, alcoholic wards, or drug rehabilitation centers. The evidence for death and destruction is overwhelming, and often the first one accused is God.

The Old Testament wisdom literature dealt with this swirling argument between man and God. What characterized the earlier stages of this literature (for example, the Book of Job) was the existential quality of the argument: God and man locked in a timeless mutual challenge; interpersonal issues of death, justice, and suffering debated with all the heat of graduate students; man fighting off craziness and God feeling sharp arrows of recrimination directed at him. Heavy stuff.

In the later stages of the wisdom literature (today's first reading stems from there), the argument moved to another plane. The issue was no longer what transpires between God and hypothetical individuals. It dealt rather with Yahweh's relationship with Israel as a people. Was his treatment of his people fair? How did Israel's worship, customs, and laws embody wisdom? Israel struggles with the fact of having been overrrun so regularly by dark forces of irreligion and tyranny. Job, as it were, is put in a historical-social framework.

Setting the argument with God in these terms does not necessarily advance it. The closer look at history could, it is true, reveal to people how much they themselves contribute to death and suffering by their superstitious and unreal faith. It could show them what fools they are for blaming God for anything.

But people always find the loophole. In today's first reading, for example, it is the devil, not people, who gets the final blame. "It was the Devil's jealousy that brought death into the world" (Wisdom 2:24). The blood-red angers of humankind, the neanderthal indifference, the offhand violence and programmed coward-ice—these are attributed to an envious superbeing of cosmic proportions. Jealousy is the word to watch. Spite and odious envy fill the air. And it comes, according to Wisdom, from some Evil One.

Whether this is just a maneuver on our part, whether we are in fact projecting our own envies out-ward—as though consciousness of our own corporate incompetence would be too much for us—it doesn't re-ally matter. For the New Testament preaches that in Jesus a new wisdom has appeared, one that cuts the argument short and ends the general recriminations. The New Testament spells out this wisdom in two ways.

First, it accepts the terms in which it has inherited the issue. It pictures Jesus as locked in a temporal com-bat with a prince of evil and as ever victorious. If there is such an instigator of evil, some one responsible on a radical, cosmic level for the woes of humankind, the New Testament presents Jesus as an equally cosmic, more radical force for good. People do not need to feel dominated and possessed by their miserable vices. All this is achieved through Jesus. "You know the grace of our Lord Jesus Christ; rich as he was, he made himself poor for your sake, in order to make you rich by means of his poverty" (2 Corinthians 8:9). What is proclaimed here is an action by God's Son so awesome in its inner dimensions that no power of evil can touch it. If God has done *this*, then let there be no more foolish talk about the inevitable power of evil.

Second, the New Testament writers attempt to watch what Jesus does, which often belies the grandiose cosmic drama described a moment ago. He heals this person, then that one. His cures are homely. They imply power, as we see in today's gospel, but the power comes forth from him in modest ways. There are almost scandalous delays. Given the general need, the harvest of health is slim. Yet, Jesus seems to credit his Father at all points with good will. He does not lead the charge against his Father's competence. He expresses wisdom in taking on one part of human life after another.

The New Testament wisdom remains a paradox. It tells us on the one hand that in Jesus, evil's day is over. On the other hand, it tells us that we must be delivered from evil on a daily basis. Above all, it tells us that the truly wise ones are those who share with the poor and comfort the sick.

Thirteenth Sunday of the Year — C

1 Kings 19:16, 19 – 21
Galatians 5:1, 13 – 18
Luke 9:51 – 62

Excuses, Excuses

"My brothers, you were called to be free" (Galatians 5:13).

Why does Jesus, in today's gospel, point the finger so rudely at our human inconsistency and hesitation? "Anyone who starts to plow and then keeps looking back is of no use for the Kingdom of God" (Luke 9:62). It is no fun to be pressed to a rigorous logic on major life decisions. Nothing can give you that trapped feeling more than the clinical, unveering observations of a friend: "If the thing is that valuable to you, what's holding you back?" "How can you say that you want to do such and such at the same time as you keep piling up obstacles to doing it?"

The gospel is talking about single-minded consistency. It reminds us that you can't dabble in Christianity the way you dabble in health kicks or avant-garde theater. A missionary friend, who had earned the right to be a bit cynical, once observed about relations between a rich North America and a destitute South America: "We're sincere, but we're not serious." By "serious" he seemed to mean that we do not draw all the implications of the real situation. We pick and choose. We deny much of what happens before our eyes. Selective remembering masks a much more energetic selective forgetting.

The picture of a frantically driving Jesus would be enough to scare most of us off. Why aren't we, then, scared off? Mostly because we think that you can't get a total picture of a person from a few isolated sayings attributed to him or her. Christianity is more than a matter of reading Scripture. It is a matter of deciphering the inspired talk coming out of a lot of people, past and present. Even in today's gospel a picture of Jesus is presented that hesitates to speak in tones of white-hot, unswerving decision. When Jesus' disciples try to impose their philosophy on the Samaritans, Jesus lets them have it. "When the disciples James and John saw this, they said: 'Lord, do you want us to call fire down from heaven to destroy them?' Jesus turned and rebuked them" (Luke 9:54–55). Apparently, there were excuses for the Samaritans that the disciples had overlooked!

How to explain this contrast between Jesus' attitude toward some and not toward others? Today's epistle offers us a clue. It suggests a way to discriminate between legitimate excuses and no excuses at all: "Stand, then, as free people, and do not allow yourselves to become slaves again" (Galatians 5:1). The difference seems to be a prior experience of freedom and responsibility that one has had in Christ. Someone who has finally found the strength to say "No" to a lot of the Mickey Mouse cannot now pretend that nonsense makes sense. Someone who has discovered that we are less in the grip of psychological, biological, or economic determinisms that we thought cannot now go back to them for support. Someone who has talked familiarly with God as a Father cannot now indulge in high speeches or cringing pleas with him. Someone who has had sure knowlegde of God as love cannot now fan rumors to the contrary.

In Saint Paul's language, we cannot pretend to be earthbound "flesh" once we have tasted what it is to be soaring "spirit." If we were always flabby and sluggish, we seem to get better treatment. But if we have experienced the mobility and alertness that "spirit" implies, then we have less excuse for our plodding ways.

In other words, the Samaritans may not have known better, but the disciples of Jesus should have.

Zechariah 9:9– 10
Romans 8:9, 11– 13
Matthew 11:25– 30

Lord of Summer

"Come to me, all of you who are tired from carrying heavy loads" (Matthew 11:28).

Many people, finding life weary and burdensom, are finally getting a chance to unbend for the summer months. Vacation means many things in our culture. If you're working two jobs, it's little enough. For many it's an opportunity to get a lot of work done around the house. It is a time for lazing or for frantic fun. Mountain people and shore people go their separate ways; the aimers and the aimless travelers head out. Vacation can be an extravaganza in which fat spending belies the poor-mouthing that normally goes on.

We owe a debt to the flesh. (Today's epistle says we don't, but it is talking about something else. Saint Paul is making his usual point there about flesh and spirit: If you engage in dull, dead, and ghastly pastimes, you'll end up dull, dead, and ghastly—and no one, especially not God, is forcing you to.) The debt we owe to the flesh is to revive its energies, to shore up its sagging walls, to get it ready for the next spiritual go-around.

Nothing revives us like people. No amount of body building, rest, fresh air, and idle toe wiggling can compare with the renewal of spirit that comes from deepening friendship, from relationships that are strengthened or resolved. Tortuous or sullen ties be-strengthened or resolved. Tortuous or sullen ties between people will offset any amount of recreation. Today's gospel does not talk directly about vacation, but it does speak of the recreational power of relationships, especially our relationship with God. A gentle and humble heart and openness to friendship with his Father is what made Jesus' own hectic life bearable. A know-it-all, saw-it-all-before attitude poses an obstacle to letting God's friendship surprise us. It cuts us off from discovering so many people in our lives and from being discovered ourselves. It is as though we cannot find joy unless we first expect joy to happen to us and we are ready to receive it with an ingenuous gratefulness. Anyhow, it's a cheap vacation.

Fourteenth Sunday of the Year — B

Ezekiel 2:2 – 5
2 Corinthians 12:7 – 10
Mark 6:1 – 6

Strong Suits

"I am most happy, then, to be proud of my weaknesses, in order to feel the protection of Christ's power over me" (2 Corinthians 12:9).

Horoscopes tend to cancel each other out: stay indoors today/go out and meet people; you are more secure in your job/you will begin a new career soon; love smiles on you/find out who your enemies are. That's why there's only one horoscope or fortune cookie to a customer. We don't want conflicting messages when our cosmic fate is being worked out.

But in real life we sometimes have to cope on several fronts at the same time. Two such fronts are described in today's readings. The epistle gives an instance of dealing with one's own limitations; the gospel an instance of how other people sometimes read limitations into us unfairly. In real life we're constantly juggling both of these issues at once. We can at least divide them up here for purposes of commenting on each.

Saint Paul's "physical ailment" (2 Corinthians 12:7) remains a mystery. Commentators have speculated on what it might have been that kept him from getting spiritually uppity. We just don't know whether it was a serious physical ailment or some moral lapse. More instructive is the fact that Saint Paul ends up boasting—a strong expression—about his limitation. Assuming that he wasn't just kidding himself, how did he get that way?

First, Saint Paul carried the reality of his limitations right into his prayer. He did not try to hide them from God. That might sound like a silly thing to say, but there are people who try to disassociate from their prayer life what most beats them down or embarrasses them. They are like people with a horrible toothache who bravely work through a conversation without ever mentioning the tooth, because they think that's the polite thing to do. Or perhaps they think that their limitations, if mentioned in prayer, might further anger an all-achieving God. Saint Paul is more candid: "Three times I prayed to the Lord about this physical ailment and asked him to take it away" (2 Corinthians 12:8).

Second, Saint Paul learned something about God by being so candid in prayer concerning his own limitations. The benevolence of God, Saint Paul discovered, was not measured out in direct proportion to his own flawless performances. The perfection God's love demanded of him was to be a human perfection after all, one in which achievement is always less than it could be, in which proper style is inevitably wanting in some respects, in which integrity is always somewhat off center.

If God did not follow this principle, then he probably would have to write off his own Son. For when Saint Paul says that his vision told him power reaches perfection in weakness, he is referring as well to Jesus, whose human limitations were no obstacle to the Father's immense love for him. So Saint Paul opts for the weak power of Christ: "When I am weak, then I am strong" (2 Corinthians 12:10).

This lesson in human imperfection is a difficult one for us to learn, especially when we have to face in ourselves the frailties that detract from our ideal self-images. It is truly comforting, on the other hand, to know that God loves us, warts and all.

In today's gospel Jesus' townspeople, when faced with his obvious ability, close their eyes to it. They attempt to level his superlative performance by direct appeals to what is totally irrelevant: "Aren't his sisters living here?" (Mark 6:3). Their lack of trust leads them to invent limitations in him that he does not have. That this happens to all of us is clear. How, then, does Jesus work with their petty, vain reaction to him?

Very simply: He doesn't. "Jesus went to the villages around there, teaching the people" (Mark 6:6). There was a bit of sniff to his departure, to be sure. The liturgical editor was probably right in paralleling his behavior with that of Ezekiel. When Jesus comments that no prophet is honored in his own country, he seems less philosophical than he sounds. Mark says, in fact, that Jesus was distressed. In any case, when he finds people *so* limited in their trust of him, he drops them. Or, better, he gives them a certain distance, which is often a good way to love some people. They lose out, but he refuses to stay chained to his distress. He does not make their lack of trust the measure of his own responsibilities or opportunities.

We are back at Saint Paul's principle, "When I am weak, then I am strong." It seems to hold even in cases in which others are rendering us powerless by their lack of faith in us. It's also a pretty good description of how God feels running the world.

Fourteenth Sunday of the Year — C

Isaiah 66:10 – 14
Galatians 6:14 – 18
Luke 10:1 – 9

Knowing the Territory

"There is a large harvest, but few workers to gather it in. Pray to the owner of the harvest that he will send out workers to gather in his harvest" (Luke 10:2).

On the theory that "the customer is always ripe," energetic businessmen down the ages have bombarded, wheedled, seduced, and stampeded consumers from Timbuktu to 42nd Street. Many of them would not admit out loud with their patron, P.T. Barnum, that "there's a sucker born every minute." Yet, however suave the come-on, however eloquent the pitch for the product, however hearty or prissy, oily or pugnacious the pitchman, selling has always been the name of the game. And you "gotta know" the territory.

Some might think it demeaning even to hint at a parallel between such salesmanship and the preaching of the Christian faith. Still less would they see that preaching as a deliberate, organized effort. Faith is seen by them too much as a me-and-Jesus thing. Even when people are convinced of the value of sharing the good news about Jesus with others, they would rather do so on a one-to-one basis.

Yet, as today's gospel indicates, Jesus' ministry was an organized and outreaching effort. The divine plan, in its human shape, took a good amount of detailed and disciplined planning. Luke's account borrows from an even earlier source. So we are not simply dealing with a picture of how Luke's contemporaries acted, as though the picture had no relation to Jesus' own mode of operation.

This early testimony will not make a dent, however, on anyone who cannot accept such a practical and hard-headed Jesus. We might argue with such people: Look, put yourself in Jesus' sandals. You want to reach a lot of people with important news, right? You are on fire with your vision of God as Father. You are sick and tired of the sick and tired you encounter around you who need help and consolation. You stand for radical surgery on the world's present condition. You only have two legs and two arms, however divine. How are you going to get yourself across? Wouldn't *you* train trainers, build leaders, make others go-getters? Wouldn't you organize?

Many of us are against organization because we have suffered much from it at one time or another in our lives. Organization connotes bureaucracy and institutionalism. It raises issues of authority, chains of command, or hierarchy. It throws us in roughly with others. We get lost in the faceless, heartless crowd. Could Jesus be in favor of that?

Yet, look at the seventy-two disciples. How many of them could Jesus have known well? How many could have had the benefit of his personal instruction and advice? How much was he at the mercy of their talent, their prayerfulness and comprehension as they set off? By our standards of perfection in all things, Jesus would still be sitting with the seventy-two, getting them ready for the first outing!

Jesus' view of the territory is not very flattering. It is inhabited by wolves. Sickness clamors for attention from all sides. Formality abounds. People will be watching where you eat and how you make your living. Everyone is busy making provision for themselves. No wonder he had to organize.

The heart of the matter is the product his disciples will have to offer. Its name is *shalom*. They are to be messengers of peace. The news is out that God has given over his supposed enmity with humankind. Everybody should relax and make peace with one another. Saint

Paul puts it with astonishing simplicity in today's epistle: "What does matter is being a new creature" (Galatians 6:15).

This newness is not always popular. The thought that we are to cooperate in our own re-creation gives us the same sinking feeling we get when we are reminded we should stop smoking or shed our paunch. The vision of our new selves—trim, snorting, and ready—dangles before us. But the very vision disheartens us, because we realize what it would take.

Re-creating ourselves as peace-people is even more complicated. A great peacemaker of the 1960s, Rabbi Heschel, used to preface his antiwar speeches with the candid admission that war was terribly exciting and in many ways more appealing than peace. No wonder the Christian who wants to sell peace has to be convinced of the product.

And organized. We are out to corner the market. We need workers, as the gospel tells us. These workers, moreover, must be teamworkers, or else the Christian ministry becomes a series of isolated gestures of charity. And if love needs an organizational chart, don't blame anybody but Jesus.

Isaiah 55:10–11
Romans 8:18–23
Matthew 13:1–23

Killing Time

"The seeds sown in the good soil stand for those who hear the message and understand it" (Matthew 13:23).

In today's epistle, Saint Paul has a striking image of the pace and progress of Christian life. He projects onto the material universe the problem that we often feel with faith. We moan and groan about the slow pace of our conversion; Saint Paul describes the physical world as heaving about futilely under its frustrations. "We know that up to the present time all of creation groans with pain, like the pain of childbirth. But it is not just creation alone which groans; we who have the Spirit as the first of God's gifts also groan within ourselves as we wait for God to make us his sons and set our whole being free" (Romans 8:22–23). The universe awaits the arrival on the scene of true "sons" of God. A son in Saint Paul's context is someone who does not cringe and scrape in the presence of God, but someone who stands on the earth erect and at ease when God is the subject at hand. It is as though the universe is embarrassed at the sight of alarmed and scurrying inhabitants and is annoyed at the level of their religious sensibility.

How far have we evolved in our religious sensibility? Are we embarrassed that we continue to act as though God were so creepy? Too often, the pace of our religious maturation rivals the miniscule pace of the physical evolution itself. Except that the rocks, stones, and animals have more excuse.

Today's gospel is more optimistic. It speaks of faith as a seed sown. Many dangers can befall the seed and these dangers are listed. But in the underlying image, faith is something that grows laboriously through time. We need a farmer's patience to tend out faith, and a farmer's expectation that the shape of things develops and changes as it grows. The gospel reminds us the evolution is underway.

Fifteenth Sunday of the Year—B

Amos 7:12–15
Ephesians 1:3–14
Mark 6:7–13

Have Faith, Will Travel

"He called the twelve disciples together and sent them out two by two. He gave them authority over the evil spirits" (Mark 6:7).

It's a shame that we get such a little snippet from the Book of Amos in today's first reading. We could use a man like him today. To get a picture of the period (eighth century B.C.) in which he lived, we would have to imagine that the South had won the Civil War, that it had gone on to unparalleled prosperity and then was lectured by some insignificant Yankee peddler on the moral and social evils that attend such prosperity. In Amos' day it was, in fact, a northern kingdom that had seceded from the union of tribes forged by King David from the south and that had gone on to great wealth and power. Amos was from the south, a Judean layman who worked at dressing sycamore trees. This meant that he went around puncturing the bark of the sycamores to let out the worms that gathered under the bark. His secular job was a good metaphor for his prophetic work in the northern kingdom. He went there to preach social justice in the name of the covenant. "You people hate anyone who challenges injustice and speaks the whole truth in court. You have oppressed the poor and robbed them of their grain. And so you will not live in the fine stone houses you build or drink wine from the beautiful vineyards you plant. I know how terrible your sins are and how many crimes you have committed. You persecute good men, take bribes, and prevent the poor from getting justice in the courts" (Amos 5:10– 12). That certainly would get the worms scurrying!

Amos turned his diatribe against religious shrines as well. In his opinion, people were using their religious affiliation, ceremonies, offerings, and religious practices to cloak over a more fundamental indifference to issues of social justice.

Prophets always seem to end up this way, preaching the same philippic to churchgoer and unchurched alike. Sinners though we all are, there's something not quite right about that. The real gougers are not going to hang around churches, where their grasping behavior is likely to be thrown up to them. And people who come to church at least are usually making a stab at social justice in their workaday lives. Perhaps it is just that prophets find more convenient audiences in churches; you can yell at them because, like Everest, they are there.

But prophets and preachers have to do more than this. They have to expose their faith, as it were, on foreign turf, as Amos did. They have to experience sharing their conviction with those who might find their message alien and remote. Like Amos, and like the Twelve in today's gospel, they have to get a feel for what their faith sounds like out on the road. This daring, missionary spirit will deepen their faith, challenge and clarify it; it will make faith more real for those to whom it is preached.

Fifteenth Sunday of the Year — C

Deuteronomy 30:10 – 14
Colossians 1:15 – 20
Luke 10:25 – 37

In the Know

"The command that I am giving you today is not too difficult or beyond your reach. . . . No, it is here with you. You know it and can quote it, so now obey it" (Deuteronomy 30:11, 14).

Do we really know what sin is, or don't we? Do we have to be taught by laws and messages, by rebukes and explanation, about how to live in charity with others? Does the slumlord need a lecture? Does the guy who "absentmindedly" spills candy wrappers in your elevator have to be told he's a slob? Does the murderer have to be reminded of his victim? Does the fast-talking charmer who loves them and leaves them need to have it pointed out to him what a self-centered clod he is?

Conversation on these matters, full of accusation and defensiveness, sometimes seems like a stylized dance of the elephants. It ill conceals a savvy awareness on all sides of where the realities beneath the surface are. While some moral issues are truly puzzling, others are the signal for a giant smokescreen. We try to lose or find each other in a cloud of moral debate. And no one ever admits to having problems in *being* moral.

In his writing, Saint Paul defends the theory that humankind conveniently loses the records of its own sinfulness. It's the old ploy, to say that the pertinent documentation has been mysteriously misplaced. Saint Paul argues that we know when we have sinned, but we try to stonewall it. More importantly, he points out the reason why people won't admit their sinfulness. It is because if they do, they think they're dead. They have previously transformed God into a judge (for the shady reason that they don't want to live with the image of God as friend). Now they have to live with the image of judge they have created. So they are caught in a bind: they know they are sinners, but they are reluctant to say so before the judge. So they keep a dreadful silence on the subject.

Or they argue about what sin is. Or they ask dumbly: "Who is my neighbor?" It's pretty tiresome. And dangerous—if there is no real sin, then no one gets any practice forgiving it. Then where are we?

315

Wisdom 12:13, 16 – 19
Romans 8:26 – 27
Matthew 13:24 – 43

Last Gasp

"We do not know how we ought to pray; the Spirit himself pleads with God for us in groans that words cannot express" (Romans 8:26).

Today's gospel makes it sound as though God is nice because he doesn't kill off sinners right away; he has the decency to wait: "Let the wheat and the weeds both grow together until harvest. Then I will tell the harvest workers to pull up the weeds first, tie them in bundles and burn them, and then gather in the wheat and put it in my barn" (Matthew 13:30). You look at the sentence twice and ask yourself what "nice" can still possibly mean.

Some would argue that the original point of Jesus in the parable was to underscore the patience of God, and nothing more. Jesus would be confronting *our* tendency to solve the problem of evil by "doing in" the people who represent evil in our lives. *We* might want to root them out because of their dragging effect on our growth. *We* might resent their presence in the field of our spiritual endeavors. Jesus would be telling us to cool it.

More than this, Jesus would be urging us to be patient and less aggressive to sinners, if only to give us time to learn that we, too, are sinners. With enough time we would perhaps revise our view that the world is divided into weeds and wheat. We would turn to the kind of merciful God described in today's first reading, in which God clearly does not want ultimate revenge on evildoers (Wisdom 12:16).

But how does this view of Jesus square with those sections of today's gospel that make him the spokesman for a Final Solution as vengeful as any we might wish on one another? Some would consider these sections to be the editorial embellishments of Saint Matthew. Why? Well, it is clear that this chapter of Matthew's Gospel contains many observations that Saint Matthew makes with an obvious eye to his own contemporary dilemma of dealing with growing opposition to the gospel from Judaism, and of coping with inconsistent behavior on the part of Christians themselves. How, Saint Matthew must ask, put some clout into the demands of the faith? Given these concerns, his preoccupation with final outcomes might be forgiven. But he may have distorted Jesus' point in the original version of the parable.

Others would disagree. They would see Jesus himself as the author of these threatening passages.

It isn't easy. We have a very patient God on the one hand and a very impatient one on the other. No wonder our prayer turns at times into groans that words cannot express.

Sixteenth Sunday of the Year—B

Jeremiah 23:1–6
Ephesians 2:13–18
Mark 6:30–34

On and On

"So they went from all the towns and ran ahead by land and arrived at the place ahead of Jesus and his disciples" (Mark 6:33).

Today's gospel describes an abortive vacation on the part of Jesus' apostles. Not really a vacation, just a rest. But then as now, there probably were those people around who pleasantly asked, after you took one miserable day off, "How was your vacation?" (They are usually just back from a three-week luxury trip themselves!) In any case, the apostles had put their time in preaching and teaching. They were tired. So Jesus suggests a little R and R. "Let us go off by ourselves to some place where we will be alone and you can rest a while" (Mark 6:31).

It doesn't come off. Work nudges its way back onto their schedule. Or, what comes to the same thing, they meet people who are on a different schedule from their own, people for whom rest may not even be a realistic category. Jesus is filled with compassion for these people; so the work goes on.

It's not a bad lesson for us. Compassion has no schedule. Vacation or not, people bring their needs to us in countless ways. Some thirst for conversation; they grasp at it with grateful intensity. Others need physical help—lifting, lugging, moving, cleaning. Many seek advice; they want to discuss some painful or puzzling experience they are going through. Many can use a smile, a laugh, some passing surcease, an excited if trivial interlude in the tense course of their ordinary lives. All need exorcism. They want greedily to find the witness of faith, hope, and true charity in us.

Jesus takes leadership in compassion: "His heart was filled with pity for them, because they were like sheep without a shepherd. So he began to teach them many things" (Mark 6:34). We may not like the shepherd/sheep imagery that conveys this fact, but we are taught here to keep our eyes open to the needs of others, to feel their hurts and reach out to them.

Sixteenth Sunday of the Year—C

Genesis 18:1–10
Colossians 1:24–28
Luke 10:38–42

Something Missing in Jesus

"And now I am happy about my sufferings for you, for by means of my physical sufferings I am helping to complete what still remains of Christ's sufferings on behalf of his body, the church" (Colossians 1:24).

In the old days, Christian meditation on the suffering of Christ was a gripping, consuming experience. Every step, every bead of sweat, every grunt, thud, swish, and crack was registered on our sensibilities. Even though tnat was a time before great introspection, preachers did succeed in capturing a lot of the psychological hammering that Jesus took as well. Throughout, the impression was conveyed (or self-administered) that Jesus' sufferings were more intense, more exquisite, rarer, and *better* than anyone else's.

So it is a bit of a shock to hear Saint Paul suggest that this wasn't quite enough. There was still something lacking. What could it have been? Paul is apparently mentioning completing Jesus' sufferings for some purpose and measuring the shortcoming by some unexpressed standard. What he might have had in mind is something like what follows:

In Jesus, God tries out the human condition. That condition at times is no fun, as we all know. Jesus got a taste of its darker side. But there is a lot that God did not personally experience in Jesus. Would God's love (in the flesh, of course) have survived if Jesus had tasted the full range of human suffering? If he were blinded, paraplegic, disturbed, haunted, sexually disjointed, inarticulate, or depressed all the time—would he have looked at faith and hope the same way he did? Would love have found a way out of his heart toward us? And what if he had lived through war or just through the ordinary bombardment of media? He never did a stretch in jail—an overnight, but no real time. He was never crammed half-knowing into an oven. He never saw his kids hooked on drugs. He was never mangled by a car driven by some pouting, distracted sot. Would his fidelity and commitment have remained the same?

In typical fashion, Saint Paul is going to prove that love and such are possible in any and all situations. He is going to dispel the lingering suspicions about Jesus. He asks Christians to give themselves in faith and love, no matter what the suffering involved. He is not promoting some sick pursuit of suffering for its own sake. It's a straight PR job for Jesus.

Seventeenth Sunday of the Year—A

1 Kings 3:5, 7–12
Romans 8:28–30
Matthew 13:44–52

Getting There

"'Do you understand these things?' Jesus asked them. 'Yes,' they answered" (Matthew 13:51).

How do we find the right language to express our faith? How do we avoid tripping over other people's language or being hurt by it? How do we get closer to a picture of Jesus that has consistency and sanity to it (if indeed we may presuppose in faith that he was not erratic and utterly offbeat)? These questions are particularly pressing when the topic happens to be God's final judgment on us. Perhaps this week's readings could give us some practical criteria for understanding God's word in this matter.

In the first reading, we find that Solomon's famed wisdom always operated in a social context: "Here I am among the people you have chosen to be your own, a people who are so many that they cannot be counted" (1 Kings 3:8). This reading reminds us that we must always see our faith in conjunction with the faith of many others. Would we think about God's final judgment the way we sometimes do if we really took a look at the people around us, at their very complex ways, their fears and sentiments? Would we be so quick with the "weeds and wheat" speech?

In the second reading, we are urged to accentuate the positive. Its topic is predestination, but without the usual overtones of who might be excluded. It concentrates on the hope that we will succeed, rather than on the possibility that we might fail. Perhaps this sense of having been chosen in love will make us look at the final judgment in a more optimistic perspective.

The third reading reminds us that we are dealing, in the formulation of our faith, with comparisons: "The Kindgom of heaven is like...." Jesus himself must at best approximate a picture of his Father's way of dealing with people. He reaches for parables and illustrations that capture his experience of God's ways in the world. Perhaps the best we can do is to hope that his comparisons about the final judgment limp a little!

2 Kings 4:42 – 44
Ephesians 4:1 – 6
John 6:1 – 15

Give or Take

*"Jesus took the bread, gave thanks to God, and distribut-
ed it to the people who were sitting there" (John 6:11).*

One of the constant anxieties of humankind is
that its resources will run out. Everyone is jittery about
oil, food, timber, coal, air, and clean water. When they
go, we go. At the slightest hint that these resources are
running low, we feel panic in our bones. A primal instinct is awakened, to smash and grab, to hoard, to look
out for number one.

And what about our inner resources? Who will
provide when number one is threatened with some final
shortage? The body wears down. Red cells wrestle with
white for hegemony. Heartbeats sound off-key; footsteps
seem more imperiled. Our spiritual powers, too, show
skittish signs. Memory sputters and slips. Reason flails
about for the next clarity. Even emotion dries up. We get
closer to final shutdown. And while this drama plays itself out, there is no one we can take from. No one can
help us as the depletion spreads.

To maintain the sense that someone is giving to
us — will give to us, even as all this depletion goes on — is
called faith. Faith flies in the face of morose prediction
and offers a view of its own about resourcing. In today's
gospel, Jesus teaches this view in the most painstaking,
step-by-step fashion (with the help of a perfect end man

in Philip): "See the shortage? Looks bad, doesn't it? Five thousand people and not much bread. Now, watch closely." And they all eat.

Whether one takes the miracle literally, or whether one thinks that Jesus' own generosity inspires the others present to dip into their hidden stocks and share them, the point is still the same. Jesus is convinced that his Father is a resourcing God. He wants others to see this, so that they will stop looking on their possessions or on themselves as threatened commodities. We must learn to stop asking God so much in prayer to *be* resourcing. Instead, we must discover in prayer the teeming, cornucopian vision of God's creativity in our regard. The confidence we gain from this vision is what will free us from anxiety and free us for generosity to others. If God, in our thinking, will not finally make something of us, how can we be expected to give of ourselves at every turn and at the expense of our own dwindling stores?

Even so, some people end up mere takers, like the crowd in today's gospel who want to keep Jesus on supply as their king. They mistake being resourced for being kept in a narcissistic dependence of take, take. Jesus will have none of that: "Jesus knew that they were about to come and seize him in order to make him king by force; so he went off again to the hills by himself" (John 6:15). He just wanted to keep giving himself away, like bread that would never run out.

Genesis 18:20–32
Colossians 2:12–14
Luke 11:1–13

What's in a Prayer

"Everyone who asks will receive" (Luke 11:10).

Today's readings sound like something out of *The Godfather*. God is foresworn to do favors for all comers. The style of our asking in prayer may vary. It may range from the haggling and shrewd flattery of Abraham (in the first reading) to the whining persistence and outright pleading of the lady in the gospel. Even the Lord's Prayer seems like a litany of gimme, gimme, gimme—with only a brief opening nod of respect and best wishes to God.

This is a truly generous picture of God. He likes to be asked. He doesn't mind all the freeloaders. He almost has to prove that he's not such a hard person to deal with. Not even sinners need hesitate to ask. The imagery in today's epistle is powerful on this score. God says: "You owe me something, because you are a sinner? Look. I take your IOU and I nail it there, near the body of my own dear Son. Now how can I even think of your debt anymore? It would be an infamy."

But somehow people aren't convinced. They immediately start to recount how prayers of petition have flopped in the past. There are those who have hounded God for blessings, only to receive further curses. They were not even asking for something for themselves but were asking for their loved ones. They were every inch as insistent as the gospel prescribes, but they got nothing for their labors.

Such complaints miss the whole point of the readings. To argue for or against the literal efficacy of prayer is out of place. It might give someone satisfaction to bring a Chase Manhattan Bank or a Con Ed to its knees on a point of accuracy and consistency. But don't try it on God. The point of the gospel is that we are praying to someone who is kind, rather than to some volatile nut, to someone who is sensitive, rather than to a stone wall. But gods, like ourselves, are in the end enigmatic. We should not press them for precision, especially when they are handing out the favors in the first place.

If we're going to get precise, then we might examine our conscience about what we in fact do pray for. Do we mention the forgotten, the stranger, the social and political outcast? Do we show in our prayers that we care beyond a narrow circle? Do we bother God about the peripheral people?

If we can't face this kind of precise inquiry, then why do we get so exact with God?

Isaiah 55:1–3
Romans 8:35, 37–39
Matthew 14:13–21

Feast or Famine

"Listen to me and do what I say, and you will enjoy the best food of all" (Isaiah 55:2).

Is religion the enemy of appetite? Many would say so. They complain that religion, with its ascetic mien and picky ways, crimps them and frustrates their zest for life. Rather than unleashing their energies, the complaint continues, religion leaves people domesticated and bored. Appetite is served but in a passive sort of way. Religion "takes care" of people. It gives them the assurance of being nourished, almost spoonfed. Why else would stories like today's gospel, in which Jesus feeds the five thousand, be held up to believers as an edifying instance of what religion does? Religion leaves people no room to dabble and dare, to taste and see. It plans the menu for you.

Well, we've heard this kind of criticism of religion before. It often comes from individuals who themselves are hardly other Zorbas. In their own behavior they seem rather to dip one toe timidly into life as if it were an overchilled pool. Sometimes, however, the criticism of religion is sincerely based. For whatever reason, people fear that divine initiatives make all other initiatives superfluous.

Why this fear should lead them to distort the character of religion is another question. After all, the "religious" hero of today's gospel is not the one who sits back and benefits from someone else's activity. It is Jesus. And there he is, letting himself be jostled by thousands, interrupted in his private griefs, feeling strongly the spiritual and physical hungers of others, trying to organize the chaos a little, and wryly giving others the sense that they can do likewise. If anyone has been let loose in life, it's Jesus.

For another example of unrestrained religious appetite, look at today's epistle. It has Saint Paul taking the full measure of time, events, possibilities—of all creation—and responding with a voracious sense of being loved personally by God: "Who then, can separate us from the love of Christ? Can trouble do it, or hardship or persecution or hunger or poverty or danger or death? . . . No, in all these things we have complete victory through him who loved us!" (Romans 8:35, 37).

So it's not that believers are timid guests at the so-called banquet of life. They're just used to better restaurants.

Exodus 16:2–4, 12–15
Ephesians 4:17, 20–24
John 6:24–35

New Look

"So get rid of your old self, which made you live as you used to —the old self that was being destroyed by its deceitful desires" (Ephesians 4:22).

Today's epistle talks about becoming someone new, of finding a new image of ourselves. That's a project many people are familiar with and undertake at different stages of their lives. Sometimes that change is limited to outward appearances: to the three-piece suit or the languid wrist bracelet; to the rimless, peering stare; to worn, down-home jeans. Joggers tell us of physical changes, of arcane transformations that result from their exertions: oxidized thinking (always preferable); alert circulation within; the pounding sense of higher and higher possibilities.

But sometimes the change in question is more personal. It may not even be profound; we may simply wish to be less of a rat than we normally are, more disciplined and autonomous. Sooner or later, however, this wish in us to change must come out into the open. If we merely had to try on this new vision of ourselves before the mirror, to strut and study it there, we would have no great problem. But we have to parade it before others, and there things get stickier. Despite our new accent and style, we have to get past that first challenging, cynical, "Hey, I know you; this is not you." At that point we have to stick to our new pattern of behaving and really test it out if it is to become settled and natural to us.

The epistle further describes when we will know it's time for us to change, at least in a spiritual context. It is when our old self deteriorates by its "deceitful desires" (4:22). Our hankerings and lusts, our cyclic fits of this or that passion reveal themselves to us as futile and frustrating. We itch for something else. We come to see the sheer incompleteness of a self-image that does not include God, as though former angles of ourselves offered us only an optical illusion. We begin to believe more, to pray more, to seek the kingdom of God in justice.

Now, if we can only survive that first "Hey, I know you."

Eighteenth Sunday of the Year—C

Ecclesiastes 1:2; 2:21–23
Colossians 3:1–5, 9–11
Luke 12:13–21

Poor Man, Rich Man

"It is useless, useless, said the Philosopher. Life is useless, all useless" (Ecclesiastes 1:2).

We were sailing along smoothly, healing winter wounds, blinking into friendlier skies, smelling the flowers, when—bang—this Sunday's readings get unexpectedly grim: "As long as you live, everything you do brings nothing but worry and heartache. Even at night your mind can't rest. It is all useless" (Ecclesiastes 2:23). "You fool! This very night you will have to give up your life" (Luke 12:20). "Keep your mind fixed on things there, not on things here on earth" (Colossians 3:2). Disruptive thoughts, as we enjoy boardwalks and lakes, kids romping at a safe (for our eardrums) distance, sticky ice-cream feasts and barbecues.

The readings seem to be challenging our leisure, but that is not the case. (Most people don't have "leisure," anyway; they are too busy simply recovering!) They are raising the broader question of our values in life. In particular, the gospel is describing the rich man who lives in each of our hearts.

What is so sour about the rich man is not the fact that his riches contributed to social injustice. We are not told that the grain bins he created were being used to drive up the market price of grain. We are told that he is a fool. Why? The rich man wants to create something and then use it solely for himself. The folly is not the desire to create; that is fine. The folly is the hope that he will enjoy his creation all by himself, when in fact it will fall to others to enjoy it—to those very others he is trying to exclude.

Saint Paul also speaks about creativity in today's episple. He speaks about our being formed anew in the image of the creator (Colossians 3:10), which comes down to saying that we ourselves are formed to *be creators*. Real creativity is the use of talent, drive, patience, sensitivity, and imagination in fashioning inner and outer worlds. It ought to lead, as it does in God, to the service of others. It ought to entertain and excite, like a song or a work of art. It ought to inspire wonder and joy.

The rich man in today's gospel is not a complete creator. He does not want to share. He is a poor image of God. And that means that he's not really rich enough.

Nineteenth Sunday of the Year—A

1 Kings 19:9, 11 – 13
Romans 9:1 – 5
Matthew 14:22 – 33

Show Business

"After sending the people away, he went up a hill by himself to pray. When evening came, Jesus was there alone" *(Matthew 14:23).*

There's the old joke about three men standing before the judgment seat. Lights flash, thunder claps, eerie music blares; the pages of the book of life corruscate (nothing less) as they are turned by the awesome Judge. When the account is finished, all three are condemned to hell. Horns blast, more flashings. Two of the men drop to their knees in liquid horror, but the third stands there smiling lopsidedly. An angel whomps him on the back with the flat side of its celestial sword: "Didn't you hear the sentence?" "Yeah," says the man, "but it's such a fantastic ceremony."

Some people expect more spactacle from God than others do. The gaudier the experience, the more they seem to see it as arranged by God. These are people who see the hand of God behind cataclysms, accidents, explosions, collapses, and other such extravaganzas. You wonder what size glove would fit that hand. You also ask why such Grand Guignol is associated with the loving and merciful Lord. Today's first reading has a delicious description of the prophet Elijah's encounter with God: "Then the Lord passed by and sent a furious wind that split the hills and shattered the rocks—but the Lord was not in the wind. The wind stopped blowing, and then there was an earthquake—but the Lord was not in the earthquake. After the earthquake there was a fire—but the Lord was not in the fire" (1 Kings 19:11–12). It turned out that the Lord was in a "soft whisper." Why, then, do we always imagine that a spiritual moment will have a stark and heavy scenario?

Today's gospel admittedly encourages such expectations. It describes a spooky encounter of Jesus with his disciples on a storm-tossed lake. The disciples apparently thought that God was telling them something with the storm. Jesus' behavior looked equally portentous to them. But whatever the facts of the matter of the walking-on-water were, it seems clear that Jesus was less interested in what threatening messages might be written into the crashing waves than his disciples were. He was interested in personal trust and confidence and inner resources for life. Perhaps his prayer on the mountain taught him that his Father sets us more prosaic tasks like these, without the Cecil B. DeMille sets.

1 Kings 19:4 – 8
Ephesians 4:30 – 5:2
John 6:41 – 51

Drooping Spirit

"Do not make God's Holy Spirit sad; for the Spirit is God's mark of ownership on you" (Ephesians 4:30).

The notion of a depressed God has always been foreign to Christianity. God was thought too serene for that, too timeless and unchanging. Eternal blissfulness better captured the divine mood, we thought. Metaphysical reasons were put forth about why this had to be so, though in presenting these reasons we might have been doing a little business of our own. For once you admit feelings of sadness in God, you also have to admit other feelings such as rage, anger, boredom (imagine a bored God!), and so forth. Better to keep God at a fairly constant level of benevolence, we said. Makes things less nerve-wracking and more predictable.

Many of us still cling to such a view of God. There is the image of the Happy Giant, who can sing gustily through imprisonment or slavery, who can cheer up the crestfallen and brighten the drabbest company, who can by dint of inner resources stave off any sadness whatsoever. Or there is the image of the Wise Queen, whose heart is so full of love (and whose supply of magic is so plentiful) that in her presence no human misfortune can truly be called such. We tell ourselves that such images, if we only plumbed them, would give us the clue we need to understand God's untrammeled joy.

When it came to God-made-man, however, Christian tradition was generous in assigning various kinds of griefs and woes to Jesus. A long road of piety stretches from the Suffering Servant to the Sacred Heart, from the crumpled figure in the Garden of Olives to the discouraged Jesus of Fatima. But here, too, a whole language and metaphysic had to be worked out to ensure that we were not saying that Jesus-in-his-divinity was actually being touched by the tragedies of his life, or of ours for that matter.

Must gods, like politicians, project such a relentless, assuring grin to the world? Or does God flinch and rebound, wince and strain, mope and storm over our individual fortunes? Some theologians are telling us that the pain reaches more nearly into the still center of God than we would like to admit—the cry on a cross, the scream from the torture chamber, the sobs of hungry children, the deflating moan of human hopelessness.

Perhaps it does. But God's Spirit does not droop for long. If it came to a contest about who cheers up whom the most, God would win every time.

Wisdom 18:6–9
Hebrews 11:1–2, 8–12
Luke 12:35–40

Seeing Something in Us

"It was faith that made Abraham able to become a father . . . From this one man came as many descendants as there are stars in the sky, as many as the numberless grains of sand on the seashore" (Hebrews 11:11 – 12).

Faith, according to today's readings, would best be described as great expectation. The Israelites in Egypt expect to be delivered and to see their enemies clobbered, besides. Abraham and Sarah expect a tangible inheritance from Yahweh—land, children, and so forth. But they do not stop there: "For Abraham was waiting for the city which God has designed and built, the city with permanent foundations" (Hebrews 11:10). The gospel describes servants who expect a reckoning with their returning master.

The common denominator in all these cases of faith-expectation is that, though the believers do not actually see what is coming, they nevertheless act on the assured knowledge that it will come. In Saint Paul's words: "To have faith is to be sure of the things we hope for, to be certain of the things we cannot see" (Hebrews 11:1).

Much has been made of the fact that faith is blind, that we act on what we do not actually see. But, in fact, some kind of "seeing" accompanies faith. You picture something that will happen, and it is this that you believe in. You first envision what is unseen. You shape something in your mind on which you pin your hopes.

This image of the future also carries with it the possibility of disillusionment, of faith deceived, but nevertheless it must be sustained. In *Man's Search for Meaning*, Victor Frankl well describes the visionary quality of faith. "When we spoke about attempts to give a man in [prison] camp mental courage, we said that he had to be shown something to look forward to in the future. He had to be reminded that life still waited for him, that a human being waited for his return. But after liberation? . . . Woe to him who, when the day of his dreams finally came, found it so different from all he had longed for!"

It is not only faith that builds on a vision of the unseen. So also does mistrust or a lack of faith. The reason why we move away from the stranger on the subway is because we picture him doing the worst. People who lose faith in a marriage or a church see a kind of behavior recurring in the future that disheartens them. Faith and mistrust, then, take a certain amount of imagination.

So faith for us becomes largely a matter of what we imagine or picture the unseen God to be up to. But might it not help to look at the matter from the other way around? For there is a kind of faith that God has in us, a faith best illustrated by Jesus. Jesus had to picture the future of his followers. He had to envision their future collaboration with him. He had to entrust himself to *that* image of things. He had to wonder what we would be up to! Perhaps if we let ourselves feel how good it is to be trusted by God, we might be more ready to trust God in return.

Isaiah 56:1, 6–7
Romans 11:13–15, 29–32
Matthew 15:21–28

Far Away Is Near

"It isn't right to take the children's food and throw it to the dogs" (Matthew 15:26).

How do we relate to people who practice a religion other than our own? Today's readings give three instances of such dealings.

In Isaiah, Israel will become a "house of prayer for the people of all nations," but the process is clearly one in which foreigners are offered the chance of leaving their own traditions and joining Israel's.

Saint Paul grieves that his former co-religionists do not share his convictions about Jesus. He even wants to make them envious of the power of the risen Lord, if that will help them. He warns them that their original call is irrevocable, and that the mercy God showed in Jesus will catch up with them anyhow.

In the gospel, Jesus attests to the great faith that can be found outside his own circle. He cures the daughter of the Canaanite woman, despite the fact that he sees his ministry as being directed primarily to the house of Israel.

In each of these cases, not everything is spelled out about how one religion is to relate to the other. In fact, the readings leave us puzzled by their abruptness and inclusiveness. Clashes seem imminent; mutual insult and odious comparison seem mixed in with welcoming overtures; issues of abandonment and feelings of invasion swirl around the dialogue; clear boundaries become murky.

If the Scriptures make us nervous, what about the following statement from Vatican II's *Declaration on the Relationship of the Church to Non-Christian Religions* (#2): "The Church therefore has this exhortation for her sons: prudently and lovingly, through dialogue and collaboration with the followers of other religions, and in witness of Christian faith and life, acknowledge, preserve, and promote the spiritual and moral goods found among these men, as well as the values in their society and culture." Acknowledge Shintoists, Sikhs, and such? Preserve Jehovah's Witnesses? Promote Moonies? Collaborate? No mention of conversion? Where are we?

It can cause great pain to reflect on the potential and actual values of other religions: the discipline, insight, technique, and embodied goodness; the heroes and teachers; the facility and conviction; the uncomplicated and persuasive productivity; the warmth and the institutional force. It takes big people to be so secure in their witness of their own Christian faith and life that they can look for what is good in those who are different. But who knows? The others might even return the compliment!

Proverbs 9:1 – 6
Ephesians 5:15 – 20
John 6:51 – 58

A Woman's Touch?

"Wisdom has build her house and made seven columns for it. She has had an animal killed for a feast, mixed spices in the wine, and set the table" (Proverbs 9:1).

Woman as nurturer is an image that will not go away. Many, though hardly all, women dislike it, because they think it denies in them other competencies they feel are theirs. In any case, given the prevailing attitudes toward women in biblical times, we can see how a woman is picked to personify Wisdom in today's first reading. Wisdom has a rhythm to it, an ebb and flow. Wisdom literally takes time. We are fools for a while and need some gentle embrace to comfort our stupidities. We have to be enticed to become wise. Wisdom is often indirect, yet sometimes quite forward. Wisdom demands communication; it likes to muse out loud a lot. Wisdom has memories and loves mementos. Wisdom is dedicated to the adornment of life and is not just a matter of survival. Attributing many of these qualities, as it does, to women, no wonder Proverbs has a woman saying; " 'Come in, ignorant people!' And to the foolish she says: 'Come, eat my food and drink the wine that I have mixed' " (Proverbs 9:4 – 5).

Funny, then, that Jesus should come across so strongly as a nurturer. He is indeed seen in the New Testament as the Wisdom of God, and this in a variety of ways. He is presented as the wise child, as the one who figures out

God's ways. He is the complete teacher, full of insight and illustration. He is no fool; he practices what he preaches. His foolish death turns out to be the height of wisdom. But this testimony to his wisdom is sometimes taken for a series of manly accomplishments. It would be easy to forget his nurturing style.

Today's gospel is full of this style. Predictably, it comes as a shock to his listeners that Jesus speaks of himself in the intimate image of sharing himself as food for others. It does not embarrass him. In fact, he looks on his own relationship to his Father as one of being nurtured. So he has no hesitation about picturing his own role toward others in terms that would normally be considered feminine.

Perhaps the important thing is the nurturing itself, and not whether a man or a woman does it. Perhaps the real wisdom is in the giving.

Twentieth Sunday of the Year—C

Jeremiah 38:4–6, 8–10
Hebrews 12:1–4
Luke 12:49–53

Up Against Love

"I came to set the earth on fire" (Luke 12:49).

The theme is opposition. There is a point at which you are supposed to dig in, to confront, to endure. Anybody can just sail along on a crest of success. It's when they're running you down, pushing you around, or threatening worse things that your true mettle appears.

Opposition crosses most people's path in life. Jeremiah got it: "This man must be put to death." By talking like this he is making the soldiers in the city lose their courage (Jeremiah 38:4– 6). Jesus got it: "Think of what he went through; how he put up with so much hatred from sinners" (Hebrews 12:4). The Christian will get it, even from his own relatives: I have come for "division" (Luke 12:51). But many people would like to think that the opposition they give is more justified than the opposition they get. How, then, can opposition be a sign of anything?

The readings do not solve this problem. But let's take another look at Jesus. How does he endure opposition?

Jesus suffers from it. He does not make others suffer. He opposes chiefly by being himself, not by running others down. He endures, without wishing to harden others in their positions. He argues, without exacting ultimate clarity from others. He opposes overtly, without the aura of sneakiness, cabal, and ritual legality that attends many professional resisters. He urges others to resist, but in the end he is the only one taken and done in. He does not snipe at his opponents, but rather confronts them and calls them names to their face.

It is clear that we are not all opponents in the same tradition as Jesus. We are catty and vindictive. We fantasize. We hit and run. We hope the war never ends. We do not argue out of a developed vision of things, but we jumble disparate issues together in clouds of fog.

The opposition that proceeds from love differs, then, from lesser kinds of opposition. The trick, if you watch Jesus, is to beat the sinner who is opposing you by taking on his sinful nature and putting yourself staunchly in his shoes. His way of overcoming opposition is to constantly wish that there were no sides to begin with.

Twenty-First Sunday of the Year—A

Isaiah 22:19– 23
Romans 11:33– 36
Matthew 16:13– 20

Rock Bottom

"I will give you the keys of the Kingdom of heaven" (Matthew 16:19).

Christians are convinced of Jesus' divinity. But they also believe that the Word of God went through a truly human experience: no capitalizing on his divine connections, no escape clauses, no end-arounds. Although we believe this in theory, the way we sometimes read Scripture indicates that in practice we think Jesus is just going through the human motions, with a conspiratorial wink of one divine eye. The exchange between Jesus and Peter in today's gospel might be illuminating if we keep in mind Jesus' full humanity.

Jesus' question to his disciples, "Who do people say the Son of Man is?" was not some kind of coy, multiple-choice test of their spiritual growth. More probably, Jesus himself was puzzled about the impression he was giving others, not to mention the impression he had of himself. Peter's answer, then, provides resolution and enlightenment for Jesus, as often only our best friends can give us. The gift of Peter to Jesus (which Jesus in turn attributes to the Father) is that he reinforces Jesus' sense of a unique mission. He becomes Jesus' rock of support. When Jesus calls Peter blessed, there's appreciation and respect in the statement. What's more, Jesus sees that this is the kind of person that his movement needs as its foundation, the one who will recognize, promote, and stoke the charisms of others.

Christian authorities would do well to see this kind of author-ing more as part of their job. As we all know, authorities can either tie people up in knots or set them free. It all depends on why authorities think they received the keys of office in the first place. Only because Peter is the type who does not go around binding up other people's charisms can Jesus say to him: "What you prohibit on earth will be prohibited in heaven; and what you permit on earth will be permitted in heaven" (Matthew 16:19).

Let's not be blind either to the fact that many of us prefer chains. We resent authorities who tell us we have capacity and talent for work in the kingdom. We can be immovable as any rock before such author-ing in us of our more authentic selves.

Joshua 24:1–2, 15–17, 18
Ephesians 5:21–32
John 6:60–69

Bite Your Tongue

"Wives, submit yourselves to your husbands as to the Lord"
(Ephesians 5:22).

Anyone who has ever been caught in an ill-conceived remark can sympathize with Saint Paul in today's epistle. We know the feeling. In the course of making a favorite point, out pops a remark that digs a grave for some of our listeners, or digs one for us! A man extols baseball as the only thing that has captured his attention in the last ten years—only his wife is standing uncomfortably next to him. A woman insists on the virtues of a small family—to a man who has six children. Another man tells his brother-in-law, a congressman, that there are nothing but crooks in Washington.

Saint Paul can be forgiven at least for the main point he is making: He is saying that Christ is consumed by the vision of other people's glorious potential (verse 27). He affirms such a close tie between Christ and people that it is hard to tell where Christ ends and others begin (29). Christ, in Saint Paul's eyes, wants only the best for people: integrity, and attractiveness (27). Submission to Christ (24) is not the same as being dominated; it denotes the way lovers surrender to one another and not the way tyrants rule one-sidely.

But in applying all these beautiful thoughts to Christian marriage, Saint Paul assigns certain roles to spouses. He identifies husbands with Christ the head, and makes wives—what else?—the body. We might indeed wonder whether the roles would have been different had a woman of that era assigned them, but no matter. Hackles rise when men are made out to be the providers, the take-charge types, and women are seen as fleshy, dependent, and possessed. Saint Paul even seems to be aware of the problem. In his summary remark (verse 33, which, alas, is not included in today's reading), he says: "Every husband must love his wife as himself, and every wife must respect her husband." He seems to think he can bank on one thing at least, that men love themselves! But he also cautions women not to lose respect for men, seeming to sense that they are sorely tempted to do so at times.

It would be a shame if we were to carp at Saint Paul's language to the point of failing to see what he was getting at. He wants married people, out of whatever roles they carry or are fantasized as carrying, to be for one another. His opening remark says it best: "Submit yourselves to one another because of your reverence for Christ" (21). He wants married people to learn love from Christ. If Christ's love for the church is to be the model for marriage, then this much both partners can learn: You have to put up with a lot, and you have to cherish a lot.

Isaiah 66:18 – 21
Hebrews 12:5 – 7, 11 – 13
Luke 13:22 – 30

Crowd Scene

"Do your best to go in through the narrow door" (Luke 13:24).

In *The Keys of the Kingdom*, A.J. Cronin's amiable priest got into trouble by advising a portly parishioner: "Eat less; the gates of heaven are narrow." Today's gospel, with its reference to "the narrow door," might have provided the inspiration for his remark. But in fact the gospel is making a somewhat different point. It speaks only indirectly about personal discipline and focuses instead on the social pressures that the individual Christian is up against. And one of these social pressures is the lure of the crowd.

Someone asks Jesus: "Sir, will just a few people be saved?" (Luke 13:23). This is a politely veiled way of asking whether there is safety in numbers, and Jesus' response indicates that he takes the question that way. For he cautions against the herd instinct. He warns us about crowds. The crowd is characterized, above all, by sameness. No one can stand out. No one can be too different. The prop that sustains the crowd is a back-slapping homogeneity. In the gospel, people are shocked when Jesus ignores their appeal to such common ties: "We ate and drank with you; you taught in our town!" (Luke 13:26). Apparently, the Lord is unimpressed by the fact that people hang out in the same bars, frequent the same restaurants, eye the same billboards, and watch the same TV programs.

A special problem exists in our contemporary culture. We are lured into the crowd through a fake appeal to our individuality. Our being exhorted to be individuals is done with an air of collusion, a hint of conspiracy, and a threat to conform. The media shout at us, "Be your own person, smoke our cigarette, wear our brand, and so on."

So how do we discipline ourselves to be individuals in an authentic way? How do we take our lead from truth rather than from slogans? How do we know when we are caught up in the crowd?

The door looks narrower and narrower.

Twenty-Second Sunday of the Year—A

Jeremiah 20:7–9
Romans 12:1–2
Matthew 16:21–27

Fooled Again

"From that time on Jesus began to say plainly to his disciples: 'I must go to Jerusalem and suffer much from the elders, the chief priests, and the teachers of the Law' " (Matthew 16:21).

Sometimes it's better to forget, to blot out the sources of our personal anguish. But since these sources exist at the same level as our best hopes and enthusiasms, we dare not forget. We might end up forgetting our best selves, as well.

The prophet Jeremiah suffers this dilemma in today's first reading. His troubled relationship with the Lord is on Jeremiah's mind. "But when I say, 'I will forget the Lord and no longer speak in his name,' then your message is like a fire burning deep within me" (Jeremiah 20:9). Jeremiah, like many of us, cannot be indifferent to God. For all the problems God causes him, Jeremiah continues to welcome God's input into his life, because God is important to him. He actually thinks God might have insight, sensitivity, and noble purpose!

That doesn't cut down, however, on the problematic side of relating with God. Peter learns this in today's gospel. "Jesus turned around and said to Peter, 'Get away from me, Satan!... These thoughts of yours don't come from God, but from man'" (Matthew 16:23). God's standards stretch us. They send us on missions that seem impossible. They disrupt our normal patterns of thinking and our comfortable ways. They put us in conflict with people with whom we would otherwise prefer to party, nice people. They land us in the company of people who seem boringly righteous.

Jesus himself had a sense that dealing with the Father was no cup of tea. It would involve suffering greatly. Jesus knew that people don't like too much realism in their religion. His commitment to faithful love of the Father would therefore make enemies of those who would rather settle for distraction, for superstition, and organized silence. In today's gospel, Jesus tries to pull back the veil on reality. You love, you pay— whether you are loving gods or people. And it's not clear that anyone is finally going to sing your praises.

For all his realism, Jesus does not descend to sullen cynicism. He is convinced that God is our main issue. "Will a person gain anything if he wins the whole world but loses his life? Of course not! There is nothing he can give to regain his life" (Matthew 16:26). With the prospect of suffering before him, Jesus no doubt wished that he were someone else. But he is Jesus, and he has to claim his own soul and the part his Father plays there. He would be a fool if he didn't. But it's nice to think that Jesus may well have made his own the words of Jeremiah: "Lord, you have deceived me, and I was deceived. You are stronger than I am, and you have overpowered me" (Jeremiah 20:7).

Twenty-Second Sunday of the Year—B

Deuteronomy 4:1–2, 6–8
James 1:17–18, 21–22, 27
Mark 7:1–8, 14–15, 21–23

Getting Personal

"Every good gift and every perfect present comes from heaven; it comes down from God" (James 1:17).

Laws have to do with our social behavior. This might sound like a truism, but it needs restating, since there are naive people around who think that laws can change the hearts and feelings of people. They would like to control internal behavior as a means of assuring social conformity and cooperation. But, thank God, things don't work that way.

The inner person must be invited and enticed. In today's first reading, for example, Moses tries to get cooperation for his laws by an appeal to people's vanity: "This will show the people of other nations how wise you are" (Deuteronomy 4:6). And in the epistle, Saint James describes the action of God on individuals in the delicate language of a creative word spoken to them, one that sparks and stirs them: "Submit to God and accept the word that he plants in your hearts, which is able to save you" (James 1:21). Laws don't help at the heart of a person; a person, being a source and center of untold freedom, goes its own way.

There is something stark about being a person. When all the layers of our roles are carefully removed and set aside with their paraphernalia of competence, authority, and recompense, we remain, as persons, a teeming hub of energetic business. Whom do we love? How do we relate? How do we feel about ourselves? What makes us us? What makes us choose or act? These are personal issues. They are matters of love and hate, praise, reverence and service, trust and alienation. No external law will make us see the deep-down worth in others or praise it. No injunction will teach us about the distances between persons or how to cope with them without casting others in our own image. No pressure will move us to put ourselves at the ready, keen to meet others where they are and to be available to them. Something must instead come out of us to achieve these tasks of personhood.

In today's gospel, Jesus invites us back to the source within us. He takes a dim view of experts in the law who fail to see the more basic stirrings of the person within. "Listen to me, all of you, and understand. There is nothing that goes into a person from the outside which can make him ritually unclean. Rather, it is what comes out of a person that makes him unclean" (Mark 7:14–15). Jesus speaks of an inner terrain, a place of striving for praise, reverence, and service. Don't talk to him about laws for the moment. He's too busy watching the life-and-death drama of persons.

Twenty-Second Sunday of the Year—C

Sirach 3:17–18, 20, 28–29
Hebrews 12:18–19, 22–24
Luke 14:1, 7–14

Low Profile

"For everyone who makes himself great will be humbled, and everyone who humbles himself will be made great"
(Luke 14:11).

It looks as though today's readings started out to be organized around the theme of humility, and then the organization collapsed. That's how difficult it is to sustain a liturgical theme with consistency and with the same meanings throughout. The first reading drips with humility, which it seems to define as knowing your limitations: "Don't try to understand things that are too hard for you, or investigate matters that are beyond your power to know" (Sirach 3:20). The second reading contrasts a showy and musclebound visitation from God with a simpler, more idyllic one. "You have not come . . . to Mount Sinai with its blazing fire. . . . Instead, you have come to. . . the heavenly Jerusalem, with its thousands of angels" (Hebrews 12:18, 22). Humility, in this case, seems to mean not throwing one's weight around.

In the first part of the gospel, the rewards of humility are stressed, to the point that humility seems to mean nothing more than hanging back before you make your own move. "When you are invited, go and sit in the lowest place, so that your host will come to you and say, 'Come on up, my friend, to a better place' " (Luke 14:10).

Yet, the second part of the gospel is more substantial. It advocates a humility that consists of actually associating with the humble: "When you give a feast, invite the poor, the crippled, the lame, and the blind; and you will be blessed, because they are not able to pay you back" (Luke 14:13–14).

We may well wonder how the average congregation would react to these four senses of humility. What do they generally understand about humility? For too many Christians, humility means the same as being humiliated, or eating humble pie. They think that God wants to cut them down to size. That is sad.

Others might be luckier. They might be familiar with the tradition that makes of humility a kind of candid acceptance of reality. Humility in that tradition is simply honoring the truth about things. In this light, the second part of today's gospel is even more convincing. It will not let us forget the reality of other people in our midst—the beggars, the blind, and the crippled—people who are readily forgotten or otherwise banished as unreal. Perhaps there is a canny logic to the gospel: contact with real beggars and cripples might reveal to us in the end that, before God, we are the beggars and cripples.

Twenty-Third Sunday of the Year—A

Ezekiel 33:7– 9
Romans 13:8– 10
Matthew 18:15– 20

Joining Forces

"Where two or three come together in my name, I am there with them" (Matthew 18:20).

Today's gospel is full of surprises. We often think that it is required of us as Christians to smart and stew over interpersonal hurts without doing something about healing them. Yet, the gospel encourages us to confront, to deal with, to eyeball others with our interpersonal griefs. "If your brother sins against you, go to him and show him his fault" (Matthew 18:15). Moreover, this confrontation is to be private. No letters to the person's boss. No roundabout revenge. No whisper campaigns. The above text continues: "But do it privately, just between yourselves." Christians are to deal with each other first, and not with third parties.

The church never relieves people of their responsibility to relate in a series of one-to-one encounters. Another way in which today's gospel indicates that religion is a matter of concrete one-to-one relationships is by envisioning people praying together—supposedly having gotten together with one another to pray. "Whenever two of you on earth agree about anything you pray for, it will be done for you by my Father in heaven" (Matthew 18:19). Perhaps what really impresses the Father is that two people actually share this intimate side of themselves—their prayer!

The quality of personal relations within it is a severe test for any institution. Parishes, religious communities, church committees—all might well squirm when the vision is offered, as it is in today's gospel, of people dealing candidly, intimately, painfully with other people. We hide so much behind our institutional membership. There is a prayer in today's liturgy that describes how God, with unparalled love, has drawn us into the circle of his life. This kind of intimacy can frighten us. But it might also encourage us to face the fact that religion begins with each individual person who approaches the circle of our lives.

Twenty-Third Sunday of the Year—B

Isaiah 35:4– 7
James 2:1– 5
Mark 7:31– 37

Aforethought

"All who heard were completely amazed. 'How well he does everything!' they exclaimed. 'He even causes the deaf to hear and the dumb to speak' " (Mark 7:31).

In today's epistle, Saint James establishes the heart as a sort of preliminary terrain on which human issues are worked out.

The context to which he refers is straightforward enough. A rich man (the Greek would even allow us to call him Goldfinger) enters a synagogue along with a poor man. The congregation gives the rich man a real hand-rubbing, heel-clicking, bowing-and-scraping reception; it snubs the poor man. Saint James barely comments on this overt behavior, on the prejudice. It is as if such behavior is too obvious for commentary. Instead, he calls attention to prior attitudes and motives in people's hearts. The force and feeling connected with these are what propel people to act the way they do.

These pre-existing attitudes are stored up in us like so many filing cards. On each one is written an attitude—about blacks or women or priests or tall people or fat people or whatever. We have things tagged this way in our hearts long before any actual external behavior is at issue. When the delicate moment comes, in which we are faced with reality—in the shape of this person or that event—what we have prejudged must be looked at again in the light of reality.

It is a moment when we need courage. Reality has a way of flashing our prejudices back into our eyes. We don't like foreigners, but this particular foreigner seems different. We see it in his eyes, in his demeanor, in the humility of his person. What, then, are we to do with our prejudgments?

This process, this challenge posed by reality, is something that happens to us a humdred times a day. It accompanies every relationship, old ones with our wives or husbands or communities or bosses, as well as new ones. Prejudice can seem a place of security and solace. People think they will find comfort there, as in a cool, dark place. The devil whom you know with prejudice often seems better than the devil whom you might get to know in reality. So reality is resisted, often with a frantic tenacity and with much self-serving.

Saint James singles out the poor as people especially discriminated against. We can hear the litany of accusations: "They're dirty; they propagate and perpetuate ignorance, superstition, and indolence; they are violent and without hope." This may well be the fantasy of many people, but reality resists this interpretation. In fact, the gospel—a vehicle of reality, if it is anything—intrudes with one other fact. And it speaks this fact in our hearts, thereby disrupting all our systems of classification and orderly prejudice. The gospel tells us that the weak are loved and lovable. It tells us that the deaf can have faith and hope and love—all the important things in life. It teaches that a little vulnerability like that of the deaf might be good for all our souls. It even hints at a divine preference for the afflicted. What do we do with our prejudices now?

Twenty-Third Sunday of the Year—C

Wisdom 9:13–18
Philemon 9–10, 12–17
Luke 14:25–33

Figuring It Out

"Who can ever learn the will of God?" (Wisdom 9:13).

The Fathers of the Church used to defend vigorously the thesis that we can know very little about God. Everything that we might say about him, we'd have to take back a little, since our language is guaranteed to fall short of expressing the mystery of God very accurately. In defending this thesis, the Fathers used an interesting argument: Why is it surprising that we know so little about God, they asked, when we can't even fully understand one another? At a certain point, each person is opaque to others; we are even enigmas to ourselves. The inner spirit that moves us is too volatile, too fine for us to espy. Still less can we grasp the Spirit of God. We are left with a lot to figure out.

Many people, to be sure, wish for a more definitive clarity. They ask incessantly for "the answers." Their request may be pathetically dependent; it may be belligerent or anxious. But their assumption is consistent: there are clear answers to all questions. If God is so smart, their reasoning seems to run, then we who have caught his Spirit should be able to come through with clinching and irrefutable answers.

But today's readings contradict such an assumption. Even when the Spirit is working overtime in us, there is still the need on our part to figure things out.

Saint Paul, for example, has to figure out how to send back Onesimus, the slave, to Philemon, his owner, without the latter wreaking the usual penalties on the runaway. So Saint Paul bows, scrapes, pulls on the heartstrings, and oozes diplomacy to make the case for mercy.

The gospel offers an even more vivid instance of figuring things out. It speaks of fitting means to ends, of measuring the moral distance between where we stand and where we aim to go.

"If one of you is planning to build a tower, he sits down first and figures out what it will cost, to see if he has enough money to finish the job" (Luke 14:28). This is logical talk, but it is a deceptive logic. It does not say, save in the most general terms, which are the means and which are the ends. So we are left to figure it out.

The gospel does, however, provide us with a norm for judging when our figuring things out is going well or badly. The norm sounds harsh when we first look at it: " 'Whoever comes to me cannot be my disciple unless he loves me more than he loves his father and his mother, his wife and his children, his brothers and his sisters, and himself as well. . . . In the same way,' concluded Jesus, 'none of you can be my disciple unless he gives up everything he has' " (Luke 14:25, 33).

The irony is that this is a picture of the incarnation itself. God in fact has "left home" in order to get in touch with us. Jesus seems to be simply asking people to do a little of the same.

Sirach 27:30 — 28:7
Romans 14:7 – 9
Matthew 18:21 – 35

What Really Counts

"Lord, if my brother keeps on sinning against me, how many times do I have to forgive him? Seven times?" (Matthew 18:21).

Vengeance seems such a simple, straightforward business. You hurt me, I hurt you—with the attendant pleasures, of course: I wallow in my hurt, I throb with indignation, I hum with plans for retribution, I play on your anxiety, I force an exhausting wariness in you and finally watch you being hurt back. No wonder the first reading today speaks of "hugging" (a better translation for "have" below) to oneself sentiments of vengeance. "Anger and a hot temper are horrible things, but sinners have both" (Sirach 27:30). From the blood feud to the vendetta to the retaliatory attack, humanity has indeed hugged a lot of vengeance to its breast.

The violence is not always out in the open. Psychologists describe passive-aggressive people who veil their violent feelings and cloak them with sweetness and light. Like the rest of us, they strike out at others, hurt them, snarl lives, trip people up, and frustrate cooperation. But they call all this awkwardness, forgetfulness, or confusion. The real aggression is totally denied.

We are offered several reasons why we should get over our anger. The first reason looks to our situation before God: "You cannot expect the Lord to pardon you while you are holding a grudge against someone else" (Sirach 28:3). The same argument is put forcefully and dramatically in today's gospel. A man with a double standard of mercy (show it to me, even if I don't show it to others) is led off screaming to torturers. "That is how my Father in heaven will treat every one of you unless you forgive your brother from your heart" (Matthew 18:35).

In some ways, this argument is badly put. It is really trying to say that God is nice, so we should be nice. But it comes out more like: Be nice or else.

The second reason we are offered for being forgiving is found in Sirach's statement: "Think about it! Some day you will die, and your body will decay" (28:6). Life is too short, it suggests, to hold grudges. To come to one's deathbed clutching nothing to one's chest but resentments, hatreds, and bitter causes is a fate too sad for words. This is true quite apart from any thought of the next life. The corrosive, self-destructive effects of vengeful and angry thinking are felt here, now.

What a workout this business of being forgiving is! First you check your own sins. Then you note how they go so gloriously unpunished. Then you let the sinner off the hook. Then the whole process starts over again. It's enough to stop a person from taking offense in the first place.

Isaiah 50:4–9
James 2:14–18
Mark 8:27–35

Faith As Flight

"Show me how anyone can have faith without actions. I will show you my faith by my actions" (James 2:18).

There is such a thing as a retreat to the heart that is the mockery of all true religion. Saint James, whose forceful insights we have been exposed to in recent readings, shows that such a retreat is a travesty of faith, however much it might borrow the same name. The temptation faces all of us: We hear that faith has to do with spirit, with soul; faith is supposed to put us in touch with invisible forces. Well, from there it's a short step to where things can get very invisible indeed! A science of the heart is constructed to deal with this new, absolute innerness. Behavioral sciences are suspect. Gurus are sought out who foster the retreat inward. Heart-reading—without benefit of fact, data, or historical materials—becomes a specialized skill. A god is postulated who works in pure privacy, with much whispering in the ear.

Perhaps that is the appeal for many pseudo-believers. They think they can find a refuge in "faith" against the realities of behavior, performance, or practice. When inner feelings and attitudes toward things become the sole criteria for assessing reality, we are in deep trouble. Saint James gives a vivid example: "Suppose there are brothers or sisters who need clothes and do not have enough to eat. What good is there in your saying to them, 'God bless you! Keep warm and eat well.' " What is notable in the example is that the pseudo-believer does not simply keep silent. Rather, the person begins to speak in an unreal manner, disassociating an inner world called "faith" from a real world of actual behavior. By creating the inner world off by itself, the pseudo-believer can then make statements in the other, real world which pretend that everything is business-as-usual. This is the most depressing aspect of pseudo-faith. There is a determined, sometimes corporate effort to defend unreality as something true, good, and beautiful.

All this is a far cry from a Jesus who himself had to deal with real people, with real issues of relationship, trust, intimacy, confrontation, and so forth. Reality came home to him in the form of a cross. What went on in his heart was inextricably connected with a personal history of involvement with other people, a feeling for their social condition and, above all, a frank communication with them in the name of faith.

Real faith—good for you, Saint James—keeps things real.

Exodus 32:7–11, 13–14
1 Timothy 1:12–17
Luke 15:1–10

Our Kind of God

"This man welcomes outcasts and even eats with them!"
(Luke 15:2).

We find ourselves somewhat back in a Lenten mood with today's readings. At least that old argument from the Lenten readings is being rehashed: Is God forgiving? Just how forgiving? We have Moses demonstrating to God that God has no alternative *except* to be forgiving. Otherwise all that God has done for his people up to that point in time will be proven a gigantic waste of divine time and energy. (Moses was always good at tripping up God with his own promises.) We have Saint Paul hammering away rhetorically at his own breast to emphasize what a great, forgiving God we have. "This is a true saying, to be completely accepted and believed: Christ Jesus came into the world to save sinners. I am the worst of them, but God was merciful to me in order that Christ Jesus might show his full patience in dealing with me, the worst of sinners" (1 Timothy 1:15–16).

The gospel, too, makes the case for divine forgiveness with the parable of the lost groat (a groat is not a relative of a sheep). More compelling is the glorious tradition concerning Jesus that the gospel passes on: "This man welcomes outcasts and even eats with them."

But it is precisely at this point that we get nervous. For, God's forgiving implies our repentance, and repentance conjures up many frightening fantasies for us. The word *repentance* denotes, by its Greek root, the price to be paid for having destroyed someone else's property. But how admit such vandalism within ourselves? We who would never think of writing graffiti on our public transport find ourselves accused of mucking up God's property with malicious abandon. Some dictionaries have even associated *repentance* with the Sanskrit root "-pu," as in *pu-rification* or, horrors, *am-pu-tation*. Hardly a cheery prospect—the purge and the poised, antiseptic pruning hook.

Contrary to these fearful fantasies, God's call to repentance is built on respect for us rather than on threat. It is certainly not God's way of driving the knife in deeper, only to twist it. It is an affirmation of our basic worth. It presupposes that we are valuable. It is as if a friend were to take you by the lapels and shake you, because he believes in you more than you believe in yourself.

The very thing that we find most difficult to claim in ourselves, the very thing that we ache to believe about ourselves, is a radical sense of our worth and dignity. It is *the* nagging question in our being, to which God alone gives the answer. Unless we are gripped by a sense of our own and others' possibility of being worthwhile objects of God's love, then we have completely missed the point of the call to repentacne. When we repent, we rue the day we ever thought so little of ourselves and of others. Our defenses come down before the realization that the Lord himself comes as friend, and we curse the fact that we ever thought otherwise.

In God's call to repentance, there is always this element of calling us to a sense of our personal worth. "This man welcomes outcasts and even eats with them." Where this welcome is missing in the church's preaching and teaching, we're simply not dealing with our kind of God.

Twenty-Fifth Sunday of the Year—A

Isaiah 55:6–9
Philippians 1:20–24, 27
Matthew 20:1–16

The Heat of Day

" 'My thoughts,' says the Lord, 'are not like yours, and my ways are different from yours' " (Isaiah 55:8).

If Jesus got killed for any single teaching, the teaching in today's gospel might have been the one. "They took their money and started grumbling against the employer. 'These men who were hired last worked only one hour,' they said, 'while we put up with a whole day's work in the hot sun—yet you paid them the same as you paid us!' 'Listen, friend,' the owner answered one of them, . . . 'don't I have the right to do as I wish with my own money? Or are you jealous because I am generous?' " (Matthew 20:11–15).

The issue is the freedom that resides at the heart of love. Is it fair for God to distribute his favors solely on the basis of his own freely determined largesse, without considering the merits of people? Does this not entail a kind of arbitrary preference on God's part, one that offends our image of divine impartiality? How can God be choosy about whom he loves?

People are used to trying to earn the right to be loved. Look at the many men and women who are trying in vain to find a marriage partner. They submit themselves to a harsh discipline. They conform in conversation and are exact in dress and manners; at great expense they make the right scenes; they try to please; they persevere in their contacts, even at the price of embarrassment and humiliation; they diet and exercise; they expand their interests; they smile, always smile, always try. And to what avail? Love seems barely to pause. It looks beyond them with a distracted air. It passes them by with forced excuses. For all their efforts, for all their undeniable deserts, love's mysterious force never connects them with another person. They toil all day in the hot sun of loneliness, and people who wander in at the last minute pick up all the eligibles.

Today's gospel points out the futility of relying totally on our own efforts to earn love where God is concerned. It makes us respect the mysterious freedom that is part of God's love. This is not to say that the point of that freedom is to keep people off balance and insecure about finally being loved. That would be far from the mark. When God proclaims the freedom of his love for people, it is not to make them more tense but more confident. Like anyone else, God is insulted when, in the midst of his favoring someone out of the goodness of his heart, that person offers further reasons why he or she should be loved! "Earning love" is a perilous way to live. There is a sense in which we allow such usage and understand it positively. But it can also be a defense mechanism against just simply being loved.

The gospel is also vivid proof that we need not be apologetic for our preferences in love. They are part and parcel of the freedom of love. Inclination is not a bad word for love. Commitment to some need not exclude others. Rather, it may be the only way in which others finally may benefit from our love, the prism through which love is refracted and diffused. God has his beloved Son. Jesus has his beloved disciple. Marriage partners have each other. Through the one we love, our dispositions improve, our sensitivity sharpens, our concern overflows. Everyone gains.

It is interesting to watch Saint Paul juggle his own preferences in love in today's gospel. He prefers Jesus. He'd even pass through the door of death sooner rather than later in order to meet the Jesus he loves. But he is strongly attracted to his friends, as well. He is torn. He ends up in a muddle, not making very much sense, sending off conflicting messages, never really as resolute as he sounds. Now that sounds like a normal picture of love. And who is to say that God doesn't go through much the same thing when he loves?

Wisdom 2:12, 17–20
James 3:16—4:3
Mark 9:30–37

New Uses of Power

"Then he took a child and had him stand in front of them. He put his arms around him and said to them, 'Whoever welcomes in my name one of these children, welcomes me; and whoever welcomes me, welcomes not only me but also the one who sent me'" (Mark 9:36–37).

A child is easily frightened. Even rambunctious, adventurous children know their limits. They can finally be overcome by the sheer size and strength of reality. They can be menaced by the newness of things. In his essay "Such, Such Were the Joys...," George Orwell tells us how a child is affected adversely even by those close to him: "People are too ready to forget the child's *physical* shrinking from the adult. The enormous size of grownups, their ungainly, rigid bodies, their coarse, wrinkled skins, their great, relaxed eyelids, their yellow teeth and the whiffs of musty clothes and beer and sweat and tobacco that disengage from them at every moment. Part of the reason for the ugliness of adults, in a child's eyes, is that the child is usually looking upward, and few faces are at their best when seen from below."

But if a child can be terrified in this way, it can also be easily delighted. It can swiggle a worm around in a puddle for hours. It can make stories out of cloud formations. It can watch rain drip on a leaf. It can make interstellar phone calls through a string attached to a tin can. It can follow relentlessly a crack in the sidewalk. It can pin flowers on dogs or cats or sheep to improve their appearance. It can stretch or jiggle its body with the greatest self-satisfaction.

When Jesus makes a hero out of a child in today's gospel, what is going on? What qualities of a child are so precious to him that the child is singled out? Certainly we cannot conclude arbitrarily that the gospel is encouraging the naivete, the dependence, the rawness and uneducated talent, the utter leisure that we normally associate with children. Nor, thank God, need we imitate their freshly scrubbed complexions! In fact, Saint Mark is not even talking about *becoming* childlike at all. Look at the text again. He is talking about *welcoming* a child. Saint Luke's version of the incident (9:46– 48) follows Saint Mark closely. It is Saint Matthew (18:3– 4) who has Jesus talk about disciples becoming children, although he, too (18:5), preserves the remark about welcoming or receiving the child.

We have to look at the context of these texts to understand what welcoming the child means. In two of the synoptic writers, the context deals with an argument going on among the disciples about which of them would be first, which would have power (Mark 9:34; Luke 9:36). Saint Matthew's context is similar, but the argument aspect is smoothed over by him. Moreover, in each case the power issue is directly prefaced (nearly so in Matthew 17:23) by a warning of Jesus to his disciples that he was going to be done in by his enemies at Jerusalem (Mark 9:31; Luke 9:44). These two issues—Jesus' powerless suffering and his disciples' concern for power—are obviously connected. And taken together they lead into the discussion of welcoming the child.

The disciples are scandalized at a powerless Jesus. Their conversation about their own power is an indirect, projective way of reflecting on him. They truly feel the power vacuum that his warnings about Jerusalem imply. In their anxiety they want to fill that vacuum fast. Jesus' point with the child is that this cannot be done. Jesus, in fact, is the one whom the child stands for. Some might have difficulty in seeing this. They tend to picture the necessity of becoming a child as purely ours, somewhat apart from that of Jesus. They would rather view themselves as children in relationship to Jesus. But that is definitely and vigorously not the point of today's gospel. When Jesus takes the child apart and shows it to his disciples, he is making a very adult statement. He is saying that we cannot escape the fact that all life, his own and that of the child's, is lived *between* terror and delight. We cannot, when the terror comes, violate our trust in a loving Father by resorting to the security that we think power might provide. Jesus is saying that he at least is willing to be a child to that degree and extent. He refuses to escape the normal course of human vulnerability by means of magical power. His statement "Whoever welcomes in my name one of these children, welcomes me" (Mark 9:37) for all its charm is a hard-nosed, adult statement about the uses of power.

Power is embodied in many ways in this life of ours; in money, in connections, in the calculated use of talent, in violence, in the security of numbers, in appealing to the worst in people, and so on. What is so beautiful is that a child wouldn't know what we were talking about by all those things.

Amos 8:4 – 7
1 Timothy 2:1 – 8
Luke 16:10 – 13

Money Talks

"If, then, you have not been faithful in handling worldly wealth, how can you be trusted with true wealth?" (Luke 16:11).

Worldly wealth, as students say, is when you steal from your customers but go bankrupt anyway. You make your pile, but your children all become ascetic creeps. You starve yourself for a new wardrobe one year, and the next some smug Frenchman surrounded by gorgeous women changes the fashion line. You work steady, back the union, and someone runs off with the whole pension fund. You have everything, but find yourself staring at the furniture a lot. You strip-mine underdeveloped countries of their natural resources, and suddenly they are outvoting you at the United Nations. Or you salt it away slowly and sparingly, and then he says you have a terminal illness.

Worldly wealth is not snobbish. Rich and poor alike can watch it astride the ponies out at the track. On Wall Street or at the stadium, it hinges on last quarter scoring. Worldly wealth is a number on a wheel or in the paper. It's a noncommittal face on a playing card. It's a hard-eyed hawker or a pink-cheeked shill. And in its honor, most of us spend a lifetime mentally arranging stacks of beautiful bills and smoothing the edges on our piles of coin.

When one person makes a killing, however, others are usually getting hurt. This is the special concern of the prophet Amos in the first reading. He attacks those who get richer at the expense of the poor and needy. The hucksters of his day fitted the product and the price to the cynical assessment they had of people: "We can sell worthless wheat at a high price. We'll find a poor man who can't pay his debts, not even the price of a pair of sandals, and we'll buy him as a slave" (Amos 8:6).

What really enraged Amos was that some people tried to make greed and religion sit easily, side-by-side, in the same pew. True, religion was at best endured by such people: "When will the Sabbath end, so that we can start selling again?" (Amos 8:5). They'd rather be out making a buck. But if religous shrines could thrive (they did so in Amos' day) at the same time as they themselves did, no harm in that.

This same attempt to make religion and greed peacefully coexist is challenged by today's gospel. "You cannot serve both God and money" (Luke 16:13). You cannot have it both ways.

But the gospel goes one step further. It attacks our proprietary mentality, the instinct we have for calling things ours in the first place. When you get down to it, the gospel says, we are always dealing with someone else's money (Luke 16:12). We might think that, because we have worked for it, it is ours. But the gospel reminds us that even our work is never just ours. It is God's creative action in us. So shouldn't God be consulted on where the profits are to go?

This kind of logic seems specious to greedy people. For if God is doing the main work by creating our work in us, how come we are doing all the sweating? How can our talents be, at the same time, his property? Their question is usually a cover story for their anger that whenever God comes on the scene, there is always an annoying reminder of the poor and the needy. There is always talk about justice and sharing and charity and that stuff.

Let's even give greedy people the benefit of the doubt. They do have trouble trusting the poor, because the poor seem so untalented to them. They do have trouble trusting a God who goes about planning people's "early retirement." How, in the face of this, can greedy people learn to trust enough to give up their greed? Perhaps they should study the financial dealings of "the man Christ Jesus, who gave himself to redeem all mankind" (1 Timothy 2:6). This transaction, we are told, took place at the very point in time when we had no assets, no collateral, no credit, nothing. . . . But we're getting into high finance here, and maybe greedy people just can't stay with the figures.

Twenty-Sixth Sunday of the Year—A

Ezekiel 18:25–28
Philippians 2:1–11
Matthew 21:28–32

That Empty Feeling

"I tell you: the tax collectors and the prostitutes are going into the Kingdom of God ahead of you" (Matthew 21:31).

"To live is to change. To be perfect is to have changed often." The words are Cardinal Newman's, but the change we are talking about here is one in which we are finally forced to say that we were wrong, that we rue a whole course of life we had previously been on and had identified with our truest self.

Oh, we might admit to mistakes in some areas of our lives. We might readily allow that the last job we had was not for us, or that moving to this or that neighborhood was ill-advised, or that we got stuck with a bad piece of goods. We might even express regret about more personal areas of our lives, such as a marriage that didn't work out or a vocation that soured.

But these changes do not yet get at our insides. Real change turns us inside out and exposes deep aspects of us to the light of day. To develop the above examples, real change has to do with our very attitudes about work and success, about marrying at all, about ourselves and God. Real change has an ally within us, a restlessness that we cannot sedate, a question that cries out.

Today's gospel offers two cases of change. In the first, a son has come to terms with his father, who sends him off to work in the fields. The son at first refuses. We are not offered much detail about the reasons. But the story smacks of the usual family drama: a son wanting to break away, to be his own man; resenting the unassailable position of his father in his home, or perhaps using his father as an excuse not to make his own decisions. Whatever the scenario, the son gets the work done, but in a way, we hope, that requires him to take fresh measure of his relationship with his father.

In the second case, prostitutes and tax collectors (both generally despised for taking your money) repent at the no-nonsense preaching of John the Baptist. They adopt John's hard-headed view that holiness is shown in the day-to-day actions of one's life. We are not told that they change their professions. Today's first reading might give the impression that religious change (conversion) is measured solely by such external performance: "When an evil man stops sinning and does what is right and good, he saves his life" (Ezekiel 18:27). We are told that the prostitutes and tax collectors came to see that their situation was not to be judged hopeless, that they were not locked into a sterile past in which they could only be victims and villains. Any change in their performance had to build on this new way in which they could picture themselves, this interior change in their image of themselves.

The real villains in today's gospel (though admittedly overdrawn by Saint Matthew) are faulted for their refusal to take a new look at their presuppositions, at their personal investment in being religious leaders in a lofty tradition. They are unwilling to face that moment which stands silently at the midway point of any personal change. It is a moment full of emptiness. What we were seems futile and desolate now, like a still photo of some aching mistake. Our past selves, which we once boasted we knew so well, are chillingly unfamiliar. There is a sense of waste. Our former worth seems called into question. What we might become is stranger still. What will our friends say? Who will recognize us without our standard props or allow us to emerge in any way altered? Who will care that we have changed?

We need models of personal change. Not the spurious kind who pass from one place to the next without the wrenching. We aren't born again all that easily. We need to rejoice when we see others change and to study the enabling mechanisms of change. All the more welcome, then, is today's epistle, in which we watch the Big Change take place: "He always had the nature of God, but he did not think that by force he should try to become equal with God. Instead of this, of his own free will he gave up all he had, and took the nature of a servant. He became like man and appeared in human likeness" (Philippians 2:6–7).

Because the Son did not cling to what he had been, he could change. But more than that is implied. For personal change also requires that we do not despise what we might become. Saint Paul tells us: "Be humble toward one another, always considering others better than yourselves" (Philippians 2:3). If we despise the thing we are to change into, there is little likelihood that change will occur. Only when we can love what we see in others as a possibility for ourselves will we become less grasping about our present state. If the Son did not humbly love humanity, he could not have changed and become human.

Numbers 11:25 – 29
James 5:1 – 6
Mark 9:38 – 43, 45, 47 – 48

Outside In

"Teacher, we saw a man who was driving out demons in your name, and we told him to stop, because he doesn't belong to our group" (Mark 9:38).

If they were toothpaste salesmen at the annual convention, you wouldn't mind. Rivalries over markets, labeling, raiding by the competition, and so forth are common there. It isn't so nice when it is Jesus' apostles who seem to be operating out of an exaggerated, even pugnacious sense of clannishness. They seem to be very possessive about Jesus.

In some ways, this is quite understandable. By forming a group apart within the mainstream of Judaism, they themselves no doubt were subjected to the usual reactions people have to such behavior: Who do they think they are? What are they up to? Why are they rejecting us? Having paid hard human prices for joining Jesus, the apostles can be excused for wanting to cash in on their separate status.

Jesus does not accept his apostles' point of view. He tells them to let the man alone. He thinks that effective action (this seems to be what he means by action taken in his name) is more important than partisan considerations. His statement, "Whoever is not against us is for us" (Mark 9:40) could be jarring for those who like to draw the lines too neatly. His generous estimate of who is "for us" remains a challenge for all Christians as they attempt to live in a pluralistic world.

As today's gospel continues, the verse immediately following the one just mentioned (v.40) does not seem at first to derive from the same incident as that of the outsider who cures in the name of Jesus. It goes: "I assure you that anyone who gives you a drink of water because you belong to me will certainly receive his reward" (Mark 9:41). Many commentators think that it is only superficially connected with what immediately precedes it.

Where the narrative really seems to take off in another direction is in the following verses (42–48), in which the issue of scandal is raised. Suddenly, we are no longer talking about reactions shown to the apostles (the "you" of v.41), but we are hearing about the way simple people should be treated. The Greek word for "simple" is *mikros*. It means ordinary, insignificant people. Saint Luke (17:2) speaks of ordinary people, not necessarily believers, whereas Saint Mark is referring to believers. Many commentators think that Saint Luke preserves the earlier version, and indeed this would bring the events behind Saint Mark's narrative back to greater coherence. For Jesus would then be returning to the question of how his apostles should act toward outsiders. He would be exhorting his apostles not only to respect talented outsiders like the man who could expel demons but ordinary ones, as well. We are back, then, to the issue of our sensitivity to those who don't belong to our own close circle.

We might wonder whether this closer kind of examination of the scriptural text is useful. People tend to live off whatever catches their ear or stirs their spirit. They can get impatient with too much picking and pecking about what Jesus said versus what Saint Mark said, and so on. But the work of pulling Scripture apart can be liberating, too. We catch nuances and even whole issues that might normally escape our eye.

Today's gospel offers an example of this. Notice that verses 44 and 46 are missing from the reading. Everyone agrees that they are late additions to the text. They occur in the description of Gehenna, the place of punishment for those who scandalize others. That description is grim enough as it stands, but some cheery soul apparently added to the description a sentence borrowed from what is called Third Isaiah (the latter part of the Book of Isaiah). The sentence read, "The worms that eat them will never die, and the fire that burns them will never be put out" (Isaiah 66:24). Just as Third Isaiah made earlier accounts of God's judgment in the Book of Isaiah more gruesome and threatening, so too a Grisly Hand was at work in doctoring Saint Mark's version of Gehenna. It just goes to show you that there are always people around who want to make you more damned than you really are. Beware of the Grisly Hand. It's not always in the original.

Amos 6:1, 4 – 7
1 Timothy 6:11 – 16
Luke 16:19 – 31

All in Good Time

"Run your best in the race of faith, and win eternal life for yourself; for it was to this life that God called you when you firmly professed your faith before many witnesses" (1 Timothy 6:12).

Some years ago, theologians discovered the future. Or, more embarrassingly, they rediscovered it. If you lived through this stirring period, you will recall how the churches were finding it difficult to budge their memberships. Social problems were mushrooming everywhere. Political alignments were shifting. New opportunities were presenting themselves. The people of God were shocked that their leaders, who had so often led the litany of praise for the past, were now suggesting change. Think of Vatican II or the work of the World Council of Churches. Many of the people of God, upon hearing the latest version of the good news, dug in their heels.

Theologians, who had to provide an imaginative rationale for all of this change, came up with the theology of the future. We could no longer rehearse the past glories accomplished by God in history. For these *mirabilia* were, at best, lessons to us that showed the true nature of God as still-to-come. God was variously described as oncoming, in-breaking, up-rushing. Or he was pictured, first, as charging ahead on his own, then

381

rushing back to call us to catch up, then tearing off again. It was all very exhilarating and somewhat exhausting. Sometimes, it seemed that God was giving us a gigantic come-hither, only to prove coy in the end. Or you got the impression that it was a case of the carrot being used now as a stick, now as a carrot.

Putting God in the future tense, then, did not guarantee a happy outcome. Some of us were confused. We knew we weren't there yet, but we thought God was better off. Still, it was difficult not to be moved by some of the better literature on the topic, such as Jürgen Moltmann's *Theology of Hope*. Why did it frequently happen that further panic ensued instead of the intended hope?

Today's readings might serve to show why. They all talk about some future doings on God's part. But these doings are basically threatening. A tense future is what we read about, and that's hard to hope in. For example, the first reading speaks of future retribution for the rich and comfortable. "So you will be the first to go into exile. Your feasts and banquets will come to an end" (Amos 6:7). Come the revolution, the soft and the sleek are always the first to go!

The gospel offers a second example of a threatening future. It is the story of the Rich Man and Lazarus. The Rich Man gets his not because he is rich but because he is gross and uncaring. All along he had all the information he ever needed to avert his fiery fate, but he did not look ahead.

The final example has Jesus showing up at some future date wanting to know whether we kept God's command without blame or reproach (1 Timothy 6:14). Here the concern is not with the rich alone, but with anyone.

All these pictures of the future are simply ominous. The future seems to be ruled by our old friend, the God of hell fire and damnation. Until theologians address themselves to *that* aspect of a Future-God, the people of God are going to stay nervous.

Some would claim that a threatening God in the future does not dishearten people. It straightens them out when nothing else could. Others would see that capital punishment is as out of place in the kingdom of God as it is in our earthly kingdoms.

We seem to be faced with a choice. Either we interpret the future threat, of which we read in the Scriptures, literally, and say that God will *treat* people who have not shaped up like the rats they are; or we will interpret it more benignly and say that people will *feel* like rats when faced finally with the clear vision of their past misdeeds (what God will be doing at that point being another matter entirely).

We lean to the latter view. It's a view better tailored to sinners, and so perhaps is self-serving. But it does avoid some of the bullying overtones of the former view. And it does clarify whether we think God wants vengeance or whether we want vengeance. In any case, it resolutely gives you something to look forward to.

Isaiah 5:1–7
Philippians 4:6–9
Matthew 21:33–43

Growing People

"Israel is the vineyard of the Lord Almighty; the people of Judah are the vines he planted" (Isaiah 5:7).

How do you "grow" people? We are saddled with this awkward imagery by today's first reading, in which God's work in the world is pictured in agricultural terms: "My friend had a vineyard on a very fertile hill. He dug the soil and cleared it of stones; he planted the finest vines" (Isaiah 5:1). Now as they say these days, agriculture is not everyone's bag. We know a great deal about human relations and how they might develop under the inspiration of God. A whole literature describes the psychological and spiritual stages of this development. Its idiom is direct and explicit. It speaks about creative capacities and lost innocence, about cultural influences and socialization in sin, about the strange gods people have before them, about conversion, sloth, hardheartedness, and egoism. It also talks in terms of growing relationships, self-transcendance, and generativity. But as if this knowledge were too complicated or too painful, we employ other images that may actually be less well known (like agriculture!) to talk about personal and spiritual growth.

Not that such imagery is all bad. When you "grow" people the way you grow vines or flowers, you have to pay attention to their individual makeup, to their peculiar needs. You must recognize the restlessness of this child, the silence of that friend. You have to try to make sure that some people can adapt to hostile environments without losing their luster. You must shelter a spouse against harsh contacts, or sometimes you must be brutally frank with people for their own protection. You have to remind many of their built-in capacity to be renewed. You have to hold out the hope that is based on the cyclic power of new life to build upon former deaths. You must tell a friend to forget a bad scene, to remember how time heals, not to let himself or herself be utterly sapped by one emotion that clings like a fungus. You have to feed people without playing up to their appetite. They must never get too far away from natural sources such as light and air and water, which feed roots in people as well as in plants. You have to prune away rough spots in them, but they must understand that you are looking out for their best interests.

If all this cultivation goes well, we are rewarded with a variety and richness of personalities, sturdy and graceful, sure of the sun, ready to give of themselves in a burst of beauty or usefulness to others. Parents, teachers, doctors, counselors all try to foster personal growth in these ways. So it's not surprising that God does.

Some might be edified by a picture of God as horticulturist. Others might find the image too crass, presupposing as it does that God is running some kind of hothouse experiment. It's bad enough when the best agricultural image of God we usually can come up with is that of the Grim Reaper.

In any case, Jesus' criticism of his enemies was that they preferred their own customs and status to other people's growth. This is the burden of today's gospel: "He will certainly kill those evil men . . . and rent the vineyard out to other tenants, who will give him his share of the harvest at the right time" (Matthew 21:41). Saint Matthew underscores the point by adding to the parallel text found in Saint Mark's gospel the following words: "The Kingdom of God will be taken away from you and given to a people who will produce the proper fruits" (21:43).

The temptation exists in any institution, even in the church, to put privilege and entrenched positions (however hard won) over the demands of personal and spiritual growth. Churchpeople, for all their talk of orthodoxy, often fall into the same trap as Jesus' enemies. They do not foster anyone's growth, even their own, but rather cling to the comfortable forms of their own religiosity. And the clergy are not the only ones prone to such a temptation. All of us can squelch new directions for growth that suggest themselves to us, because we are timid or resentful of them. And then to justify ourselves, we can bad-mouth these same directions for growth when others take them.

That leaves us with one key question: How do we distinguish between the person who is in a rut and the person who is growing? One distinction that comes to mind is that the former seldom give long speeches about growing, but the latter, like Jesus, do. That should tell us something.

Twenty-Seventh Sunday of the Year — B

Genesis 2:18 – 24
Hebrews 2:9 – 11
Mark 10:2 – 12

Suitable Partners

"So he took some soil from the ground and formed all the animals and all the birds. Then he brought them to the man to see what he would name them; and that is how they all got their names. So the man named all the birds and all the animals; but not one of them was a suitable companion to help him" (Genesis 2:19 – 20).

There is something poignant about the picture of humanity presented above. In its poetic fashion, the passage is speaking about all people, men and women, when it describes the restless and perfunctory way in which "the man" behaves until he finds a suitable partner. The restlessness, to be sure, takes the form of great, talented activity.

Humanity has always been good at naming the animals. A visit to the card catalogue of any library reveals the manifold ingenious ways in which humanity has pursued this task: *The Beastly Gazette*, *The Happy Beast in French Thought of the Seventeenth Century*, *The Uses of Animals in Relation to the Industry of Man*, *Grzimek's Animal Life* (by Grzimek himself). Naming animals, of course, is but one symbolic instance of humanity's impressive scientific capacity to sort and classify, to order and regulate all the forces of the material universe. But in the midst of all this achievement, humanity is constantly trying to put its finger on something else. There is a hollow, unsettled sensation in the human heart that calls for something. . . for more.

This is the context in which the Book of Genesis speaks of marriage. Men and women seek to find in each other a kind of sharing that makes all the work, all the use of one's talents, all the technical mastery of life both meaningful and complete. They find in the eyes, the touch, the words, the bodies, the challenge, and sheer stimulus of each other, energies that stoke their hope and ambition in life. They practice with each other the divine art of giving in anticipation of another's needs. And the Book of Genesis says that all this is great!

But marriage is not always a matter of being in tune with each other even before the music is heard. The stresses and strains of marriage are all too familiar. Divorces, separations, mutual cruelty, both physical and psychological, abandonings, and infidelities are daily occurrences. Or an awful silence grows between the partners. They watch each other from a wary, recriminating distance. Hurts are noted and filed away. Mannerisms are magnified; actions are typed; motives are supplied endlessly.

When this happens, how can we speak of two becoming one flesh? In the New Testament, how can Jesus take such a firm moral stance on the matter of divorce and remarriage? "A man who divorces his wife and marries another woman commits adultery against his wife. In the same way, a woman who divorces her husband and marries another man commits adultery" (Mark 10:11 – 12). Jesus does seem to want to drive people back to the original vision of things that he read in Genesis. He is demanding that people try to recapture that vision and live by it. He probably sensed that people themselves, moral teachers aside, hungered for that sort of vision anyway. They wanted someone to tell them what they already believed in their hearts, namely, that a "suitable" partnership is one that goes on and on, that grows, is broken and healed, rests and surges forward again. Still, Jesus' position seems harsh.

What enables him to maintain it is not some naivete or insensitive idealism. Jesus' position on male–female relationships can be maintained and preached by him only because at the same time and with equal vigor he preaches about the more fundamental partnership that exists between his Father and people. If people have not explored their basic dissatisfactions, their unexamined longings, their upsets and seekings around God in their personal lives, then no amount of talk will reach them about how they should relate to their spouses.

What kills a lot of married people (in many senses) is that the official church monitors their matching and mating very vigorously, indeed, but frequently without at the same time supplying a vision of God that is worth pursuing as far as the corner drugstore. And yet *that* suitable partnership is the standard and measure of all others.

Perhaps we should try to name God with the same vigor with which we name the animals.

Habakkuk 1:2–3; 2:2–4
2 Timothy 1:6–8, 13–14
Luke 17:5–10

No Cowardly Spirit

"Hold firmly to the true words that I taught you, as the example for you to follow, and remain in the faith and love that are ours in union with Christ Jesus. Through the power of the Holy Spirit, who lives in us, keep the good things that have been entrusted to you" (2 Timothy *1:13*–14).

What happened to the deposit of the faith shouldn't happen to anything. For many Christians, the expression conjures up the image of a strongbox, its contents carefully listed, appropriately surrounded by guards and custodians, carefully closed, padlocked, and sealed. Years later, does anyone remember what's inside?

Today's epistle will not allow faith simply to be deposited. Faith is entrusted to us in a very personal way. We do not satisfy the demands of that trust if we merely dump the faith in a corner of our lives and check it from time to time to see whether it has been tampered with. We must keep it alive.

This is not always easy. Faith is something that can engage our emotions. It can embarrass us terribly before others. It can make us bolder than we ever thought we could be. "The Spirit that God has given us does not make us timid" (2 Timothy 1:7). Faith also brings us our share of grief. In one of the epistle's beautiful expressions, we must suffer the evil things that go with believing in this gospel. Faith goes into things with eyes wide open. It restores vision, as we see God restoring vision to the prophet Habakkuk in today's first reading: "Write down clearly on tablets what I reveal to you, so that it can be read at a glance. Put it in writing, because it is not yet time for it to come true. But the time is coming quickly, and what I show you will come true" (Habakkuk 2:2–3).

This confidence in faith's effectiveness in the world is mirrored in today's gospel. Jesus says, "If you had faith as big as a mustard seed, you could say to this mulberry tree, 'Pull yourself up by the roots and plant yourself in the sea!' and it would obey you" (Luke 17:6).

Occasionally, television gives us David Lean's *Lawrence of Arabia*. Lawrence, played by Peter O'Toole, is poignantly torn between a lofty vision of the future and a more humdrum passage through life. On the one hand, he burns hotly with faith in Arab unity. His vision places him literally and figuratively upon God's anvil. On the other hand, he says with grief and near despair: "I want to be an ordinary man." He longs for the comfort of the officer's club, the small gossip, the camaraderie, the trivial enthusiasms. He dreads his own vision, its frustrations, its tearing demands, and especially the strange mixture of lust and power that accompanies his faith. In order to believe, Lawrence also has to fight the encrustments of written law and tradition. "Nothing is written," he says in the name of his vision. He would probably even suspect Habakkuk for writing down a vision, as though it would thereby lose its fierceness.

Lawrence is admittedly an instance of faith written large. There are, however, similarities with every believer's situation. We, too, are drawn to a vision, a vision of God bringing about a kingdom of justice and peace. But this very preposterous quality of Christian faith makes us long for something more banal and within our grasp. The believer does not seem to be an "ordinary man."

On the other hand, Christian faith departs from Lawrence's "faith" in important respects. His battlefield of faith was an extraordinary terrain. Christianity differs in that it makes the ordinary itself the landscape of faith. While it may fall to the lot of some few Christians to unite nations, bridge oceans, and get whole peoples to see themselves in the new light, by and large the task of Christianity is to get us to embrace our own ordinary humanity with an extraordinary fidelity. The incarnation illustrates this with a vengeance. In terms of performance, Jesus hardly rises above the ordinary. He certainly did not go around transplanting mulberry trees into the sea. He did not act, as many of us do, as though he were deposited here until judgment day. His vision put him to work for the kingdom now.

Isaiah 25:6– 10
Philippians 4:12– 14, 19– 20
Matthew 22:1– 14

The Party Spirit

"The Kingdom of heaven is like this. Once there was a king who prepared a wedding feast for his son" (Matthew 22:2).

Could there be some playful and mischievous providence at work in the fact that a banquet has become the symbol of good times in the kingdom of God? The banquet image is offered by Isaiah in today's first reading: "Here on Mount Zion the Lord Almighty will prepare a banquet for all the nations of the world—a banquet of the richest food and the finest wine" (Isaiah 25:6). We can easily relate to this image. People at banquets are supposed to have happy, flushed faces, sparkling eyes, intense, though pleasant, conversation, nice clothes, a sense of euphoria, laughter, exquisite toilette, dancing, one delectable plate after the next, satiety, and a generally excited hum. And the waiters are really professional. Whatever speeches are given are to be short and heartwarming. For the poor among us, it's a living, and its free. We belong. No wonder we're flushed.

Isaiah's point is not so much to tell us that good things like this will happen to us; it is rather to indicate what sort of person God is. Isaiah creates his image in such wise that attention focuses on the gracious host of the banquet, a person of quality, largesse, a person whose first inclination is to have a rip-roaring party.

Thus, the banquet is not only a symbol of good times in God's kingdom, it is also a symbol of God himself.

Jesus took up this image and made it his own, but with his own special nuances. First, he protested that such festive relations with God need not wait until some distant, rosy point in time. If God is basically a genial host, then people could start dealing with him as such right now. Secondly, Jesus backed up this belief by the way he behaved. He incorporated his appreciation of the Old Testament banquet image in his practice of fellowship meals. He ate with various categories of Jews who normally would be excluded from one's table fellowship: sinners, prostitutes, tax collectors. For how would such people ever learn that God wants to have a banquet with them if no one else wanted to eat with them?

Moreover, under Jesus' inspiration (though not his personal example), his followers extended table fellowship to the Gentiles. After all, if you can't eat with "them," then you can hardly hope to share joy in the same Lord with them.

Thirdly, as we see in today's gospel, Jesus added the insight that some people are basically party poopers. They find excuses not to join the banquet circuit. Perhaps they are too timid to celebrate relationships. Perhaps they think the host has something up his sleeve in inviting them. They prefer duller pastimes such as work. They resent, too, those who represent a less pragmatic, more devil-may-care way of life. "The invited guests paid no attention and went about their business: one went to his farm, another to his store, while others grabbed the servants, beat them, and killed them" (Matthew

22:5– 6). Jesus certainly was aware that it's hard to cheer some people up!

We might be overdoing the image of the Christian-as-banqueter. But when seen over against the alternatives to it, the image is a stirring one. It keeps in focus a picture of God that unfortunately is foreign to many of us. It places the burden back on us to ask ourselves who, after all, is being the glum one in our relationship with God.

Still, no one would pretend that we can sustain the party spirit amid all the harsh realities of life. In today's epistle, Saint Paul gives a more balanced picture of someone who knows how to tighten the belt when things go wrong. "I know what it is to be in need and what it is to have more than enough. I have learned this secret, so that anywhere, at any time, I am content, whether I am full or hungry, whether I have too much or too little" (Philippians 4:12). Saint Paul is sustained by the thought that it is God's way to be interested in revelry. That thought loosens him in every workaday situation. But he also knows there is work to do. Besides, the logical thing is not to eat for a long time before any banquet.

As if to destroy the image of the banquet he had previously built up, Saint Matthew adds four verses (11 – 14), in which the king suddenly becomes quite ungracious. After inviting in everyone and his brother from the byroads, the king now starts worrying about how people are dressed. Some commentators see in this section a reference to early Christian baptism (the baptismal robe). Saint Matthew's "many are invited, but few are chosen" does seem to be part of his usual anti-Jewish polemic. The invited would be the Jews who do not accept Jesus; the elect would be the Christian communities (to be entered through baptism) who accept him. The king in these verses would be pointing out that the Jews have missed the spirit of the messianic banquet. At any rate, it's a sour note to end on, because the last four verses seem to present a picky God. This simply encourages Christians to fall into the same trap of exclusiveness that mars the image of the gracious banquet host who is so interested in having a party that he invites people off the road. That certainly is one way to postpone the party: to haggle about who is invited, how they should dress, and so on. Sometimes you wonder why the king doesn't move the whole party out onto the road.

Twenty-Eighth Sunday of the Year—B

Wisdom 7:7–11
Hebrews 4:12–13
Mark 10:17–27

Keeping Company

"The word of God is alive and active, sharper than any double-edged sword. It cuts all the way through, to where soul and spirit meet, to where joints and marrow come together. It judges the desires and thoughts of man's heart" (Hebrews 4:12).

Although the above image is that of a sword, it sounds more like a scalpel at work. The anatomical shaving away of all our parts, mind as well as matter, is a frightening prospect. It recalls a C. S. Lewis phrase about "God's surgery."

But the trick is that Jesus does not perform the operation himself. He leaves that to the church. For it is by being joined to others who are similarly engaged with Jesus in the church that we experience much of the healthy dissection described in Hebrews.

The first proof of this is seen in that very first expression of a gathered church, the New Testament writings themselves. What first jostles us is the mind-boggling diversity of style and personality, the conflicting emphases, the alternating magnaminity and narrowness of the New Testament writers. They mix legend with fact, recollection with rumor, pious invention with tenacious conviction, quirk with insight, pet peeve with wise proposal. Reading Scripture is like having your mind and nerves rearranged, because the word of God comes to us in the words of men who differ so much from one another and from us.

The second proof is seen in the events and issues these same writers describe. The churches they speak of are storm centers. Challenge, emotion, growth, controversy, and excitement mark their ordinary calendar of events. They are stuck with every conceivable human issue from moral integrity to political status, from scrounging for funds to authority disputes, from persecution to planning charitable works. Any individual caught in the middle of this scene would surely feel that his joints and marrow where being tampered with, that his soul was being penetrated and divided!

Today's gospel deals with one such divisive, troublesome issue that confronted the early churches. It is the issue of the rich versus the poor. Jesus himself seems to throw up his hands when he confronts the tug that money has, even on good people. "How hard it is to enter the Kingdom of God! It is much harder for a rich person to enter the Kingdom of God than for a camel to go through the eye of a needle" (Mark 10:24–25). The scandal is not so much what money does to the individual who has it, though there are certainly problems there. It is that wealth creates a wall of separation from poorer people who are also Christians. Once that wall has risen, those on either side, rich or poor, seem foreign and distasteful to one another. The quality of our unity in the kingdom seems fraudulent and strained. Jesus believes that his Father can forge unity out of this mess, anyway. But he does seem to be disturbed by the whole affair.

It seems worth repeating here that it is *because* we are attempting to create Christian community with others that most of the upset comes. It is not our direct relationship with Jesus that causes us pain. It is because Jesus associates us with others. For all the sword-wielding imagery, most of us continue to trust him personally, even as he sends us into that circus of community that we call the church. He certainly gets us into some searing situations there, but that does not seem to touch our personal relationship with him. In fact, we realize that it is this personal relationship that is supposed to sustain and transform all our other relationships. Today's gospel reminds us that when we give up cherished and comfortable ties for him, we receive "a hundred times more houses, brothers, sisters, mothers, children and fields — and persecution as well" (Mark 10:30). That is to say, a solid dedication to him enables us to discover more friends and more affinity all around us than we ever expected or hoped for. We forge charity despite a lack of comfort in doing so, and suddenly the whole world is truly our home.

There are many these days who have, for one reason or another, opted out of being formal members of the Christian community. They are called the unchurched. They are safe from the two-edged swords that flail about in a normal parish situation. They are seldom challenged. They are never irked by this doctrinal debate or that god-awful liturgical experience or by any other contact with a church in the crisis of growth. They do not have to listen any longer to the babble that even sincere believers can indulge in. Some of the unchurched, moreover, are satisfied that they have "met the Lord" in their private lives. That is enough for them, they say: they have found peace in him. Maybe. But with no church to shake up their joints and marrow from time to time, we may wonder whether they have found peace or simply have shut their eyes to his reality.

2 Kings 5:14– 17
2 Timothy 2:8– 13
Luke 17:11– 19

One Leper Thanks You

"There were ten men who were healed; where are the other nine?" (Luke 17:17).

Has anyone else noticed a great deal of ungraciousness and awkwardness in our culture about showing gratitude? We don't mean how nephews find it hard to write thank-you notes to generous aunts. Problems with gratitude certainly exist with young people. But there are enough instances of adult discomfort with gratitude to keep the discussion at that level.

Why is it that some of us feel knotted and constrained if another person picks up the tab? Why is it humiliating when others go out of their way to serve us? Why do teachers and other entertainers feel that audiences are so demanding? Why do counselors who work through painful questions with their clients feel that when some resolution has come, those clients never want to see them again. Why do doctors say that some patients are more ready to sue than to celebrate the small victories that medicine can provide?

Today's gospel, the story of the ten lepers, raises this issue of gratitude squarely. "Why is this foreigner the only one who came back to give thanks to God?" (Luke 17:18). If you believe, as we do, that Jesus' cures took something out of his hide, that they proceeded from his prayer and sweating faith and were not simply a display of divine power, then his remark is all the more poignant. Jesus' complaint has an edge of personal hurt about it. He seems to be asking what we all ask from time to time: How do people get that way?

One explanation of our difficulty with gratitude is our own low self-image. We simply don't believe we are worthy of being favored by others. Despite cures, some people are going to go on feeling like lepers, anyway. They cannot be touched by sentiments of gratitude, because no sentiment is capable of penetrating the hard and fixed coating of their unworthiness.

A second explanation is that people fear the intimacy that is part and parcel of sincere gratitude. We cover up our embarrassment in situations in which we receive favors by paying enormous attention to the thing given us. We remark on its size, price, shape, detail, packaging, mechanisms, utility, anything. We hide behind *it* so we won't be touched by the person who hovers behind the gift as our potent and loving benefactor. This turning from person to thing happens in the life of grace, as well. In fact, it happens with a vengeance where God's favors are concerned. We have transformed the grace of God into the most amorphous, utile, quantified, and thingified glob of all. We can say when you get it, lose it, are in it or out of it. It remains firmly an "it." If others have confused us with notions of grace that made it so impersonal, this did not happen without our cooperation. We know a lot more about keeping our distance from God than we let on. We know that gratitude takes a certain alertness about who is doing what. So we numb ourselves with talk of grace, and manage thereby not to let God get too close.

A third explanation is that it is difficult for us to be grateful to a God who seems to have allowed the leprosy in the first place.

A fourth explanation is less flattering to us. We often do favors for the wrong reasons (one-upmanship, showing off, an obsessive need to look good, guilt, controlling others, pity, and so forth). So, we think others are acting just as aggressively or obliquely when they do us favors. Kindness, we suspect, is a contest, and the one who has to say thank you has already lost. Or we fear that to show gratitude is to compromise our independence. This is especially the case in our relationship with God, in which we wonder whether God is merely out to reinforce his sovereignty through his favors to us.

A section of today's epistle could be misleading on this score. It says, "If we deny him, he will also deny us" (2 Timothy 2:12). The statement hardly makes God out to be a gracious bestower of favors. On the contrary, it gives the impression of a very touchy God. But the very next phrase corrects this impression when it says: "If we are not faithful, he remains faithful, because he cannot be false to himself." In other words, while we might not take advantage of the favors God does for us, that will never change the nature of God from being generous and giving. Even God's "denial" of us is the gesture of a friend who is pointing out to us what we already know, that ingratitude is bad for our personalities!

If we could only see that it is not undignified to be needy, we would be less insulted when someone meets our need out of a generous heart. Even better, we might even come to see that neediness is not even the issue. Someone might even like us.

Isaiah 45:1, 4– 6
1 Thessalonians 1:1– 5
Matthew 22:15– 21

The Powers
That May Not Be

"Pay to the Emperor what belongs to the Emperor, and pay to God what belongs to God" (Matthew 22:21).

Government has always been a looming presence and power in the lives of common people. Sometimes that presence is benevolent, sometimes menacing; often it is irritating. Governments can arrest us, tax us, exile us, enlist us, bombard us with forms to fill out, harangue us, and generally leave us off balance. Government so quickly becomes a self-subsisting organism with a life of its own. It breathes heavily, forages ravenously. It makes decisions that descend on our humdrum lives with force. We feel removed from this omnipotent side of government, despite all our theoretical convictions that it is, after all, our government, the collected expression of our wishes. Government remains, at least as an emotional experience, a province apart. It is peopled by shadowy figures, pols, lobbyists, pork-barrelers, backroom types, polished buck passers, former high school debaters, wheelers and dealers, old men with wizened memories, sycophants, users.

So it is doubly interesting to conjecture what a God-man's reaction to the psychological colossus of government might be. Will he bow or bristle? Will he partake or stand aloof? Will he serve or look the other way? Will he oppose or ignore? Will he be strong or will he knit his brow like the rest of us? The questions are intriguing because of all we know from history about the churches' checkered fate in the face of governments. Yet, it is always easy to criticize religion for not being able to tame or modulate the forces of government. Even today, when such heroic stands are taken by the churches in the face of shady and compromised governments, the barstool atheists still point with pride at the apparent impotence of the churches to effect political renewal.

Today's gospel finds Jesus himself confronted with government. His situation is particularly delicate for two reasons. First, the government in question is an armed occupation force of Romans who fatten the coffers of their mother city by taxing conquered lands. Second, Jesus cannot even have the comfort of grappling with this difficult issue from a shared perspective among religious people. For it is his own coreligionists who are putting the question to him in a devious and compromising way. There is an attempt underway to put him down, and not to find the truth. The question is put squarely: How well does Jesus come off?

Not badly, but with no astonishing revelations and certainly with no hint that religion provides any magical cure against the force of government. Jesus says that Caesar should get what he deserves and so should God. While the first part of the statement might be dripping with irony, irony does not seem to have been the burden of the remark. Rather, Jesus seems to be saying that the religious man has to be *discriminating* in his reactions to government.

A passage from Romans (13:1 – 10) that is sometimes used to help interpret this one from Saint Matthew (and even employs some of the same key Greek words) supports this notion of discrimination. Saint Paul has no doubts about the presence of government. He says that it's power to punish is real (13:4). But he adds (7 – 8) that the Christian's main obligation is not taxes but charity. No one can make government an excuse for avoiding charity. That's what discrimination is all about.

Many would have wanted something more trenchant from Jesus on this matter. Discrimination seems so . . . balanced. Jesus does not go as far as Saint Paul (13:6) and say that government authorities "are working for God." Nor does Jesus echo Isaiah, in today's first reading, who describes Cyrus II, king of Persia, as being used by God to free Israel from the Babylonian yoke. "I appoint you. . . ." says the Lord to Cyrus II. "I have given you great honor, although you do not know me" (Isaiah 45:4). Jesus makes no such case for governments. Perhaps he took governments on their own terms and saw them as the fragile, mixed expression of the good and the bad in all people. Perhaps he found it hard to be impressed by governments when they have fallen so regularly and resoundingly throughout history.

You wonder whether Jesus had ever heard the story of Cyrus I, grandfather of the Cyrus mentioned by Isaiah. The story is found in Herodotus. The old Cyrus once lectured a delegation of his fellow Persians on the fate of a government that gets too fat and powerful. "Soft countries," he said, "breed soft men." Herodotus goes on: "The Persians had to admit that this was true, and chose rather to live in a rugged land and rule than to cultivate rich plains and be slaves." Cyrus II wasn't so wise. Jesus, on the other hand, chose to live in a rugged land.

Twenty-Ninth Sunday of the Year—B

Isaiah 53:10–11
Hebrews 4:14–16
Mark 10:35–45

Uncommon Good

"Our High Priest is not one who cannot feel sympathy for our weaknesses. On the contrary, we have a High Priest who was tempted in every way that we are, but did not sin. Let us be brave, then, and approach God's throne, where there is grace. There we will receive mercy and find grace to help us when we need it" (Hebrews 4:15–16).

The epistle pictures humanity lined up like shoddy, hopeful freeloaders at the door of someone who knew hard times himself. The scene smacks of sheer neediness and embarrassment. Humanity down-at-the-heels, "Buddy, can you spare a dime?" In this crowd, everyone knows quite well that life means coming up short, means never getting there, means taking it and taking it some more with no let up.

But the hope comes from the fact that we are dealing with one of our own. We won't have to search around for words that describe our neediness. We won't have to turn our pockets out in a grand gesture of emptiness. We won't have to spell out all our circumstances to the nth degree. We won't have to display our pain like so much collateral. He's been there.

This is a heartwarming reminder of God's solidarity with us in Jesus. It lifts us up. Today's gospel, however, concentrates on one specific area in which he joined our human condition. It depicts him caught in the wake of other people's struggle for power. It describes an incident in which James and John ask Jesus for a commanding spot in his entourage. No hanging back for them! There is a moment of preliminary sparring, in which Jesus tests them for their seriousness and realistic assessment of the personal risks involved. "Can you drink the cup of suffering that I must drink? Can you be baptized in the way I must be baptized?" (Mark 10:38). But personal heroism is not the point, and Jesus seems to have known this even before they got out their firm response "We can." All that their boasting about their capacity for endurance succeeds in doing is to get the other disciples angry at James and John. So Jesus must take the matter further. He does so by contrasting leadership and command among the Gentiles with the kind that he envisions: "You know that the men who are considered rulers of the heathen have power over them. . . . This, however, is not the way it is among you. If one of you wants to be great, he must be servant of the rest; and if one of you wants to be first, he must be the slave of all" (Mark 10:42 – 44).

The text indicates a progression: greatness is said to consist in serving the rest; but the height of greatness is reserved for the one who serves the needs of *all*. Even if we stop being self-serving and reach out to select others, it is a long way from there to feel a responsibility beyond that for the way *everything* is going. Just the stretching, intense exercise of letting oneself be aware of a wider circle of events and people can be exhausting. To note in a vast number of others what is diverse and complex about them is an energetic pastime. To be open to such awareness makes for a special kind of bath of pain. Moreover, the kind of action that is called for when we are committed to serve *everyone* seems to be different. The process of judging one's course differs when the common good is the issue. No one is fully pleased; no one fully agrees; not all cooperate. Jesus states his conviction to James and John and the others that the highest authority must be the widest and most painful.

We might wonder if suddenly, as he stated it, he thought of himself in a new, frightening way.

Twenty-Ninth Sunday of the Year — C

Exodus 17:8 – 13
2 Timothy 3:14 — 4:2
Luke 18:1 – 8

Staying Power

"As long as Moses held up his arms, the Israelites won"
(Exodus 17:11).

Even if Aaron and Hur cheated a little by holding Moses' arms up, Moses demonstrated remarkable endurance in prayer, according to today's first reading. The same kind of endurance is praised in the gospel. The mean old judge in Jesus' story gives in to the relentless entreaties of a widow woman. Jesus draws the moral: "Will God not judge in favor of his own people who cry to him day and night for help?" (Luke 18:7).

Prayer as an endurance contest has been the experience of many of us, though perhaps not in the same sense as in today's readings! One thing that these readings can teach us is that prayer should be focused or pointed. Exhortations to prayer that do not take note of this fact can be very misleading. Prayer is not a matter of prolonged, blank staring. If it is to last, prayer should have a focus, even if that focus is no more specific than a deliberate attempt to bat the breeze. Some might find talk of setting oneself a task in prayer too businesslike. But to know what we are up to in prayer is half the battle.

There is a difference, however, between prayer that is focused and prayer that drives toward resolution. The latter wants something settled. It is not only pointed, but it is in pursuit.

But what kind of resolution can it expect? Does it mean that I always get what I want? Hardly. More likely, we should expect the kind of resolution that normally takes place in relationships between people, in which it is not required that one party wins or the other party gives in. What matters is that the relationship is clarified, strengthened, and enabled to move forward, because something has been decisively said and candidly accepted.

Most of our prayer falls into this category. A person might begin to pray seriously about a specific moral problem. Say he is trying to kick a mean habit of unchasteness. He is hurting women by his sexual aggressiveness. He prays. The resolution of his problem, however, can come in a different shape than he anticipated.

He might, for instance, abruptly learn what this God he prays to is like. He might discover that he has been using his relationship with Christ as some sort of amulet or good-luck charm that protects him against unnamed misfortunes. He might come to realize that Christ is not all that anxious to scare the hell out of him with ultimate threats. He might be surprised to find that Christ is interested in other things besides his sex life. He might come to see Christ's own relationship to women in a more serious, less insulting light.

Or he might learn more about himself. In the quiet of prayer, he might hear more loudly now the small, mocking voice (his own) that he frequently heard in the midst of his sins: "This is ridiculous." Or he might see his sexual behavior as part of a larger skein of values and concerns. He might start to ask himself what the Garden of Allah deodorants, the hair wavers and capped teeth, the suits with the tight armpits, the macho pants and chest-baring shirts, the Teutotnic finger rings all add up to. Or—prayer can do this, too—what they cost.

Through prayer, he might also begin to espy other people's needs, their struggles and strengths. He might come to see woman's search for dignity, her economic anxiety, the pressures on her to conform, her desperations and talents.

Some blunt and direct reader might ask: Well, did he or didn't he ever resolve his problem of sexual aggression? Did his endurance at prayer ever pay off? The question is legitimate, but overhasty. It looks for a resolution along the lines of today's readings, in which the

410

Israelites clearly mow down Amalek and his people, or where the judge collapses before the widow's barrage. It forgets that even after victorious battles, bodies must be buried and more widows appear. Our hero may or may not succeed in throwing over his tendency to be the town bull. The resolution he gets through prayer may be that his problem is broken down into its several parts. In each one of them, he finds himself more able to be sensitive and decisive, so each becomes a step in his growth and healing. Perseverance in prayer brings self-knowledge. It makes us give up old gods for new, energetic ones. It's such a workout that we may not have any strength left for our sins.

This kind of prayer better apes the rugged pace of Scripture itself, which today's epistle urges us to learn from. "All Scripture is inspired by God and is useful for teaching the truth, rebuking error, correcting faults, and giving instruction for right living" (2 Timothy 3:16). On the whole, the Scriptures present us with an endless list of heroes who hoped and prayed for one thing but got another. Sometimes it seems that the only one in the book who begins and ends praying for the same thing is God.

411

Exodus 22:20–26
1 Thessalonians 1:5–10
Matthew 22:34–40

Dear Me

"The whole Law of Moses and the teachings of the prophets depend on these two commandments" (Matthew 22:40).

We all have little tricks to remind ourselves of things we have come to see as important or valuable. We jot down messages to ourselves—lest we forget. We pin a note on the refrigerator or paste a picture on the bathroom mirror. We carry an item in our purse or wallet. The astounding thing is that these reminders often deal with fairly momentous issues, with the rise and fall of our own personalities: "Improve your mind today." "Put someone at his ease." "Which will it be, your posture or your posterior?" "Are the clouds of depression gathering?" "The tears will pass." "The humble are mighty."

While it's humiliating to have to treat such important aspects of our lives this way, it's a fact of life that this is the way we keep ourselves going. Our personal development, our professions, our key relationships with others—each of these has its appropriate reminders with which we decorate the walls of our minds.

The people of Israel had its own version of such reminders. The Book of Deuteronomy (6:4–5) contains the Shema (from the Hebrew word for "hear," or "pay attention," which begins with verse 4). It bids the people to love the Lord with all their energies and talents, with their very selves. This commandment was not, however, something that the Israelites were to hear once and file away. "Never forget these commands that I am giving you today. Teach them to your children. Repeat them when you are at home and when you are away, when you are resting and when you are working. Tie them on your arms and wear them on your foreheads as a reminder. Write them on the doorposts of your houses and on your gates (Deuteronomy 6:6–9). Have we left any place out?

In today's gospel, Jesus cites this Shema as the first major responsibility of his people. Jesus the Jew knows that this kind of message has to be absorbed by a long, steady effort. He, too, would be in favor of writing it down somewhere, anywhere—lest we forget. He, too, would realize that it is especially humiliating for us to have to say, as the Israelites found it necessary to say, "Oops, I forgot that I'm supposed to love God; I'll have to make note of that for the future." Jesus would not be embarrassed at our awkwardness.

The second major responsibility Jesus mentions in today's gospel is the golden rule: "Love your neighbor as you love yourself" (Matthew 22:39). Again, his precedent is the Old Testament. Today's first reading from Exodus lists some particularly offensive ways of dealing with our neighbor: picking on foreigners, cheating widows, making money off orphans, loan-sharking among the poor, taking collateral without consideration of the needy situation of the person you take it from. Whether we ourselves do or don't do these particular things is not the point. For the kernel of the commandment is to get us to imagine ourselves as the victims of other people's viciousness: What if poeple did such things to you? The

413

golden rule is almost an invitation to us to discover compassion by the route of self-interest or self-pity. Or rather, it tries to picture our most tender, most dogged and noblest feeling for our own dignity, and then to apply that feeling to others. It focuses us on the fact that others feel the way we feel, hurt the way we hurt, fear the way we fear, need love the way we need love.

The golden rule, however, is a two-step mechanism. It works only if its basic assumption is verified, namely, that we love ourselves. That is half the problem. Much of the violence we deal out is the overflow of our self-hatred. More often than not, we strike out blindly at others from our interior pain. The golden rule invites us to fix on our own lovableness and sense of dignity. Without this first step, nothing happens.

This is where the two great commandments come together. Only a person with the sense of being loved by God is free to look more benevolently on the neighbor. We have to pin that on our refrigerators and see that on our bathroom mirrors. We have to work at the realization that we are really dear to someone. Only then will we be free to share joy with our neighbors, instead of the surly, suspicious contacts we often have with them. The only embarrassing drawback is that someone might find in our wallet or purse the note we wrote to ourselves: "Dear me: God, at least, loves you."

Jeremiah 31:7–9
Hebrew 5:1–6
Mark 10:46–52

Seldom Heard

"Every high priest is chosen from his fellow-men and appointed to serve God on their behalf, to offer sacrifices and offerings for sins. Since he himself is weak in many ways, he is able to be gentle with those who are ignorant and make mistakes" (Hebrews 5:1 – 2).

It would be a rare day that a parish priest gave a sermon about himself. But if he did, would he be ready to make use of the words of today's epistle that speak of the priest as beset by weaknesses?

The question is somewhat illegitimate and fanciful. The Epistle to the Hebrews is not primarily a manual on clerical duties. It is an exploration of the unique role of Jesus in salvation history. Even its sustained comparison between Jesus and the high priest of the Old Testament can be misleading, for it is a comparison that creates the image of Jesus as priest as much as it clarifies what this means. Jesus himself probably would have been surprised by it. Anyway, would our modern priest sermonize on his priesthood in terms of his own sinful weaknesses?

Some would certainly not. They would distance themselves from such a topic, and they would cover their tracks with a lot of exhortation (to others) about being strong in the Lord and living manfully (sorry about that, ladies). They would defend the righteousness of their role at all costs. They would confront their personal weakness with a loud speech about strength, because any real sign of weakness has to be downplayed—even beyond our normal American reluctance to appear incompetent or flawed. Their person, they feel, must remain submerged in and leave intact the sacredness of their role.

Other priests would blame themselves, but for the wrong reasons. They would bewail the fact that they are not the most prayerful in the parish, the most unselfish with their time, the best read in spiritual matters, the wisest of counselors, the liveliest at liturgy. The premise of this lamentation is, of course, finally self-serving. These priests rake themselves over the coals in a way that ends up flattering to themselves, since what they are supposedly failing in is their superiority to everyone else. Their role, when you press them, is to be a sacred person.

Whether one locates sacredness in the role or in the person of the priest, the same problem seems to linger on: sacredness is the name of the game. Any admission of personal weakness is made or not made within this context. Priests who live off this conviction borrow heavily from the words of today's epistle: "Every high priest is chosen from his fellow-men and appointed to serve God in their behalf, to offer sacrifices and offerings for sins." And you don't get close to God unless you are sacred, right?

Still other priests would say bother to the whole discussion. They would hope, with the rest of us, that people don't zero in too diligently on their personal vices. They would not wish to get into a futile contest with their parishioners about who is weaker than whom. While they do see a sacred aspect to their priesthood, they identify that sacredness with the fact that God creates in them the ability to do a very humdrum work for the community. They play down the who's-closer-to-God argument in order to concentrate on what they see their *job* as priests to be. That God deals gently with their person through it all, they piously hope. But they do not confuse priesthood with a kind of leadership based on personal performance or on privileged ties with God. Rather, they see their work as priests along the following lines: They have the authority to get people's attention. They do not have to beg for this, nor to parade themselves in such an appealing fashion that they command it; the faithful themselves should accord it out of a mature sense of *their own* membership in the community of Christ. Second, when the priest gets people's attention, he can then raise the issue of people's *own* responsibilities and opportunities in Christian living. Third, he can coordinate and focus the striving of his many parishioners and can help them come to some *shared* definition of their own Christian faith.

There are, to be sure, dilemmas for the priest in doing this task. These would make for an excellent sermon, indeed. How do you get people's attention without being the man with a thousand faces, each one capable of winning over attention? How do you get people's attention, when many people resent the fact that you can get it by virtue of your official status, while they can't? How do you call people to the responsibilities they already have, when by doing so you seem to be creating those very responsibilities for them? How do you focus people on one another, when they may not like all that much contact with one another? How do you move people toward definition, when blurred edges suit them better?

Because of this authority, the priest is a walking reminder of the state, not of himself, but of the community. Less sophisticated parishioners do not advert to this fact. All they know is that there is something about the priest that makes them uncomfortable. But they never trace their discomfort to its real sources, namely, to problems with themselves or with other parishioners whom the priest reminds them of. The priest, by reason of his job, evokes in people *their own* questions about God, about Jesus, about salvation in its major and minor forms. Where such soul-shaking questions arise and are posed by the very role and presence of the priest, it is easy to see why some might want to change the topic by introducing the issue of the priest's personal character!

The priest has to return people to their own responsibilities. Any priest who is not still playing the sacred person will tell you that.

Sirach 35:12– 14, 16– 18
2 Timothy 4:6– 8, 16– 18
Luke 18:9– 14

Big Deal

" 'But the tax collector stood at a distance and would not even raise his face to heaven, but beat on his breast and said, "God, have pity on me, a sinner!" I tell you,' said Jesus, 'the tax collector. . . was in the right with God when he went home' " (Luke 18:13 – 14).

Ever since the story of the Pharisee and the publican was first told, the back pews have been filled with would-be publicans, proudly crowing about their sinfulness. No fasting for them, no tithes, but straightforward crookery and even a little adultery. The back pews, it seems, have turned into a kind of muscle beach for "honest" sinners. The remake seems to have lost something of the original. We seem to have forgotten what it was the original had that made the Pharisee the villain and the publican the hero.

The most obvious difference between the two is that the Pharisee measured himself against the performance of others, while the publican measured his own performance alone, as he stood before God. It was not self-assessment that got the Pharisee into trouble. It was the odious comparisons he made of himself with others. Our second-rate modern imitators of the publican slip into the same error the Pharisee made. They, too, make secret comparisons of their behavior with others. (Look, Ma, I'm in the back pew. . .not like those others.) So they lose the charm of the original publican, who simply didn't look around at all. He looked within, and he looked at the holiness of God. That was all it took.

In the epistle, Saint Paul offers another image that describes the right kind of self-assessment. It is the image of the athlete: "I have done my best in the race, I have run the full distance, and I have kept the faith. And now there is waiting for me the prize of victory" (2 Timothy 4:7–8). He, too, is not comparing his performance with others', but is looking at it as it is in itself, before the Lord. We have seen athletes, in professional settings, give this same kind of self-measured report on their own performance. Media commentators may reach for comparisons with other athletes; the press may talk up the charismatic glow of the star. But the professionals are politely uncomfortable with all that. They are thinking about the integrity of their own performance—whether the body reacted, the nerves wavered, the terrain was gauged, the right pressure exerted. If Saint Paul thinks he won, he is also oblivious that there were others in the race. That's not being a big deal; that's class.

The case of Saint Paul, however, brings out a major dilemma that faces us in our solitary self-assessments. While self-assessment might lead us, like the publican, to see ourselves as sinners, it might also lead us to see ourselves as talented, faithful, sincere, and—would you believe—nice. Yet, many people have such a low self-image that *any* self-assessment ends up on a note of dull desperation. Bankers, teenagers, bartenders, bishops, housewives, and nuns share this affliction. It is counter-Christian and devastating. It consists of the gnawing habit of running oneself down. It is a parody of the publican's stance. It prevents a person from ever seeing himself as loved, even by God. It is, at bottom, hopeless. The person who constantly runs his finger this way over the flaw in his being, feels scarred and hampered in all his relationships. This person is ill equipped even to look at his own sinfulness.

How do we avoid this morose downgrading of ourselves that is so bereft of hope? We cannot curry God's favor by adopting a bleak and despairing attitude toward ourselves. Our declarations of sinfulness are supposed to lead us to hope in God's deep respect for us and his adult confidence in us.

God does not make his own name for justice by turning us into greater villains than we are. Once we see that God is a God who makes a big deal of publicans and such, the pressure is off us to be anything but honest in our self-assessments. We might even end up saying nice things about ourselves.

Thirty-First Sunday of the Year—A

Malachi 1:14—2:2, 8—10
1 Thessalonians 2:7—9, 13
Matthew 23:1—12

Favorite Enemies

"The greatest one among you must be your servant"
(Matthew 23:11).

Why can't we be for one thing without being against something else? We are moved and excited at the idea of maintaining a warm, encompassing benevolence toward all people. We want to exude charity and touch everyone we meet with our concern and understanding. This is, after all, the standard image of the good and gentle Jesus. And besides, we need all the help we can get to control the torrent of explosive emotions within us.

We are perplexed, then, to find Jesus in overtly explosive situations. We are shocked to find him engaged in confrontation, sniping, caricature, and violent generalization. If Saint Matthew's account is at all accurate, Jesus could really turn it on when he wanted to arouse the crowds to partisan fervor against his enemies. In today's gospel he goes after the scribes and Pharisees: "They tie onto people's backs loads that are heavy and hard to carry, yet they aren't willing even to lift a finger to help them carry those loads" (Matthew 23:4).

There is some difficulty with the interpretation of this statement. Is Jesus saying that the burdens, though heavy, are legitimately imposed? Or is he saying that they are unfairly imposed? In the former case, Jesus would be charging the Pharaisees with hypocrisy in not carrying out what they tell others to do. This is certainly the traditional understanding. It seems to be borne out in the statement: "Do not. . .imitate their actions, because they don't practice what they preach" (Matthew 23:3). Important to this traditional understanding is that no criticism would be leveled at the Pharisees' basic authority to interpret the Law: "The teachers of the Law and the Pharisees are the authorized interpreter's of Moses' Law. So you must obey and follow everything they tell you to do" (Matthew 23:2 – 3).

However, a second interpretation remains a possibility, namely, that Jesus is attacking the Pharisees' very authority to make rules the way they do. In this interpretation, Jesus' criticism of the "heavy loads" would be that they are unfair, and hence unauthorized. This position is certainly more consistent with his frequent rejection of their authority (for example, on such issues as curing on the Sabbath, eating with unwashed hands, consorting with sinners, and so on) and with his abetting those who do the same.

But in fact it would be too simplistic to speak of an either/or attitude toward the Pharisees' authority. The context of today's gospel, it must be remembered, is diatribe, attack, conflict. Precision, neat distinctions, and niceties of speech yield to the anger of such moments. It is the kind of anger that makes you suspect motives and make sweeping statements ("They do everything so that people will see them"). It is the kind of anger that has you fixated on the way your enemies dress and how they look ("Notice. . .the tassels on their cloaks"). It is the kind of anger that makes you accuse others of feeding off their professional titles ("They love to have people call them 'Teacher' "). Jesus' anger stems, no doubt, from a frustrating tension, the same kind of tension that we feel when we are torn between preserving authority and telling it off. We don't seem to be getting his calmest or clearest thoughts on the subject.

His annoyance even seems to extend to his disciples. For it is the haste of ordinary people to exalt authorities that sustains the Pharisees in power in the first place. The masses enthrone rabbis, fathers, teachers, gurus—but not always for the best reasons. They seek to hand over their personal authority and responsibility to someone else, because it saves them the emotional trouble of thinking or deciding in their own lives. The urge to have idols and heroes is seldom free from such murky or naive purposes.

A real authority will reject this false kind of exaltation. The last person to agree that "father knows best" should be father himself. A real authority will see through the silly, unsubstantial, fanciful praise that comes his way. He will refuse to let people hypnotically base their allegiance to him on the way he smiles, his demeanor, his dress, or, God forbid, his "style." He will measure his effectiveness, instead, by the degree to which he shows people the way to their own initiative and responsibility.

Jesus' experience in todays' gospel is in vivid contrast with simplistic ways of viewing authorities. He suffers through our *full* human experience of dealing with authorities: the itching, if not peevish, demand for certain personality traits in them that have little or nothing to do with their job; the agitation about how far their authority extends; the doubts about excepting ourselves from their judgments; the having to cope with needy feelings in us that make us want authorities to do it all; the guilt over the way we keep their job description blurred for our own ends; the temptation to lose respect for the person of those in authority just because the operation isn't going well. No doubt, in cooler moments Jesus wondered how his own operation was doing.

Deuteronomy 6:2 – 6
Hebrews 7:23 – 28
Mark 12:28 – 34

In a Nutshell

"Love the Lord your God with all your heart, with all your soul, and with all your strength" (Deuteronomy 6:5).

If someone handed you a Bible, the Code of Canon Law, and a few thick catechetical commentaries and asked you to pick out four or five lines that summed them all up, the remarkable thing is that you would probably plunge right in to try to find them. We take on a tall order like that partly out of naivete but partly, too, out of a justifiable conviction that anything worth saying should be said in a nutshell. We like our wisdom in manageable chunks. We need quick and catchy reminders of what really counts. So we are always ready to boil things down to a more simplified form.

We're not the only ones. In Jesus' day, rabbis were accustomed to debate whether some one principle could be discovered in the Torah from which every other commandment in it could be deduced. Some rabbis were nervous with this pastime. They thought it dangerous to reduce the Torah to any one principle, since once that principle was named, people might get the mistaken impression that they could forget about the rest of the commandments.

It is possible that this rabbinic debate serves as the background to today's gospel, in which Jesus and a scribe trade summations of the traditional wisdom of

Israel with each other. The friendly fashion of their exchange is itself surprising, since this dialogue is found in a larger section of Saint Mark's Gospel, in which Jesus' controversies with his enemies are underscored. Perhaps the scribe agreed with the nervous school of rabbis described above and was trying to find out where Jesus lined up on the question. In any case, Jesus is the first to pick out his favorite lines. The scribe has just asked him, "Which commandment is the most important of all?" (Mark 12:28). In response, Jesus cites the passage beginning with Deuteronomy 6:4, but then adds, "The second most important commandment is this: 'Love your neighbor as you love yourself' " (Mark 12:31, referring to Leviticus 19:18). Jesus does two things with this answer. He shows that he has nothing against the practice of making summaries of the Torah. He also admits to the scribe that you can't boil down the Law so much that important things are forgotten, such as love of neighbor. The scribe seems to like this. In giving his summary, he adds one slight nuance of his own. He throws in 1 Samuel 15:22 to the effect that love of neighbor is worth more than any burnt offering or sacrifice (Mark 12:33). Would he have preferred that Jesus had taken a dig at the temple liturgy crowd? The thought is enticing.

Saint Mark's version credits Jesus with combining love of God and love of neighbor into one summary statement of the Torah. Saint Luke (10:25–28) has someone else making the statement, with Jesus then approving it afterward. Saint Mark probably has the more authentic version of the event. Many commentators point out how original, even genial, the combining would have seemed to a contemporary listener. Apparently not too many would have added love of neighbor to their summary!

Summing up the faith has, down the ages, gotten a lot more tense than it was for Jesus in today's gospel. Preferences run from the simplest slogan ("All for Jesus") to the Oath Against Modernism, in triplicate. You wish sometimes that we'd all just settle for Jesus' version.

Thirty-First Sunday of the Year — C

Wisdom 11:22 — 12:1
2 Thessalonians 1:11 — 2:2
Luke 19:1 — 10

Short Story

"Hurry down, Zacchaeus, because I must stay in your house today" (Luke 19:5).

Zacchaeus was a rich man. That qualified him, in the eyes of his contemporaries, as a sinner. He takes Jesus to his house and is impressed, even moved. He does a moral turnabout, letting even his wallet feel the effects of the change. Jesus praises him. Though short in stature, Zacchaeus is a big man and a true son of Abraham. Blush, smile, fade out.

The story is so simple that it defies commentary. It is one of those stories, reported only in the writings of Saint Luke, that underscore the warmth of Jesus.

The first reading offers a different image. It pictures God as a loving artisan of his own creatures. It plays on God's professionalism and vanity as a craftsman. God is excited by his handiwork. He wants it to be a work of art that endures. We have seen something like this in great painters, architects, filmmakers, and writers. We have watched auto mechanics and carpenters smile and nod when the work is done and it's a good job.

But God is not just some cheery, whistle-while-you-work tinkerer. God's professionalism is such that he stays with the product. He does not let his creation run to seed or collapse. He is solicitous to keep his creation going. This, too, takes skill and artfulness, given the sinfulness of man, who tends to ruin everything. "You have allowed it all to exist, O Lord," says Wisdom, "because it is yours, and you love every living thing" (11:26—12:1). The way God does this is by a determined, energetic effort to look the other way. "You overlook our sins and give us time to repent" (Wisdom 11:23).

Note the sequence: The overlooking precedes the repentance. It takes a real artist not to try to reverse the process. Only amateurs remain aloof until the repentance has been exacted. This same sequence is the point of the Zacchaeus story. Jesus first associates with sinners, and through that contact they cease to be sinners. He makes this initial contact without making Zacchaeus feel like a moral leper. It does not deter Jesus that his conduct is taken by the crowd as giving aid and comfort to the enemy or as being soft on sin.

If we think of our own contacts with people who are supposed to be sinners (we could always use a mirror for this one), we know how difficult it is to fight down a tendency to be judgmental. We know what it is to stand up to the opinion of others. Above all, we wonder whether the sinner's association with us could really bring about a change in him. All these sentiments, Jesus, too, must face in himself. That is why his artistry at forgiving is all the more impressive.

The story of Zacchaeus has had a further inteptetation in biblical circles. It is thought to typify the kind of generous conversion that would be expected of the early Christian at baptism. The life of faith is called *work* by Saint Paul in today's epistle. *Workout* would be closer to the sense. Baptism puts claims on our time, our money, our past ways and future plans. It signals a big change in what we are to expect of ourselves and in what we are to be for others.

In our age of infant baptism, this sense of an important passage in the life of the one baptized is easily lost sight of. Forgetting that the work of faith only begins with the baptismal ceremony, we invent ethereal or trivial passages that we suppose the infant to be going through now, during the ceremony. But the truth is that big changes do not happen all at once in baptism, either for adults or for infants. Rather, baptism directs us to a hardheaded assessment of our lives on an ongoing basis, to a deliberate organization of ourselves to meet the call of Christ in concrete, realistic ways. Like Zacchaeus, we often find ourselves up a tree in the effort. But we get a better view of Jesus that way.

Wisdom 6:12–16
1 Thessalonians 4:13–18
Matthew 25:1–13

No Fooling

"Wisdom shines bright and never grows dim" (Wisdom 6:12).

Two of this week's readings are strung loosely around the theme of wisdom. In the first reading, we find Wisdom personified as a mysterious woman who lingers in front of people's houses waiting to be consulted. She's eager enough, all right, but she *never* gives unsolicited advice. We could pass her a hundred times at our door, but she would remain practically invisible if we really weren't interested in what she had to say. If we feel that we have nothing to learn in the way of wisdom, if we deny our proneness to mistakes and stupidity in our life decisions, then her presence will make no impression on us.

This little vignette from the wisdom literature is as alluring as the woman herself, who embodies wisdom. Her presence is insistent. It may seem like a rebuke to us or a constant itch. We feel challenged by her. We are deathly afraid that she might become less retiring and begin to ask us embarrassing questions. But we know she's out there! Pretty soon we'll be peeking out through the blinds to see if she's still there!

In the second reading, ten maidens are waiting for a bridegroom to arrive for a wedding feast. Five aren't so smart; in fact, our word *moron* comes from the

Greek word used for them. They fail to put oil in the lamps that must light the way for the bridegroom when he comes. Five are more provident. (The word in Greek isn't quite the same as "wisdom," but the tradition does speak about "the wise and foolish virgins," so we may allow the liturgical pairing.) They have sufficient oil to greet the bridegroom in style, when he finally arrives.

All this is not presented as the earliest New Testament account of a Middle East oil crisis. The reference throughout this passage is to the second coming of Jesus. In the primitive church consciousness of this second coming was much more vivid than it is today. Notice, for example, in today's second reading, how they have gotten down to such minor items as who profits most from the second coming, the dead or the living. Saint Paul even adds a scenario for the second coming: "Then we who are living at that time will be gathered up along with them in the clouds to meet the Lord in the air" (1 Thessalonians 4:17). Notice, too, that the theme of the second coming can be used differently by different scriptural writers for their own purposes. Saint Paul uses it for purposes of consoling: "And so we will always be with the Lord. So then, encourage one another with these words" (4:17 – 18). Saint Matthew, on the other hand, uses it to keep people on their toes in a general sort of way: "Watch out, then, because you do not know the day or the hour" (25:13).

But when we have put these readings together, we still haven't said much more than that it's better to be wise than to be stupid, and that we should keep our oil wicks dipped. What then?

The trouble is that the theme of wisdom scares us off. Wisdom means different things when applied to different people. A wise politician is not the same as a wise judge. The wisdom called for in raising children is not quite the wisdom of the very old. Wisdom comes to some through suffering and to others at the moment they refuse to suffer any longer. Wisdom can be expressed in silence or in honed and painstaking phrases. Wisdom is equated with common sense, and yet common sense is often the enemy of wisdom. Wisdom is associated with not knowing and with knowing a lot. In much of our literature, wisdom is played by fools. Everybody volunteers to set everybody else wise. Clearly, we are dealing with an obscure commodity when we are dealing with wisdom.

It seems, however, that God has prepared a way out of our dilemma. In the course of the scriptural tradition, wisdom becomes less identified with a personification, and still less with a body of doctrine, and more with a concrete person, Jesus. Wisdom is achieved in relationship with him. That pins things down a great deal. Where questions of wisdom are posed out of this basic personal relationship, there is an anchor, a foundation that can support much fog and ambiguity in life. Even follies can be shared, along with the scars. The only question is whether we are dumb enough to try to make it without such a relationship.

Thirty-Second Sunday of the Year—B

1 Kings 17:10–16
Hebrews 9:24–28
Mark 12:38–44

Widow's Might

"The others put in what they had to spare of their riches; but she, poor as she is, put in all she had —she gave all she had to live on" (Mark 12:44).

Most of us have suffered the ill effects of some-one else's piety. At least that is how we would formulate the way we have sometimes fared at others' hands. We were bidden to sit through some utterly boring sermon. We were lectured on the virtues of various and sundry medals, amulets, chains, rosaries, pictures, pendants, scapulars, bones, slivers, and such. We were harangued about this or that vision, appearance, sign, omen, or epiphany. We might even have exhausted ourselves with other people's methods of spiritual self-improvement, following this sequence of prayer and breathing or that battery of concentration and palpitation.

Other people's piety has sometimes been an obstacle to our own. What our gurus sometime forgot to tell us is the fact that while *they* might have needed such things to get in touch with *their* spirit (let alone with their emotions, bodies, memories, environments, and so forth), others are in touch with their spirit by the very fact of getting out of bed in the morning! The gurus tend to hog the name of piety for themselves. The forms of piety are infinite, despite a prevailing hegemony that limits them to a few. If our own forms of piety are not chosen, we feel relegated to exterior darkness. We feel cheap, ungenerous, marginal, and, yes, impious.

What we need in the midst of these competing claims to piety is a relatively unassailable image of it. God bless today's gospel for giving us a nice, black-and-white version of things. First, it gives us an example of the pious fraud. It describes an instance of blatant spiritual fakery: the scribes "who like to walk around in their long robes and be greeted with respect in the market place, who choose the reserved seats in the synagogues and the best places at feasts" (Mark 12:38–39). They really play to the crowd! In some ways, Jesus' observation on the statement above is overkill. If the scribes were that obvious about it, their behavior hardly seems to have deserved commentary. But Jesus was not exercised so much about their vanity as he was about the dirty dealing that went on beneath the surface and tried to pass for piety. He continues: "They take advantage of widows. . .and then make a show of saying long prayers" (12:40). The scribes are described as pitiless money grubbers who, on religious grounds of course, hit the poorest and the weakest for contributions, while they themselves drone on with prayers that are thought to justify their grasping and insensitive methods. Disassociation is such a delightful state—*if* you can carry it off! What galls Jesus is using religious forms and practices for ulterior purposes, instead of entering into them with soul and heart. He seems to prefer that people take their sins (greed, vanity), their practical needs (money), and their religion (prayer) neat, rather than serving them up in some distasteful concoction.

An ideal version of piety is found in the gospel's portrayal of a poor widow. She is destined to strike an authentic chord in generations of believers. You simply can't knock her. We don't know if she was, in other respects, the sorriest and most ineffective creature God ever made. We aren't sure she wasn't already beginning to dodder. On the contrary, she might have been quite aware of the parameters, as they say, of her action. In any case, she had a woman's sense of giving it *all* away, not for show and certainly, not for duty, but for love. If her modern counterparts are any indication—and God knows she has many—it might have been on behalf of a sick child or in memory of some promise made long ago. She might simply have been arming herself for future demands on her fidelity and generosity. She might have been defending the pride of the poor, who do not want to seem less capable of giving than others.

Her divesting herself, her thinking of others is the solid stuff of which piety is made. The giving need not always be measured in money. It can surface in a kind word dredged up out of our parched interior silence to help someone needier than ourselves. It can appear in a smile given when there's only one more left in us. It can consist of an outpouring of sophisticated talent, or of brawn or humor or tears. What marks the widow's might is that she gives of her substance and not just of her abundance. We got a speech to that effect from John Paul II during his visit to the United States. It would be a shame if the speech got lost because some people were using the occasion of his visit to parade their own versions of piety for vindication and support. When we are asked to give of our substance, we are being asked to join the ranks of the needy. Being truly needful before the Lord might well be the secret of piety. Do you think the widow in the gospel knew something we don't know?

Thirty-Second Sunday of the Year—C

2 Maccabees 7:1–2, 9–14
2 Thessalonians 2:16—3:5
Luke 20:27–38

For the Cause

"He is the God of the living, not of the dead, for to him all are alive" (Luke 20:38).

What do young people today want to die for? Most of us had a whole list to choose from when we were younger: We could die for our country in World War II or in Korea. We could go down fighting for the faith under Communism. We could save people from burning buildings or push them from the paths of oncoming trains. Not that we actually faced death, nor would we have taken any concrete steps in that direction. But there were moments in the mind when we were the heroes, and no enemy could stop us in our cause. These days, alas, wars are trickier, and faith is less bellicose. And you could be sued if your rescue missions misfire.

A good cause, as many governments have discovered, requires a good enemy. A villain is part of the scenario. Sometimes enemies are invented, but most of the time the opposition is already there. In today's epistle, for example, Saint Paul warns us: "Pray also that God will rescue us from wicked and evil people; for not everyone believes the message" (2 Thessalonians 3:2). Locating enemies this way may not seem a suitable religious stance, but the cause of fidelity in faith may require as much.

The seven heroic brothers in today's first reading were convinced that they had a cause. Their pearl of great price was fidelity to the religious laws of Israel. Torture, mutilation and death did not matter. The brothers were not simply being pugnacious. Their tradition was at stake; that is what inspired them. Their cause had a content and shape and familiarity about it.

Note that the story is taken from Second Maccabees. First Maccabees held a different theory, more like the one attributed to General Patton: "No one becomes a hero by dying for his country; he becomes one by making another s.o.b. die for *his* country." But our seven heroes in 2 Maccabees looked at their own suffering almost as something desirable, something to match themselves against. It was as if their sincerity in the cause could be tested only by their own dying for it.

The theme of dying leads to the theme of life-after-death. Today's liturgy ties the seven Maccabee brothers to the seven husbands mentioned in Jesus' debate with the Sadducees concerning the resurrection. The parallel is forced, but there it is. Both groups are interested in the afterlife. Thus, one of the brothers says, "The King of the universe will raise us from the dead and give us eternal life" (2 Maccabees 7:9). Jesus, too, defends a view of the next world against those traditional disbelievers in resurrection, the Sadducees. First, he resolves the dilemma presented by the Sadducees. They offer the case of seven brothers married to the same woman in this life. Whose wife will she be in some resurrected world? Jesus argues that, because the propagation of the race will not be an issue in the next life, marriage won't be necessary, either. Second, Jesus scores a debating point on a phrase of Scripture. He says that if God is described by Scripture as *being* the God of Abraham, Isaac, and Jacob, then these people must, in some sense, now *be*.

We suggest, however, that resurrection was not the predominant issue, either for Jesus or for the heroes of the Maccabees. Or at least we should not think that resurrection was their chief motivating force. Their cause was here and now, and the courage they poured into that cause should not be lost sight of. We have met many people who lead good lives almost for no other purpose than to be raised by God to some future happiness. But they are often singularly untouched by what they are doing in this life; they do not seem to care what its intrinsic value, its drama, its excitement or service to others might be. It is difficult to interest such people in causes, sometimes even the cause of Jesus!

The issue, then, is not simply whether we will face death with hope in a future life. The issue is whether our way of facing life now is valid and true and effective. Perhaps young people would be more ready to die for a cause if we stopped making resurrection itself the only cause and believed them when they tell us they are called to live now.

Proverbs 31:10–13, 19–20,30–31
1 Thessalonians 5:1–6
Matthew 25:14–30

Autumn Hopes

"We do not belong to the night or to the darkness" (1 Thessalonians 5:5).

An unresigned poet once wrote about death: "When I go out, I want to go out like autumn, in an aching blaze of color and interwoven light, where my last voice leaps forth like sharp sun on autumn trees, and my finger points, without accusation, at such an array of joy as stills all doubt." As the current liturgical year grinds down to its demise, we get no such exuberant finale. It's more like kicking through thick brown leaves. But there is some flair in today's readings, and we will try to extract it.

The gospel is the parable of the talents. In it, Saint Matthew describes how God reacts to people on the day of judgment, or, as we would say, in the final analysis. The parable pictues God as some sort of rich business-man who enjoys making money. If he goes off on a trip (as some say he has!), he wants his subordinates to make his money work for him. For besides being good at business, he is also lucky. If his subordinates don't trust his luck, they haven't understood him. This explains the severity of his reaction to one of them: "You bad and lazy servant!. . . You knew, did you, that I reap harvests where I did not plant, and gather crops where I did not scatter seed? Well, then, you should have deposited my money in the bank, and I would have received it all back with interest when I returned" (Matthew 25:26– 27).

We could begin to make the usual edifying application of all this to our moral lives, as is frequently done with this parable. We could discourse on the need to develop our talents, to bring out of them a proportionate amount of good works and service, an equitable return. If we are gifted with attractiveness, brains, psychological stamina, artistic or organizational ability, insight, or simply a broad back, the point would be to ask: How responsibly are we using them in the kingdom of God? But this approach misses the spirit of the gospel. It fails to capture the flavor of the gospel, which has us engaged with God in an exciting gamble, a go-for-broke common enterprise based on daring, mutual trust and luck.

In this light, the use of our talents is not some plodding dutifulness. God is not only doing his thing through us but is hoping that we might do our thing, as well, with the talents he has given us. In the relationship of trust with God, we not only may, but should, bring initiative and imagination to bear. People who don't have this sense of adventure are faced with a built-in penalty. Unable or unwilling to dare, they become more and more isolated and impoverished. The windows of their personality remain shuttered against the noise and clamor of other people. Or as the gospel puts it: "For to every person who has something, even more will be given. . .; but the person who has nothing, even the little that he has will be taken away from him" (Matthew 25:29). Talent suffocates, unless it is exercised in an atmosphere of trust in God and in others.

Today's first reading is paired with the gospel in order, it seems, to give a concrete instance of someone who uses her talents well. It is an Old Testament picture of the ideal wife. In some ways it is a bit breathless and chauvinistic. It could also give the impression that the wife's value is being measured solely by her achievements. But in fact the passage rejoins the spirit of today's gospel. For the Old Testament writer does try to point out that a deep basic relationship of trust exists between the ideal wife and her husband. The husband does not simply entrust her with things to do. "Her husband puts his confidence in her" (Proverbs 31:11). The same principle is at work, then, as above. The atmosphere of trust creates an explosion of talented doings.

It is so easy to look at God as the monitor of our talents and as their harsh assessor. In some ways, many of us feel robbed, either because we have no talents to speak of or because we have done so little with them. It may not help, then, to hear Saint Paul saying that the Lord will come "as a thief comes at night" (1 Thessalonians 5:2). The statement simply reinforces our anxiety and depression.

We should not feel that the Lord is returning in order to rob us of anything. Our trust in him goes beyond that. It is a complete trust. In our memory of him on earth he is open and clear like an autumn day. And so he will remain in the final analysis.

Daniel 12:1 – 3
Hebrews 10:11 – 14, 18
Mark 13:24 – 32

The Living End

"Heaven and earth will pass away, but my words will never pass away" (Mark 13:31).

"How will it all turn out?" Up and down the trenches, the troops philosophize. Humanity seems so sore, so worn down at times that the question comes out like a cry of pain or like an accusation. It is as though we can't do another thing or bear up under one more sling or arrow, unless we get a picture in our heads of the End of it all. We plead with our wise men and consult our wise women for some small peek at the finale. We want to read the last pages of history first; otherwise, turning the pages can be exhausting.

From early time, a form of literature existed whose purpose was to offer such prognoses. It is called *apocalyptic*. In stunning imagery and explosive symbols, writers displayed their views on the subject of the Last Days. Not blessed with a direct vision of those events, their descriptions were necessarily rather vague. But the genre enabled them to dispose of many of their contemporary enemies by assigning horrible fates to them in the Last Analysis. Dante did no less in his *Inferno*. They also made lush provision for their friends. Apocalyptic is full of vindication, scores settled, good and bad guys, hurrahs and fury. But the question about apocalyptic is: Will it hold water?

The thirteenth chapter of Mark's Gospel is such a piece of apocalyptic writing. Out of a hodgepodge of small items, one-liners and snippets that he had picked up from the tradition about Jesus, Saint Mark strung together a stirring sequence of apocalyptic events. Like other Jewish-Christian apocalyptic writers—and no doubt like Jesus himself—Saint Mark borrowed much of his imagery, characters, tone, and even plot from earlier apocalyptic passages in Scripture (such as today's first reading). But he wove them together into his own vision of the last times.

First, he pictured massive destruction on earth (13:5–8). This destruction is so violent that it reaches right into the religious institutions of humankind and corrodes them (13:14). Then, in the section we have for today's reading, he extends this cataclysmic vision to the heavens themselves: During that period, "the sun will grow dark, the moon will no longer shine, the stars will fall from heaven, and the powers in space will be driven from their courses" (13:24–25). Finally, a colossal figure, the Son of Man, will arrive in the midst of this destruction. He will take up a position literally between earth and heaven and begin meting out final justice. For Saint Mark, that figure is clearly none other than Jesus.

Christian apocalyptic writers such as Saint Mark were not content simply to describe these end-time events. They drew lessons for the present from such projections about the future. Much of what we find in Chapter 13 is this kind of pointed exhortation about the here-and-now. The hope of the apocalyptic writer is that people will be better able to face their contemporary challenges when these challenges are seen to be leading somewhere, when the end of it all is clearly laid out for all to see.

As far as we can judge, this never works. The first question everyone asks is: When will the resolution of humanity's problems come? Saint Mark comes unstuck when faced with that question. He cites contradictory views in his sources: "All these things will happen before the people now living have all died" (13:30) as against "No one knows, however, when that day or hour will come—neither the angels in heaven, nor the Son; only the Father knows" (13:32). For all the colorful fireworks the apocalyptic writers provide us, humanity is again herded back into the trenches unconsoled and still worrying whether it is all worth the effort.

Saint Mark, however, adds one touch to his apocalyptic portrait that does provide the spark of hope. "Heaven and earth will pass away, but my words will never pass away." It's the kind of statement we might retrieve from memories of long-dead parents or hear from struggling loved ones or recall from favorite old-timers in our lives. It brings the whole matter back to a trust in Jesus' word: Do Christians really believe that Jesus' promise can survive, can overcome the multiple destructions that life offers? Will the word of Jesus remain meaningful despite threat, pain, terror, and persecution?

No reasoned answer can be given to such questions. If anything, they sound a retreat from an apocalyptic perspective. To answer them, we would have to look not forward but backward, at our actual experiences of Jesus and what they have meant to us. That is perhaps why the next chapter of Mark's gospel deals with the passion, in which Jesus faces his own historical apocalypse of pain, destruction, and judgment. Jesus' personal universe collapses with as much shuddering and terror as is usually found in apocalyptic writing. Any man's death really comes down to that same kind of thing. But, in the midst of suffering, Jesus' word of promise and fidelity to his followers remains the same.

Thirty-Third Sunday of the Year — C

Malachi 3:19 – 20
2 Thessalonians 3:7 – 12
Luke 21:5 – 19

Sorry I Mentioned It

"Some of the disciples were talking about the Temple, how beautiful it looked with its fine stones and the gifts offered to God" (Luke 21:5).

Whoever remarked on the beauties of the Temple probably regretted that they had done so. "Look at the nice colored stones. Aren't the candles stunning?" By Saint Luke's account, it brought forth from Jesus a head-splitting speech on how things are more complicated than they seem. Jesus seems to drive them beyond the superficial, the aesthetic, the trimmings, the nonessentials. It's not certain that this is a blow-by-blow account of an actual speech of Jesus. Nor do we know the manner in which such a speech might have been given, whether with heavy foreboding or pedantic correction, or, more modestly, with delicate, foot-shuffling hesitancy. In any case, Saint Luke has Jesus piling on everything but the kitchen sink.

If we may paraphrase the points Jesus makes in response to the comments on the Temple's beauty, we see how almost comical the contrast of interests is. The first point is his reminder not to be disappointed when religion does not seem to work, when it takes too long for things to happen, when the desire for an instant savior becomes overwhelming. "Many men, claiming to speak for me, will come and say, 'I am he!' and 'The time has come!' " (Luke 21:8). The second point is the presence of powerful forces, such as the scandal of war, that escape our control and mock our attempts to bring charity into the world. "Don't be afraid when you hear of wars and revolutions" (Luke 21:9). The third point is the necessity of living under what look like enigmatic omens, without clarity and helpless against the irrational and rude powers of nature. "There will be terrible earthquakes, famines, and plagues everywhere; there will be strange and terrifying things coming from the sky" (Luke 21:11). The fourth point is opposition from government, in which law and persecution seem to intertwine. "You will be arrested and persecuted" (Luke 21:12). The fifth point is the rejection of our naive conviction that things should come naturally and spontaneously between people. "You will be handed over by your parents, your brothers, your relatives, and your friends" (Luke 21:16).

The gospel certainly shows how we tend to cloak over the grimmer aspects of faith. This does not mean that we should be too hard on our own versions of temple-gazing: our creches, confirmation outfits, stoles and banners, displays and icons, soaring arches and refined statuary. Everyone has an aesthetic and emotional investment in such things. Many sweat and pay good money for the adornment of churchs and the arrangement of striking ritual. But the gospel gives us courage to imagine our own forms of temple-gazing. The appointments of church and sanctuary are important and worthy of all our taste and sensitivity. But there is a time when they don't matter any more. The gospel encourages us to let other, more painful, issues into our religious consciousness before they break in, anyhow.

Our habits are not always helpful in this effort. Rosy is better in many aspects of our lives, even religion apart. The rot of cities is disguised by the gleaming marble of our municipal centers or by flashy pockets of fashion boutiques. Many of our partisan, compromised politicians keep up an oily pretense of hail-fellow-well-met that mocks the common good supposedly being served. As they used to say about Hollywood: "Scratch the veneer and you get to the real veneer underneath."

Above all, it is in interpersonal relationships that we keep up the polite exterior, the self-possessed sheath. Our response in the presence of someone else's emotion is like the stylized moves in a chess game. We deny the pain and struggle in others and in ourselves with an incredible array of defenses, strategies, camouflages, and distractions. We do this on the theory that one shouldn't interfere, or that someone else is handling the problem, or that it's better not ot dig too deeply. A lot of business is going on in each one of us, but we sit around and sharpen and resharpen our pencils, because we do not know how to raise the real issues that preoccupy us.

For many, religion is the last defense against complexity. They want "healing like the sun's rays" (Malachi 4:2) but they don't want to burn! How pleasant to his readers, for example, was Saint Paul's blunt kind of religion that we see in today's epistle. "Whoever refuses to work is not allowed to eat" (2 Thessalonians 3:10). How would they react to his sharp observation that there would be fewer religious busybodies around if people concentrated more on work and on the integrity of their own faith? Saint Paul does not see much contradiction between charity and the uncovering of more realistic issues within us.

The Spirit's realm is this complex reality within us and around us. The Spirit is a Spirit of reality. To try to simplify things or to smooth them over is understandable. But we should not be surprised to get a head-splitting speech in return.

Solemnity of Christ the King—A

Ezekiel 34:11 – 12, 15 – 17
1 Corinthians 15:20 – 26, 28
Matthew 25:31 – 46

Crowning Point

"I will bring them back from all the places where they were scattered on that dark, disastrous day" (Ezekiel 34:11).

As a crowning piece to the liturgical cycle, the Solemnity of Christ the King calls our attention to the person and work of the founder of the Christian community. But this is not just any good old founder, nor is his work any common work.

We may think of the personalities of other founders and trace their influence on the ongoing life of their organizations. Joseph Smith, Cesar Chavez, Ignatius of Loyola, Elizabeth Seton, Lenin—all magnetic, galvanizing personalities who were capable of eliciting enthusiasm and cooperative action from large numbers of people. But with the passage of time you don't have their followers going around saying that they have offended Joseph Smith, or personally vindicated Elizabeth Seton, or betrayed more than the memory of Lenin. Christians, on the other hand, see Jesus everywhere. They find him in marriage partners and business partners, in children and old people, in colleagues and bosses. He is the one who is touched by their actions. He is in the members of his community in a resistant and stubborn way that no other founder has achieved.

Some might try to explain this conviction of Christians by the fact that they believe all people are made in the image of God who is the divine Son. Seeing Jesus in others, then, would come back to the respect they have for this divine element in all people. But is this the reason? The force of Christ was also the force of his humanity. It was his human achievement to have communicated to his followers how much and how far he chose to identify with each one of them. He fostered a vigorous, intimate sense of solidarity among his followers precisely by making their relating to one another a condition for relating to him. He turned people away from too great a personal attraction to him and said in effect that they would find each other equally attractive, if only they looked more closely. His identification with others was blunt and eloquent: "I tell you, whenever you did this for one of the least important of these brothers of mine, you did it for me" (Matthew 25:40). With one genial and resolute stroke he loosed a tide of mutual respect and fraternal concern among people that will never fully be fathomed. Humanity will always wear the hypnotic imprint of his humanity. We are still trying, in his name, to look at one another with new eyes.

Jesus' identification with humanity was not sanitized and bourgeois. He gave special attention to areas of humanity where many of us fear to tread. "I was hungry and you fed me, thirsty and you gave me a drink; I was a stranger and you received me in your homes, naked and you clothed me; I was sick and you took care of me, in prison and you visited me" (Matthew 25:35–36). His descent takes him among the seamier and darker recesses of humanity. We can discover in his life a pattern of selective concern for the marginal people. He is king of the cons, the pushovers, the sheep. He is king of the lost and of the losers. He sides with the dregs, the decaying, skeletal masses who are forced to scratch and starve. He is Lord and leader of the strange and the questionable.

All this is to say that he takes reality as he finds it. He makes the present condition of humankind his starting point. Ideology yields to hard fact. His affiliation with humankind is not so selective that it is guaranteed to look good in the end. He never looked good as a king, anyway.

Many are scandalized by these preferences of his for the poor and the underdog. Given the trouble most of us have with these categories of people, we have to ask, "Is he serious? Is he indulging in some cosmic venture, some final suicidal charge against the fixed, unwavering phalanx of human evils?" Well, if he is, he's going all the way. Today's epistle reads, "The last enemy to be defeated will be death" (1 Corinthians 15:26). He even identifies with this sorry, deflated crew who daily slip out of reach of the living. He goes with them on their mute, cringing journey to the grave. And here again he makes a condition of our relating to him that we relate to these dead and to our own death with compassion and hope. He has some program!

Where does he get his motivation for it? Today's epistle tells us, "Christ will overcome all spiritual rulers, authorities and powers, and will hand over the Kingdom to God the Father. . . . God will rule completely over all" (1 Corinthians 15:24, 28). His purpose throughout is to give people what he himself had learned, the sense of God's presence in human life. He wants to cut through all the hierarchies, the determinisms, the who's-in-charge games, the impotencies, the threats, the inferiority complexes, and to convince people of God's own desire to relate to them as to his own image in a mirror. Not a bad cause to go down fighting for.

Daniel 7:13 – 14
Revelation 1:5 – 8
John 18:33 – 37

Visions During the Night

"My kingdom does not belong to this world" (John 18:36).

There have been many attempts to exalt human-kind to the skies. Poets, artists, and architects have traced the contours of humanity's greatness, and philosophers have provided the reasons why. Yet, it all rings hollow when, in a darker vision, we see the prison walls, the slums, the starvation, the stockpiles, the torture chambers, the relentless dying and killing. Our nightmares walk abroad in daylight, and we pretend not to know the difference. The kings of earth seem firmly in place.

One of Dostoevsky's characters says that we are torn by an "inextinguishable desire to achieve a purpose and at the same time the denial of that purpose." Even where we are great, our greatness seems to carry with it a certain guilt, almost a loathing, that we have stood out too starkly from the evolutionary mass. Our heat and rutting, unlike that of our animal ancestors, produce intelligent offspring. But to what avail? Who wants the ability to reflect analytically and theoretically on pain? Who wants insight into the causes and effects of misery? Who cares to look knowingly into darkness?

The gospel for the Solemnity of Christ the King describes a dark moment in Jesus' life. The process of his destruction has been set in motion. His meeting with

Pilate is just a part of a larger sequence of events in which his hopes are unhinged one by one and he is propelled along a sure downward course. But the meeting is instructive. It shows us how, in the real order, you get exalted to the skies. And it teaches us how to behave when the darkness comes.

No one is freed from personal responsibility to the truth when the crunch comes. Our grisly circumstances, we say, provide us with many excuses to skirt that responsibility: "You have to look out for yourself; you can't buck the system; what one person does doesn't matter in the long run." In the midst of his own crisis, Jesus thinks otherwise. He calls Pilate to be responsible to the truth as he sees it: "Does this question come from you or have others told you about me?" (John 18:34). Pilate has become a symbol of expediency and compromise, a larger symbol perhaps than he deserved. That he could have altered the course of events is speculative at best. What he was being offered by Jesus was a chance to own his part in the inevitable fiasco taking place. What Jesus is convinced of is that when we lose contact with small truths about ourselves, we gradually lose the habit of truth altogether. A commitment to truth is a precondition to recognizing Jesus whenever he appears before us. If Pilate can pretend that he has no personal opinion on Jesus' style and competence as a religious leader, if he can lie to himself about what his usual estimate of Jesus' hot-breathed enemies would be, then what is left of his personal truth?

Jesus also has to face the issue of his own personal truth. As the kingdom of darkness engulfs him, he has to ask himself where all his efforts have led him. He, too, could easily have hedged. He could have concentrated on the unforgivable malice of his enemies. He could have accused the well-intentioned incompetence of his disciples. He could have denied the validity of his youthful hankerings after a better world that he and the Baptist had thought of as the Kingdom Now. He could have succumbed to dark thoughts about his Father. But what he knows for certain is his own commitment to the truth and the apparent failure of that commitment. His words "My kingdom does not belong to this world" contain a jolting realization that he didn't succeed as well as the dogged conviction that his day will come. Amid the babble of accusation and recrimination, it is Jesus' simple trust in his Father's providence that stands out as his greatest personal truth. He is a faithful witness to that truth. Beyond the night visions he sees a day of brightness dawning. From the ruins he sees a kingdom of justice rising. It is this faith of his that he offers to us to be our personal truth and our way out of the darkness.

2 Samuel 5:1–3
Colossians 1:12–20
Luke 23:35–43

Going to Glory

"We are your own flesh and blood" (2 Samuel 5:1).

It is difficult not to be ambivalent about the word *king*. Perhaps it is our American memory of our colonial days, when we corporately wrenched ourselves away from a king and a country, that makes the word flat for us. There are versions of kingship that caution us against enthusiasm. The word reminds us of feudal subservience. It speaks of the enforced homage paid to a stranger who, while we are told he is our better, appears simply to be more heavily armed. It smacks of the dependency we see in those subject to kings. It underscores their helplessness and inability to do for themselves. In their abject state they exalt the king in various ways. The king is in his court, a segregated place of privilege and manners. Moreover, from his isolated and exalted position the king is expected to take all the responsibility for peace and justice in the realm. This being impossible, he often must settle for making violent examples of those who disturb that peace and justice.

You will say that's a description of bad kings, the ones with a George Zucco or Basil Rathbone at their elbow. Yes, yes, we all know what people mean by a good king. They mean someone who galvanizes others into responsible and satisfying action and firmly cuts the dependency ties. They mean someone who is attractive enough to support general initiatives. They mean someone who is not distant, who is collegial in suffering and humor, work and hope, in all the things that count. They mean someone who faces the real odds against peace and justice, promises a kingdom, anyway, and almost makes you believe. But all these qualities are true of many kinds of leaders: presidents, premiers, chieftains. They are not synonymous with *king*.

These picky observations on the way we hear the word *king* should not distract us from the main business of today's feast, which is, after all, to salute Christ at the end of the liturgical year. Let us search the liturgical readings for the way they see Christ's kingship.

Some would find in the readings the theme of Christ's sovereignty, of his awesome power. They would cite today's epistle to this purpose: "Christ is the visible likeness of the invisible God. He is the first-born Son, superior to all created things. For through him God created everything in heaven and on earth, the seen and the unseen things. . . . God created the whole universe through him and for him. Christ existed before all things, and in union with him all things have their proper place" (Colossians 1:15–17). We must recall the context in which these words were written. Saint Paul was contesting errors in the church at Colossae, which maintained that certain intermediary powers and elemental forces gripped humankind and accounted for patterns of existence that are fixed and inevitable. (Think of your modern versions of astrology, life forces, spiritism, and so forth.) Saint Paul is not talking about Jesus' power *over* people. Rather, he is saying that postulating power-figures is futile to begin with. Jesus offers freedom and responsibility. His reign means that people are *not* subject to the forces they think they are under. They are more free than they think from the determinisms that seem to control them. *Sovereignty* hardly expresses this concern on God's part for autonomy in his creatures. If anything, it gives the opposite impression.

Others would underscore the majesty of Jesus in the liturgical readings. Majesty in kings is something easily overlooked. Our democratic prejudice resists it, but it is there. Whether it is there by tradition or blood or self-contained hauteur, common people like ourselves draw back. Today's liturgy would supposedly be celebrating the person of God in Jesus, the awesome eternal one, the splendor, the noble strain that differentiates him. Majesty, however, is not enough. For on the Solemnity of Christ the King, it is God in *our* flesh that we are celebrating. It is the unheralded bond that God has forged with our humanity that makes Christ so appealing.

If we must talk about kings, then what today's feast is all about is a mattter of *allegiance*. First, there is his allegiance to us, the fact that he has pledged his sweat and blood to our human cause. He calls us to a do-or-die togetherness and mutual fidelity. He swears the same oath to us that his Father has always sworn, that he will be our God and we will be his people. Second, there is our sense of solidarity with him. The Israelites say to David: "We are your own flesh and blood." What greater allegiance can we imagine? Saint Paul uses a similar, but paler, expression when he speaks of the church as the body of Christ. But the idea is the same, the abiding sense that we are in it with him to the end.

Nowhere does this solidarity appear more vividly than in today's gospel, when Jesus goes down bloodily under the ironic banner of his enemies: "This is the King." His vulnerability to the human condition has finally caught up with him. He goes the route of all suffering, confused, maltreated, hurting humanity. He meets that final judgment that all of us face, when some will call us worthless and some will call us true. And, at that moment, he can still mutter to another soul in pain: We're going to glory—together.

Index of Themes